Alfred Hitchcock's
SPELLBINDERS
in SUSPENSE

"These are mystery-suspense stories. Some will keep you on the edge of your chair with excitement. Others are calculated to draw you along irresistibly to see how the puzzle works out. I have even included a sample or two of stories that are humorous, to show you that humor and mystery can also add up to suspense.

"So here you are, with best wishes for hours of good reading."

—*Alfred Hitchcock*

Alfred Hitchcock's

SPELLBINDERS
in SUSPENSE

Illustrated by Harold Isen

Random House   **New York**

The editor gratefully acknowledges the invaluable assistance of Robert Arthur in the preparation of this volume.

The editor wishes to thank the following for permission to reprint:

Doubleday & Company, Inc. and Curtis Brown, Ltd. for "The Birds" from *Kiss Me Again Stranger* by Daphne du Maurier. Copyright 1952 by Daphne du Maurier.

A. Watkins, Inc. for "The Man Who Knew How" from *Hangman's Holiday*. Copyright, 1933, by Dorothy L. Sayers. © Renewed 1961 by Anthony Fleming.

Paul R. Reynolds, Inc. for "Black Magic" by Sax Rohmer. First published in *Collier's*. Copyright 1938 by Sax Rohmer.

Harry Altshuler for "Yours Truly, Jack the Ripper" by Robert Bloch. Copyright, 1943, by *Weird Tales*.

Curtis Brown, Ltd. for "Puzzle for Poppy" by Patrick Quentin. Copyright 1946 by Davis Publications, Inc. Originally printed in *Ellery Queen's Mystery Magazine*.

Robert Arthur for "Eyewitness." Original version copyright 1939 by Red Star News Co., renewed 1967 by Robert Arthur. Revised version copyright 1951 by Grace Publishing Co., Inc.

Dodd, Mead & Company for "The Veiled Lady" from *Poirot Investigates* by Agatha Christie. Copyright 1923, 1924, 1925 by Dodd, Mead & Company, Inc. Renewed 1953 by Agatha Christie Mallowan.

Collins-Knowlton-Wing, Inc. for "The Treasure Hunt" by Edgar Wallace. Copyright © 1965 by Penelope Wallace.

Brandt & Brandt for "The Most Dangerous Game" by Richard Connell. Copyright, 1924, by Richard Connell. Copyright renewed, 1952, by Louise Fox Connell. And for "Treasure Trove" by F. Tennyson Jesse, Copyright, 1928, by The McCall Corp.

Clayre Lipman for "The Dilemma of Grampa Dubois" by Clayre and Michel Lipman. Copyright, 1952, by Emil Jungell and reprinted by permission of *American Family Magazine* and *Family Publications, Inc.*

Harold Matson Company, Inc. for "P. Moran, Diamond Hunter" by Percival Wilde. Copyright, 1947, by Percival Wilde.

Alfred A. Knopf, Inc. for "Man from the South" by Roald Dahl from *Someone Like You*. Copyright © 1948 by Roald Dahl.

This title was originally cataloged by the Library of Congress as follows:
Hitchcock, Alfred Joseph, 1899–   *comp.*
Alfred Hitchcock's spellbinders in suspense.   Illustrated by Harold Isen.   New York, Random House [1967]   206 p.   illus.   27 cm.
1. Detective and mystery stories.   I. Title.   II. Title: Spellbinders in suspense.
PZ1.H53Am   67–20603
ISBN: 0-394-81665-X   ISBN: 0-394-91665-4 (lib. ed.)

A BRIEF MESSAGE FROM OUR SPONSOR

If you have been keeping pace with this series of books that I have been bringing you, you know that in the past I have gathered for your enjoyment tales of ghosts, spooks and spirits. I have given you a group of ingenious solve-them-yourself mysteries. I have paraded before your eyes a collection of monsters who took my fancy. This time I have assembled for your entertainment a choice group of stories of suspense.

But what, indeed, *is* suspense? I prefer the simplest definition—suspense is that quality in a story which makes you want to keep on reading it to find out what happens. By this definition any good story, of course, has suspense in it. A love story can have suspense—does it end happily? A mountain climbing story can have suspense—does the hero get to the top or does he slip and fall over a cliff?

I can assure you, however, that you will find neither love stories nor mountain-climbing stories in this collection. These are mystery-suspense stories. Some will keep you on the edge of your chair with excitement. Others are calculated to draw you along irresistibly to see how the puzzle works out. I have even included a sample or two of stories that are humorous, to show you that humor and mystery can also add up to suspense.

So here you are, with best wishes for hours of good reading from your perennial host——

ALFRED HITCHCOCK

Contents

Alfred Hitchcock's
SPELLBINDERS
in SUSPENSE

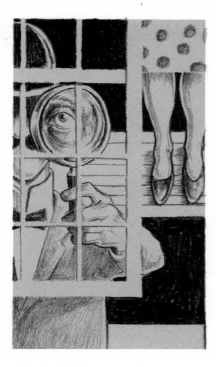

The Chinese Puzzle Box

Agatha Christie

I had noticed that for some time Hercule Poirot had been growing increasingly dissatisfied and restless. We had had no interesting cases of late, nothing on which my little friend could exercise his keen wits and remarkable powers of deduction. This July morning he flung down the newspaper with an impatient *"Tchah!"*—a favorite exclamation of his which sounded exactly like a cat sneezing.

"They fear me, Hastings—the criminals of your England they fear me! When the cat is there, the little mice they come no more to the cheese!"

"I don't suppose the greater part of them even know of your existence," I said, laughing.

Poirot looked at me reproachfully. He always imagines that the whole world is thinking and talking of Hercule Poirot. He had certainly made a name for himself in London, but I could hardly believe that his existence struck terror into the criminal world.

"What about that daylight robbery of jewels in Bond Street the other day?" I asked.

"A neat *coup*," said Poirot approvingly, "though not in my line. *Pas de finesse, seulment de l'audace!* A man with a loaded cane smashes the plate-glass window of a jeweler's shop and grabs a number of precious stones. Worthy citizens immediately seize him; a policeman arrives. He is caught red-handed with the jewels on him. He is marched off to the police station, and then it is discovered that the stones are paste. He has passed the real ones to a confederate—one of the aforementioned worthy citizens. He will go to prison—true; but when he comes out, there will be a nice little fortune awaiting him. Yes, not badly imagined. But I could do better than that. Sometimes, Hastings, I regret that I am of such a moral disposition. To work against the law, it would be pleasing, for a change."

"Cheer up, Poirot. You know you are unique in your own line."

"But what is there on hand in my own line?"

I picked up the paper. "Here's an Englishman mysteriously done to death in Holland," I said.

"They always say that—and later they find that he ate the tinned fish and that his death is perfectly natural."

"Well, if you're determined to grouse!"

"*Tiens!*" said Poirot, who had strolled across to the window. "Here in the street is what they call in novels a 'heavily veiled lady.' She mounts the steps; she rings the bell—she comes to consult us. Here is a possibility of something interesting. When one is as young and pretty as that one, one does not veil the face except for a big affair."

A minute later our visitor was ushered in. As Poirot had said, she was indeed heavily veiled. It was impossible to distinguish her features until she raised her veil of black Spanish lace. Then I saw that Poirot's intuition had been right; the lady was extremely pretty, with fair hair and large blue eyes. From the costly simplicity of her attire, I deduced at once that she belonged to an upper stratum of society.

"Monsieur Poirot," said the lady in a soft, musical voice, "I am in great trouble. I can hardly believe that you can help me, but I have heard such wonderful things of you that I come literally as a last hope to beg you to do the impossible."

"The impossible, it pleases me always," said Poirot. "Continue, I beg of you, mademoiselle."

Our fair guest hesitated.

"But you must be frank," added Poirot. "You must not leave me in the dark on any point."

"I will trust you," said the girl suddenly. "You have heard of Lady Millicent Castle Vaughan?"

I looked up with keen interest. The announcement of Lady Millicent's engagement to the young Duke of Southshire had appeared a few days previously. She was, I knew, the fifth daughter of an impecunious Irish peer, and the Duke of Southshire was one of the best matches in England.

"I am Lady Millicent," continued the girl. "You may have read of my engagement. I should be one of the happiest girls alive, but oh, M. Poirot, I am in terrible trouble! There is a man, a horrible man—his name is Lavington; and he—I hardly know how to tell you. There was a letter I wrote—I was only sixteen at the time; and he—he—"

"A letter that you wrote to this Mr. Lavington?"

"Oh, *no*—not to him! To a young soldier—I was very fond of him—he was killed in the war."

"I understand," said Poirot kindly.

"It was a foolish letter, an indiscreet letter, but indeed, M. Poirot, nothing more. But there are phrases in it which—which might bear a different interpretation."

"I see," said Poirot. "And this letter has come into the possession of Mr. Lavington?"

"Yes, and he threatens, unless I pay him an enormous sum of money, a sum that it is quite impossible for me to raise, to send it to the Duke."

"The dirty swine!" I exclaimed. "I beg your pardon, Lady Millicent."

"Would it not be wiser to confess all to your future husband?"

"I dare not, M. Poirot. The Duke is a very jealous man, suspicious and prone to believe the worst. I might as well break off my engagement at once."

"Dear, dear," said Poirot with an expressive grimace. "And what do you want me to do, milady?"

"I thought perhaps that I might ask Mr. Lavington to call upon you. I would tell him that you were empowered by me to discuss the matter. Perhaps you could reduce his demands."

"What sum does he mention?"

"Twenty thousand pounds—an impossibility. I doubt if I could raise even a thousand."

"You might perhaps borrow the money on the prospect of your approaching marriage—but *eh bien*, it is repugnant to me that you should pay! No, the ingenuity of Hercule Poirot shall defeat your enemies! Send me this Mr. Lavington. Is he likely to bring the letter with him?"

The girl shook her head.

"I do not think so. He is very cautious."

"I suppose there is no doubt that he really has it?"

"He showed it to me when I went to his house."

"You went to his house? That was very imprudent, milady."

"Was it? I was so desperate. I hoped my entreaties might move him."

"Oh, *lá lá!* The Lavingtons of this world are not moved by entreaties! He would welcome them as showing how much importance you attached to the document. Where does he live, this fine gentleman?"

"At Buona Vista, Wimbledon. I went there after dark—" Poirot groaned. "I declared that I would inform the police in the end, but he only laughed in a horrid, sneering manner. 'By all means, my dear Lady Millicent, do so if you wish,' he said."

"Yes, it is hardly an affair for the police," murmured Poirot.

" 'But I think you will be wiser than that,' he said. 'See, here is your letter—in this little Chinese puzzle box!' He held it so that I could see. I ried to snatch at it, but he was too quick for me. With a horrid smile he folded it up and replaced it in the little wooden box. 'It will be quite safe here, I assure you,' he said, 'and I keep the box itself in such a clever place that you would never find it.' My eyes turned to the small wall safe, and he shook his head and laughed. 'I have a better safe than that,' he said. Oh, he was odious! Do you think you can help me?"

"Have faith in Papa Poirot. I will find a way."

These reassurances were all very well, I thought, as Poirot gallantly ushered his fair client down the stairs, but it seemed to me that we had a tough nut to crack. I said as much to Poirot when he returned. He nodded ruefully.

"Yes—the solution does not leap to the eye. He has the whip hand, this M. Lavington. For the moment I do not see how we are to circumvent him."

Mr. Lavington duly called on us that afternoon. Lady Millicent had spoken truly when she described him as an odious man. I felt a positive tingling in the end of my boot, so keen was I to kick him down the stairs.

He was blustering and overbearing in manner, laughed Poirot's gentle suggestions to scorn, and generally showed himself as master of the situation. I could not help feeling that Poirot was hardly appearing at his best. He looked discouraged and crestfallen.

"Well, gentlemen," said Lavington, as he took up his hat, "we don't seem to be getting much further. The case stands like this: I'll let the Lady Millicent off cheap, as she is such a charming young lady. We'll say eighteen thousand. I'm off to Paris today— a little piece of business to attend to over there. I shall be back

on Tuesday. Unless the money is paid by Tuesday evening, the letter goes to the Duke. Don't tell me Lady Millicent can't raise the money. Some of her gentlemen friends would be only too willing to oblige such a pretty woman with a loan—if she goes about it the right way."

I took a step forward, but Lavington had wheeled out of the room as he finished his sentence.

"My God!" I cried. "Something has got to be done. You seem to be taking this lying down, Poirot."

"You have an excellent heart, my friend—but your gray cells are in a deplorable condition. I have no wish to impress Mr. Lavington with my capabilities. The more pusillanimous he thinks me, the better."

"Why?"

"It is curious," murmured Poirot reminiscently, "that I should have uttered a wish to work against the law just before Lady Millicent arrived!"

"You are going to burgle his house while he is away?" I gasped.

"Sometimes, Hastings, your mental processes are amazingly quick."

"Suppose he takes the letter with him?"

Poirot shook his head. "That is very unlikely. He has evidently a hiding place in his house that he fancies to be impregnable."

"When do we—er—do the deed?"

"Tomorrow night. We will start from here about eleven o'clock.

At the time appointed I was ready to set off. I had donned a dark suit and a soft dark hat. Poirot beamed kindly on me.

"You have dressed the part, I see," he observed. "Come, let us take the underground to Wimbledon."

"Aren't we going to take anything with us? Tools to break in with?"

"My dear Hastings, Hercule Poirot does not adopt such crude methods."

It was midnight when we entered the small suburban garden of Buona Vista. The house was dark and silent. Poirot went straight to a window at the back of the house, raised the sash noiselessly, and bade me enter.

"How did you know this window would be open?" I whispered, for really it seemed uncanny.

"Because I sawed through the catch this morning."

"What?"

"But yes, it was most simple. I called, presented a fictitious card and one of Inspector Japp's official ones. I said I had been sent, recommended by Scotland Yard, to attend to some burglar-proof fastenings that Mr. Lavington wanted fixed while he was away. The housekeeper welcomed me with enthusiasm. It seems they have had two attempted burglaries here lately—evidently our little idea has occurred to other clients of Mr. Lavington's—with nothing of value taken. I examined all the windows, made my little arrangement, forbade the servants to touch the windows until tomorrow, as they were electrically connected up, and withdrew gracefully."

"Really, Poirot, you are wonderful."

"*Mon ami*, it was of the simplest. Now, to work! The servants sleep at the top of the house, so we will run little risk of disturbing them."

"I presume the safe is built into the wall somewhere?"

"Safe? Fiddlesticks! There is no safe. Mr. Lavington is an intelligent man. You will see, he will have devised a hiding place much more intelligent than a safe. A safe is the first thing everyone looks for."

Whereupon we began a systematic search. But after several hours' ransacking of the house, our search had been unavailing. I saw symptoms of anger gathering on Poirot's face.

"*Ah, sapristi,* is Hercule Poirot to be beaten? Never! Let us be calm. Let us reflect. Let us reason. Let us—*enfin!*—employ our little gray cells!"

He paused for some moments, bending his brows in concentration; then the green light I knew so well stole into his eyes.

"I have been an imbecile! The kitchen!"

"The kitchen," I cried. "But that's impossible. The servants!"

"Exactly. Just what ninety-nine people out of a hundred would say! And for that very reason the kitchen is the ideal place to choose. It is full of various homely objects. *En avant,* to the kitchen!"

I followed him, completely skeptical, and watched while he dived into bread bins, tapped saucepans, and put his head into the gas oven. In the end, tired of watching him, I strolled back to the study. I was convinced that there, and there only, would we find the *cache.* I made a further minute search, noted that it was now a quarter past four and that therefore it would soon be growing light, and then went back to the kitchen regions.

To my utter amazement, Poirot was now standing right inside the coal bin, to the utter ruin of his neat light suit. He made a grimace.

"But yes, my friend, it is against all my instincts so to ruin my appearance, but what will you?"

"Lavington can't have buried it under the coal!"

"If you would use your eyes, you would see that it is not the coal that I examine."

I then saw that on a shelf behind the coal bunker some logs of wood were piled. Poirot was dexterously taking them down one by one. Suddenly he uttered a low exclamation.

"Your knife, Hastings!"

I handed it to him. He appeared to insert it in the wood, and suddenly the log split in two. It had been neatly sawed in half and a cavity hollowed out in the center. From this cavity Poirot took a little wooden box of Chinese make.

"Well done!" I cried.

"Gently, Hastings! Do not raise your voice too much. Come, let us be off before the daylight is upon us."

Slipping the box into his pocket, he leaped lightly out of the coal bunker, and brushed himself down as well as he could. After leaving the house by the same way as we had entered, we walked rapidly in the direction of London.

"But what an extraordinary place!" I expostulated. "Anyone might have used the log."

"In *July*, Hastings? And it was at the bottom of the pile—a very ingenious hiding place. Ah, here is a taxi! Now for home, a wash, and a refreshing sleep."

After the excitement of the night, I slept late. When I finally strolled into our sitting room just before twelve o'clock, I was surprised to see Poirot, leaning back in an armchair, the Chinese box open beside him, calmly reading the letter he had taken from it.

He smiled at me affectionately, and tapped the sheet he held.

"She was right, the Lady Millicent—never would the Duke have pardoned this letter! It contains some of the most extravagant terms of affection I have ever come across."

"Really, Poirot," I said, "I don't think you should have read the letter. That sort of thing isn't done."

"It is done by Hercule Poirot," replied my friend imperturbably.

"And another thing," I said. "I don't think using Japp's official card yesterday was quite playing the game."

"But I was not playing a game, Hastings. I was conducting a case."

I shrugged—one can't argue with a point of view.

"A step on the stairs," said Poirot. "That will be Lady Millicent."

Our fair client came in with an anxious expression on her face which changed to one of delight on seeing the letter and box which Poirot held up.

"Oh, M. Poirot, how wonderful of you! How did you do it?"

"By rather reprehensible methods, milady. But Mr. Lavington will not prosecute. This is your letter, is it not?"

She glanced through it.

"Yes. Oh, how can I ever thank you! You are a wonderful, wonderful man. Where was it hidden?"

Poirot told her.

"How very clever of you!" She took up the small box from the table. "I shall keep this as a souvenir."

"I had hoped, milady, that you would permit me to keep it—also as a souvenir."

"I hope to send you a better souvenir than that—on my wedding day. You shall not find me ungrateful, M. Poirot."

"The pleasure of doing you a service will be more to me than a check—so you permit that I retain the box."

"Oh, no, M. Poirot, I simply must have that," she cried laughingly.

She stretched out her hand, but Poirot's closed over it. "I think not." His voice had changed.

"What do you mean?" Her voice seemed to have grown sharper.

"At any rate, permit me to abstract its further contents. You observe that the original cavity has been reduced by half. In the top half, the compromising letter; in the bottom—"

He made a nimble gesture, then held out his hand. On the palm were four large glittering stones, and two big milky white pearls.

"The jewels stolen in Bond Street the other day, I rather fancy," murmured Poirot. "Japp will tell us."

To my utter amazement Japp himself stepped out of Poirot's bedroom.

"An old friend of yours, I believe," said Poirot politely to Lady Millicent.

"Nabbed, by the Lord!" said Lady Millicent, with a complete change of manner. "You nippy old devil!" She looked at Poirot with almost affectionate awe.

"Well, Gertie, my dear," said Japp, "the game's up this time—fancy seeing you again so soon! We've got your pal, too, the gentleman who called here the other day *calling himself* Lavington. As for Lavington himself, alias Croker, alias Reed, I wonder which of the gang it was who stuck a knife into him the other day in Holland? Thought he'd got the goods with him, didn't you? And he hadn't. He double-crossed you properly—hid 'em in his own house. You had two fellows looking for them, and then you tackled M. Poirot here, and by a piece of amazing luck he found them."

"You do like talking, don't you?" said the late Lady Millicent. "Easy there, now. I'll go quietly. You can't say that I'm not the perfect lady. *Ta-ta*, all!"

"The shoes were wrong," said Poirot dreamily, while I was still too stupefied to speak. "I have made my little observations of your English nation, and a lady, a born lady, is always particular about her shoes. She may have shabby clothes, but she will be well shod. Now, this Lady Millicent had smart, expensive clothes, and cheap shoes. It was not likely that either you or I should have seen the real Lady Millicent; she has been very little in London, and this girl had a certain superficial resemblance which would pass well enough. As I say, the shoes first awakened my suspicions, and then her story—and her veil—were a little melodramatic, eh? The Chinese box with a bogus compromising letter in the top must have been known to all the gang, but the log of wood was the late Mr. Lavington's own idea. *Eh, par exemple,* Hastings, I hope you will not again wound my feelings as you did yesterday by saying that I am unknown to the criminal classes. *Ma foi,* they even employ me when they themselves fail!"

2

The Most Dangerous Game

Richard Connell

"Off there to the right—somewhere—is a large island," said Whitney. "It's rather a mystery—"

"What island is it?" Rainsford asked.

"The old charts call it 'Ship-Trap Island,'" Whitney replied. "A suggestive name, isn't it? Sailors have a curious dread of the place. I don't know why. Some superstition—"

"Can't see it," remarked Rainsford, trying to peer through the dank tropical night that was palpable as it pressed its thick warm blackness in upon the yacht.

"You've good eyes," said Whitney, with a laugh, "and I've seen you pick off a moose moving in the brown fall bush at four hundred yards, but even you can't see four miles or so through a moonless Caribbean night."

"Nor four yards," admitted Rainsford. "Ugh! It's like moist velvet."

"It will be light enough in Rio," promised Whitney. "We should make it in a few days. I hope the jaguar guns have come from Purdey's. We should have some good hunting up the Amazon. Great sport, hunting."

"The best sport in the world," agreed Rainsford.

"For the hunter," amended Whitney. "Not for the jaguar."

"Don't talk rot, Whitney," said Rainsford. "You're a big-game hunter, not a philosopher. Who cares how a jaguar feels?"

"Perhaps the jaguar does," observed Whitney.

"Bah! They've no understanding."

"Even so, I rather think they understand one thing at least— fear. The fear of pain and the fear of death."

"Nonsense," and Rainsford laughed. "This hot weather is making you soft, Whitney. Be a realist. The world is made up of two classes—the hunters and the hunted. Luckily, you and I are hunters. Do you think we've passed that island yet?"

"I can't tell in the dark. I hope so."

"Why?" asked Rainsford.

"The place has a reputation—a bad one."

"Cannibals?" suggested Rainsford.

"Hardly. Even cannibals wouldn't live in such a God-forsaken place. But it's got into sailor lore, somehow. Didn't you notice that the crew's nerves seem a bit jumpy today?"

"They were a bit strange, now you mention it. Even Captain Nielsen—"

"Yes, even that tough-minded old Swede, who'd go up to the devil himself and ask him for a light. Those fishy blue eyes held a look I never saw there before. All I could get out of him was, 'This place has an evil name among seafaring men, sir.' Then he said to me very gravely, 'Don't you feel anything?'—as if the air about us was actually poisonous. Now, you mustn't laugh when I tell you this—I did feel something like a sudden chill.

"There was no breeze. The sea was as flat as a plate-glass window. We were drawing near the island then. What I felt was a— a mental chill—a sort of sudden dread."

"Pure imagination," said Rainsford. "One superstitious sailor can taint the whole ship's company with his fear."

"Maybe. But sometimes I think sailors have an extra sense that tells them when they are in danger. Sometimes I think evil is a tangible thing—with wave lengths, just as sound and light have. An evil place can, so to speak, broadcast vibrations of evil. Anyhow, I'm glad we're getting out of this zone. Well, I think I'll turn in now, Rainsford."

"I'm not sleepy," said Rainsford. "I'm going to smoke another pipe up on the afterdeck."

"Good night, then, Rainsford. See you at breakfast."

"Right. Good night, Whitney."

There was no sound in the night as Rainsford sat there but for the muffled throb of the engine that drove the yacht swiftly through the darkness, and the swish and ripple of the wash of the propeller.

Rainsford, reclining in a steamer chair, indolently puffed on his favorite brier. The sensuous drowsiness of the night was on him. "It's so dark," he thought, "that I could sleep without closing my eyes; the night would be my eyelids—"

An abrupt sound startled him. Off to the right he heard it, and his ears, expert in such matters, could not be mistaken. Again he heard the sound, and again. Somewhere, off in the blackness, someone had fired a gun three times.

Rainsford sprang up and moved quickly to the rail, mystified. He strained his eyes in the direction from which the reports had come, but it was like trying to see through a blanket. He leaped upon the rail and balanced himself there, to get greater elevation; his pipe, striking a rope, was knocked from his mouth. He lunged for it; a short, hoarse cry came from his lips as he realized he had reached too far and had lost his balance. The cry was pinched off short as the blood-warm waters of the Caribbean Sea closed over his head.

He struggled up to the surface and tried to cry out, but the wash from the speeding yacht slapped him in the face and the salt water in his open mouth made him gag and strangle. Desperately he struck out with strong strokes after the receding lights of the yacht, but he stopped before he had swum fifty feet. A certain cool-headedness had come to him; it was not the first time he had been in a tight place. There was a chance that his cries could be heard by someone aboard the yacht, but that chance was slender, and grew more slender as the yacht raced on. He wrestled himself out of his clothes, and shouted with all his power. The lights of the yacht became faint and ever-vanishing fireflies; then they were blotted out entirely by the night.

Rainsford remembered the shots. They had come from the right, and doggedly he swam in that direction, swimming with slow, deliberate strokes, conserving his strength. For a seemingly endless time he fought the sea. He began to count his strokes desperately; he could do possibly a hundred more and then—

Rainsford heard a sound. It came out of the darkness, a high, screaming sound, the sound of an animal in an extremity of anguish and terror.

He did not recognize the animal that made the sound; he did

not try to; with fresh vitality he swam toward the sound. He heard it again; then it was cut short by another noise, crisp, staccato.

"Pistol shot," muttered Rainsford, swimming on.

Ten minutes of determined effort brought another sound to his ears—the most welcome he had ever heard—the muttering and growling of the sea breaking on a rocky shore. He was almost on the rocks before he saw them; on a night less calm he would have been shattered against them. With his remaining strength he dragged himself from the swirling waters. Jagged crags appeared to jut up into the opaqueness; he forced himself upward, hand over hand. Gasping, his hands raw, he reached a flat place at the top. Dense jungle came down to the very edge of the cliffs. What perils that tangle of trees and underbrush might hold for him did not concern Rainsford just then. All he knew was that he was safe from his enemy, the sea, and that utter weariness was on him. He flung himself down at the jungle edge and tumbled headlong into the deepest sleep of his life.

When he opened his eyes he knew from the position of the sun that it was late in the afternoon. Sleep had given him new vigor; a sharp hunger was picking at him. He looked about him, almost cheerfully.

"Where there are pistol shots, there are men. Where there are men, there is food," he thought. But what kind of men, he wondered, in so forbidding a place? An unbroken front of snarled and jagged jungle fringed the shore.

He saw no sign of a trail through the closely knit web of weeds and trees; it was easier to go along the shore, and Rainsford floundered along by the water. Not far from where he had landed, he stopped.

Some wounded thing, by the evidence a large animal, had thrashed about in the underbrush; the jungle weeds were crushed down and the moss was lacerated; one patch of weeds was stained crimson. A small, glittering object not far away caught Rainsford's eye and he picked it up. It was an empty cartridge.

"A twenty-two," he remarked. "That's odd. It must have been a fairly large animal, too. The hunter had his nerve to tackle it with a light gun. It's clear that the brute put up a fight. I suppose the first three shots I heard was when the hunter flushed his quarry and wounded it. The last shot was when he trailed it here and finished it."

He examined the ground closely and found what he had hoped to find—the print of hunting boots. They pointed along the cliff in the direction he had been going. Eagerly he hurried along, now slipping on a rotten log or a loose stone, but making headway; night was beginning to settle down on the island.

Bleak darkness was blacking out the sea and jungle when Rainsford sighted the lights. He came upon them as he turned a crook in the coastline, and his first thought was that he had come upon a village, for there were many lights. But as he forged along he saw to his great astonishment that all the lights were in one enormous building—a lofty structure with pointed towers plunging upward into the gloom. His eyes made out the shadowy outlines of a palatial château; it was set on a high bluff, and on three sides of it cliffs dived down to where the sea licked greedy lips in the shadows.

"Mirage," thought Rainsford. But it was no mirage, he found, when he opened the tall spiked iron gate. The stone steps were real enough; the massive door with a leering gargoyle for a knocker was real enough; yet about it all hung an air of unreality.

He lifted the knocker, and it creaked up stiffly, as if it had never before been used. He let it fall, and it startled him with its booming loudness. He thought he heard footsteps within; the door remained closed. Again Rainsford lifted the heavy knocker, and let it fall. The door opened then, opened as suddenly as if it were on a spring, and Rainsford stood blinking in the river of glaring gold light that poured out. The first thing Rainsford's eyes discerned was the largest man Rainsford had ever seen—a gigantic creature, solidly made and black-bearded to the waist. In his hand the man held a long-barrel revolver, and he was pointing it straight at Rainsford's heart.

Out of the snarl of beard two small eyes regarded Rainsford.

"Don't be alarmed," said Rainsford, with a smile which he hoped was disarming. "I'm no robber. I fell off a yacht. My name is Sanger Rainsford of New York City."

The menacing look in the eyes did not change. The revolver pointed as rigidly as if the giant were a statue. He gave no sign that he understood Rainsford's words, or that he had even heard them. He was dressed in uniform, a black uniform trimmed with gray astrakhan.

"I'm Sanger Rainsford of New York," Rainsford began again. "I fell off a yacht, I am hungry."

The man's only answer was to raise with his thumb the hammer of his revolver. Then Rainsford saw the man's free hand go to his forehead in a military salute, and he saw him click his heels together and stand at attention. Another man was coming down

the broad marble steps, an erect, slender man in evening clothes. He advanced to Rainsford and held out his hand.

In a cultivated voice marked by a slight accent that gave it added precision and deliberateness, he said, "It is a very great pleasure and honor to welcome Mr. Sanger Rainsford, the celebrated hunter, to my home."

Automatically Rainsford shook the man's hand.

"I've read your book about hunting snow leopards in Tibet, you see," explained the man. "I am General Zaroff."

Rainsford's first impression was that the man was singularly handsome; his second was that there was an original, almost bizarre quality about the general's face. He was a tall man past middle age, for his hair was a vivid white; but his thick eyebrows and pointed military mustache were as black as the night from which Rainsford had come. His eyes, too, were black and very bright. He had high cheekbones, a sharp-cut nose, a spare, dark face, the face of a man used to giving orders, the face of an aristocrat. Turning to the giant in uniform, the general made a sign. The giant put away his pistol, saluted, withdrew.

"Ivan is an incredibly strong fellow," remarked the general, "but he has the misfortune to be deaf and dumb. A simple fellow, but I'm afraid, like all his race, a bit of a savage."

"Is he Russian?"

"He is a Cossack," said the general, and his smile showed red lips and pointed teeth. "So am I.

"Come," he said, "we shouldn't be chatting here. We can talk later. Now you want clothes, food, rest. You shall have them. This is a most restful spot."

Ivan had reappeared, and the general spoke to him with lips that moved but gave forth no sound.

"Follow Ivan, if you please, Mr. Rainsford," said the general. "I was about to have my dinner when you came. I'll wait for you. You'll find that my clothes will fit you, I think."

It was to a huge, beam-ceilinged bedroom with a canopied bed big enough for six men that Rainsford followed the silent giant. Ivan laid out an evening suit, and Rainsford, as he put it on, noticed that it came from a London tailor who ordinarily cut and sewed for none below the rank of duke.

The dining room to which Ivan conducted him was in many ways remarkable. There was a medieval magnificence about it; it suggested a baronial hall of feudal times with its oaken panels, its high ceiling, its vast refectory table where twoscore men could sit down to eat. About the hall were the mounted heads of many animals—lions, tigers, elephants, moose, bears; larger or more perfect specimens Rainsford had never seen. At the great table the general was sitting, alone.

"You'll have a cocktail, Mr. Rainsford," he suggested. The cocktail was surpassingly good; and, Rainsford noted, the table appointments were of the finest, the linen, the crystal, the silver, the china.

They were eating *borsch*, the rich, red soup with sour cream so dear to Russian palates. Half apologetically General Zaroff said, "We do our best to preserve the amenities of civilization here. Please forgive any lapses. We are well off the beaten track, you know. Do you think the champagne has suffered from its long ocean trip?"

"Not in the least," declared Rainsford. He was finding the general a most thoughtful and affable host, a true cosmopolite. But there was one small trait of the general's that made Rainsford uncomfortable. Whenever he looked up from his plate he found the general studying him, appraising him narrowly.

"Perhaps," said General Zaroff, "you were surprised that I recognized your name. You see, I read all books on hunting published in English, French, and Russian. I have but one passion in my life, Mr. Rainsford, and it is the hunt."

"You have some wonderful heads here," said Rainsford as he ate a particularly well cooked filet mignon. "That Cape buffalo is the largest I ever saw."

"Oh, that fellow. Yes, he was a monster."

"Did he charge you?"

"Hurled me against a tree," said the general. "Fractured my skull. But I got the brute."

"I've always thought," said Rainsford, "that the Cape buffalo is the most dangerous of all big game."

For a moment the general did not reply; he was smiling his curious red-lipped smile. Then he said slowly, "No. You are wrong, sir. The Cape buffalo is not the most dangerous big game." He sipped his wine. "Here in my preserve on this island," he said in the same slow tone, "I hunt more dangerous game."

Rainsford expressed his surprise. "Is there big game on this island?"

The general nodded. "The biggest."

"Really?"

"Oh, it isn't here naturally, of course. I have to stock the island."

"What have you imported, General?" Rainsford asked. "Tigers?"

The general smiled. "No," he said. "Hunting tigers ceased to interest me some years ago. I exhausted their possibilities, you see. No thrill left in tigers, no real danger. I live for danger, Mr. Rainsford."

The general took from his pocket a gold cigarette case and offered his guest a long black cigarette with a silver tip; it was perfumed and gave off a smell like incense.

"We will have some capital hunting, you and I," said the general. "I shall be most glad to have your society."

"But what game—" began Rainsford.

"I'll tell you," said the general. "You will be amused, I know. I think I may say, in all modesty, that I have done a rare thing. I have invented a new sensation. May I pour you another glass of port, Mr. Rainsford?"

"Thank you, General."

The general filled both glasses, and said, "God makes some men poets. Some He makes kings, some beggars. Me He made a hunter. My hand was made for the trigger, my father said. He was a very rich man with a quarter of a million acres in the Crimea, and he was an ardent sportsman. When I was only five years old he gave me a little gun, specially made in Moscow for me, to shoot sparrows with. When I shot some of his prize turkeys with it, he did not punish me; he complimented me on my marksmanship. I killed my first bear in the Caucasus when I was ten. My whole life has been one prolonged hunt. I went into the army —it was expected of noblemen's sons—and for a time commanded a division of Cossack cavalry, but my real interest was always the hunt. I have hunted every kind of game in every land. It would be impossible for me to tell you how many animals I have killed."

The general puffed at his cigarette.

"After the debacle in Russia I left the country, for it was imprudent for an officer of the Czar to stay there. Many noble Russians lost everything. I, luckily, had invested heavily in American securities, so I shall never have to open a tearoom in Monte Carlo or drive a taxi in Paris. Naturally, I continued to hunt—grizzlies in your Rockies, crocodiles in the Ganges, rhinoceroses in East Africa. It was in Africa that the Cape buffalo hit me and laid me up for six months. As soon as I recovered I started for the Amazon to hunt jaguars, for I had heard they were unusually cunning. They weren't." The Cossack sighed. "They were no match at all for a hunter with his wits about him and a high-powered rifle. I was bitterly disappointed. I was lying in my tent with a splitting headache one night when a terrible thought pushed its way into my mind. Hunting was beginning to bore me! And hunting, remember, had been my life. I have heard that in America businessmen often go to pieces when they give up the business that has been their life."

"Yes, that's so," said Rainsford.

The general smiled. "I had no wish to go to pieces," he said. "I must do something. Now, mine is an analytical mind, Mr. Rainsford. Doubtless that is why I enjoy the problems of the chase."

"No doubt, General Zaroff."

"So," continued the general, "I asked myself why the hunt no longer fascinated me. You are much younger than I am, Mr. Rainsford, and have not hunted as much, but you perhaps can guess the answer."

"What was it?"

"Simply this: hunting had ceased to be what you call 'a sporting proposition.' It had become too easy. I always got my quarry. Always. There is no greater bore than perfection."

The general lit a fresh cigarette.

"No animal had a chance with me any more. That is no boast; it is a mathematical certainty. The animal had nothing but his legs and his instinct. Instinct is no match for reason. When I thought of this it was a tragic moment for me, I can tell you."

Rainsford leaned across the table, absorbed in what his host was saying.

"It came to me as an inspiration what I must do," the general went on.

"And that was?"

The general smiled the quiet smile of one who has faced an obstacle and surmounted it with success. "I had to invent a new animal to hunt," he said.

"A new animal? You are joking."

"Not at all," said the general. "I never joke about hunting. I needed a new animal. I found one. So I bought this island, built this house, and here I do my hunting. The island is perfect for my purposes—there are jungles with a maze of trails in them, hills, swamps—"

"But the animal, General Zaroff?"

"Oh," said the general, "it supplies me with the most exciting hunting in the world. No other hunting compares with it for an instant. Every day I hunt, and I never grow bored now, for I have a quarry with which I can match my wits."

Rainsford's bewilderment showed in his face.

"I wanted the ideal animal to hunt," explained the general. "So I said, 'What are the attributes of an ideal quarry?' And the answer was, of course, 'It must have courage, cunning, and, above all, it must be able to reason.'"

"But no animal can reason," objected Rainsford.

"My dear fellow," said the general, "there is one that can."

"But you can't mean—" gasped Rainsford.

"And why not?"

"I can't believe you are serious, General Zaroff. This is a grisly joke."

"Why should I not be serious? I am speaking of hunting."

"Hunting? Good God, Zaroff, what you speak of is murder."

The general laughed with entire good nature. He regarded Rainsford quizzically. "I refuse to believe that so modern and civilized a young man as you seem to be harbors romantic ideas about the value of human life. Surely your experiences in the war—" He stopped.

"Did not make me condone cold-blooded murder," finished Rainsford stiffly.

Laughter shook the general. "How extraordinarily droll you are!" he said. "One does not expect nowadays to find a young man of the educated class, even in America, with such a naïve, and, if I may say so, mid-Victorian point of view. It's like finding a snuffbox in a limousine. Ah, well, doubtless you had Puritan ancestors. So many Americans appear to have had. I'll wager you'll forget your notions when you go hunting with me. You've a genuine new thrill in store for you, Mr. Rainsford."

"Thank you, I'm a hunter, not a murderer."

"Dear me," said the general, quite unruffled, "again that unpleasant word. But I think I can show you that your scruples are quite ill founded."

"Yes?"

"Life is for the strong, to be lived by the strong, and, if needs be, taken by the strong. The weak of the world were put here to give the strong pleasure. I am strong. Why should I not use my gift? If I wish to hunt, why should I not? I hunt the scum of the earth—sailors from tramp ships—lascars, blacks, Chinese, whites, mongrels—a thoroughbred horse or hound is worth more than a score of them."

"But they are men," said Rainsford hotly.

"Precisely," said the general. "That is why I use them. It gives me pleasure. They can reason, after a fashion. So they are dangerous."

"But where do you get them?"

The general's left eyelid fluttered down in a wink. "This island is called Ship-Trap," he answered. "Sometimes an angry god of the high seas sends them to me. Sometimes, when Providence is not so kind, I help Providence a bit. Come to the window with me."

Rainsford went to the window and looked out toward the sea.

"Watch! Out there!" exclaimed the general, pointing into the night. Rainsford's eyes saw only blackness, and then, as the general pressed a button, far out to sea Rainsford saw the flash of lights.

The general chuckled. "They indicate a channel," he said, "where there's none: giant rocks with razor edges crouch like a sea monster with wide-open jaws. They can crush a ship as easily as I crush this nut." He dropped a walnut on the hardwood floor and brought his heel grinding down on it. "Oh, yes," he said casually, as if in answer to a question, "I have electricity. We try to be civilized here."

"Civilized? And you shoot down men?"

A trace of anger was in the general's black eyes, but it was there for but a second, and he said, in his most pleasant manner: "Dear me, what a righteous young man you are! I assure you I do not do the thing you suggest. That would be barbarous. I treat these visitors with every consideration. They get plenty of good food and exercise. They get into splendid physical condition. You shall see for yourself tomorrow."

"What do you mean?"

"We'll visit my training school." The general smiled. "It's in the cellar. I have about a dozen pupils down there now. They're from the Spanish bark *San Lucar* that had the bad luck to go on the rocks out there. A very inferior lot, I regret to say. Poor specimens, and more accustomed to the deck than to the jungle."

He raised his hand, and Ivan, who served as waiter, brought thick Turkish coffee. Rainsford, with an effort, held his tongue in check.

"It's a game, you see," pursued the general blandly. "I suggest to one of them that we go hunting. I give him a supply of food and an excellent hunting knife. I give him three hours' start. I am to follow, armed only with a pistol of the smallest caliber and range. If my quarry eludes me for three whole days, he wins the game. If I find him—" the general smiled—"he loses."

"Suppose he refuses to be hunted?"

"Oh," said the general, "I give him his option, of course. He need not play that game if he doesn't wish to. If he does not wish to hunt, I turn him over to Ivan. Ivan once had the honor of serving as official knouter to the Great White Czar, and he has his own ideas of sport. Invariably, Mr. Rainsford, invariably they choose the hunt."

"And if they win?"

The smile on the general's face widened. "To date I have not lost," he said.

Then he added, hastily, "I don't wish you to think me a braggart, Mr. Rainsford. Many of them afford only the most elementary sort of problem. Occasionally I strike a tartar. One almost did win. I eventually had to use the dogs."

"The dogs?"

"This way, please. I'll show you."

The general steered Rainsford to a window. The lights from the windows sent a flickering illumination that made grotesque patterns on the courtyard below, and Rainsford could see moving about there a dozen or so huge black shapes; as they turned toward him, their eyes glittered greenly.

"A rather good lot, I think," observed the general. "They are let out at seven every night. If anyone should try to get into my house—or out of it—something extremely regrettable would occur to him." He hummed a snatch of song from the Folies Bergère.

"And now," said the general, "I want to show you my new collection of heads. Will you come with me to the library?"

"I hope," said Rainsford, "that you will excuse me tonight, General Zaroff. I'm really not feeling at all well."

"Ah, indeed?" the general inquired solicitously. "Well, I suppose that's only natural, after your long swim. You need a good, restful night's sleep. Tomorrow you'll feel like a new man, I'll wager. Then we'll hunt, eh? I've one rather promising prospect—"

Rainsford was hurrying from the room.

"Sorry you can't go with me tonight," called the general. "I expect rather fair sport—a big, strong black. He looks resourceful—Well, good night, Mr. Rainsford; I hope that you have a good night's rest."

The bed was good and the pajamas of the softest silk, and he was tired in every fiber of his being, but nevertheless Rainsford could not quiet his brain with the opiate of sleep. He lay, eyes wide open. Once he thought he heard stealthy steps in the corridor outside his room. He sought to throw open the door; it would not open. He went to the window and looked out. His room was high up in one of the towers. The lights of the château were out now, and it was dark and silent, but there was a fragment of sallow moon, and by its wan light he could see, dimly, the court-yard; there, weaving in and out in the pattern of shadow, were black, noiseless forms; the hounds heard him at the window and looked up, expectantly, with their green eyes. Rainsford went back to the bed and lay down. By many methods he tried to put him-self to sleep. He had achieved a doze when, just as morning began to come, he heard, far off in the jungle, the faint report of a pistol.

General Zaroff did not appear until luncheon. He was dressed faultlessly in the tweeds of a country squire. He was solicitous about the state of Rainsford's health.

"As for me," sighed the general, "I do not feel so well. I am worried, Mr. Rainsford. Last night I detected traces of my old complaint."

To Rainsford's questioning glance the general said, "Ennui. Boredom."

Then, taking a second helping of crepes suzette, the general explained, "The hunting was not good last night. The fellow lost his head. He made a straight trail that offered no problems at all. That's the trouble with these sailors; they have dull brains to begin with, and they do not know how to get about in the woods. They do excessively stupid and obvious things. It's most annoying. Will you have another glass of Chablis, Mr. Rainsford?"

"General," said Rainsford firmly, "I wish to leave this island at once."

The general raised his thickets of eyebrows; he seemed hurt. "But, my dear fellow," the general protested, "you've only just come. You've had no hunting—"

"I wish to go today," said Rainsford. He saw the dead black eyes of the general on him, studying him. General Zaroff's face suddenly brightened.

He filled Rainsford's glass with venerable Chablis from a dusty bottle.

"Tonight," said the general, "we will hunt—you and I."

Rainsford shook his head. "No, General," he said. "I will not hunt."

The general shrugged his shoulders and delicately ate a hot-house grape. "As you wish, my friend," he said. "The choice rests entirely with you. But may I not venture to suggest that you will find my idea of sport more diverting than Ivan's?"

He nodded toward the corner to where the giant stood, scowling, his thick arms crossed on his hogshead of chest.

"You don't mean—" cried Rainsford.

"My dear fellow," said the general, "have I not told you I always mean what I say about hunting? This is really an inspiration. I drink to a foeman worthy of my steel—at last."

The general raised his glass, but Rainsford sat staring at him.

"You'll find this game worth playing," the general said enthusiastically. "Your brain against mine. Your woodcraft against mine. Your strength and stamina against mine. Outdoor chess! And the stake is not without value, eh?"

"And if I win—" began Rainsford huskily.

"I'll cheerfully acknowledge myself defeated if I do not find you by midnight of the third day," said General Zaroff. "My sloop will place you on the mainland near a town."

The general read what Rainsford was thinking.

"Oh, you can trust me," said the Cossack. "I will give you my word as a gentleman and a sportsman. Of course you, in turn, must agree to say nothing of your visit here."

"I'll agree to nothing of the kind," said Rainsford.

"Oh," said the general, "in that case— But why discuss it now? Three days hence we can discuss it over a bottle of Veuve Clicquot, unless—"

The general sipped his wine.

Then a businesslike air animated him. "Ivan," he said to Rainsford, "will supply you with hunting clothes, food, a knife. I suggest you wear moccasins; they leave a poorer trail. I suggest too that you avoid the big swamp in the southeast corner of the island. We call it Death Swamp. There's quicksand there. One foolish fellow tried it. The deplorable part of it was that Lazarus followed him. You can imagine my feelings, Mr. Rainsford. I loved Lazarus; he was the finest hound in my pack. Well, I must beg you to excuse me now. I always take a siesta after lunch. You'll hardly have time for a nap, I fear. You'll want to start, no doubt. I shall not follow till dusk. Hunting at night is so much more exciting than by day, don't you think? *Au revoir*, Mr. Rainsford, *au revoir.*"

General Zaroff, with a deep, courtly bow, strolled from the room.

From another door came Ivan. Under one arm he carried khaki hunting clothes, a haversack of food, a leather sheath containing a long-bladed hunting knife; his right hand rested on a cocked revolver thrust in the crimson sash about his waist. . . .

Rainsford had fought his way through the bush for two hours.

"I must keep my nerve. I must keep my nerve," he said through tight teeth.

He had not been entirely clear-headed when the château gates snapped shut behind him. His whole idea at first was to put distance between himself and General Zaroff, and, to this end, he had plunged along, spurred on by the sharp rowels of something very like panic. Now he had got a grip on himself, he had stopped, and was taking stock of himself and the situation.

He saw that straight flight was futile; inevitably it would bring him face to face with the sea. He was in a picture with a frame of water, and his operations, clearly, must take place within that frame.

"I'll give him a trail to follow," muttered Rainsford, and he struck off from the rude path he had been following into the trackless wilderness. He executed a series of intricate loops; he doubled on his trail again and again, recalling all the lore of the fox hunt, and all the dodges of the fox. Night found him leg-weary, with hands and face lashed by the branches, on a thickly wooded ridge. He knew it would be insane to blunder on through the dark, even if he had the strength. His need for rest was imperative and he thought, "I have played the fox, now I must play the cat of the fable." A big tree with a thick trunk and outspread branches was nearby, and, taking care to leave not the slightest mark, he climbed up into the crotch and, stretched out on one of the broad limbs, rested after a fashion. Rest brought him new confidence and almost a feeling of security. Even so zealous a hunter as General Zaroff could not trace him there, he told himself; only the devil himself could follow that complicated trail through the jungle after dark. But, perhaps, the general was a devil—

An apprehensive night crawled slowly by like a wounded snake, and sleep did not visit Rainsford, although the silence of a dead world was on the jungle. Toward morning when a dingy gray was varnishing the sky, the cry of some startled bird focused Rainsford's attention in that direction. Something was coming through the bush, coming slowly, carefully, coming by the same winding way Rainsford had come. He flattened himself down on the limb, and through a screen of leaves almost as thick as tapestry, he watched. The thing that was approaching him was a man.

It was General Zaroff. He made his way along with his eyes fixed in utmost concentration on the ground before him. He paused, almost beneath the tree, dropped to his knees and studied the ground. Rainsford's impulse was to hurl himself down like a panther, but he saw that the general's right hand held something small and metallic—an automatic pistol.

The hunter shook his head several times, as if he were puzzled. Then he straightened up and took from his case one of his black cigarettes; its pungent incense-like smoke floated up to Rainsford's nostrils. Rainsford held his breath. The general's eyes had left the ground and were traveling inch by inch up the tree. Rainsford froze there, every muscle tensed for a spring. But the sharp eyes of the hunter stopped before they reached the limb where Rainsford lay; a smile spread over his brown face. Very deliberately he blew a smoke ring into the air; then he turned his back on the tree and walked carelessly away, back along the trail he had come. The swish of the underbrush against his hunting boots grew fainter and fainter.

The pent-up air burst hotly from Rainsford's lungs. His first thought made him feel sick and numb. The general could follow a trail through the woods at night; he could follow an extremely difficult trail; he must have uncanny powers; only by the merest chance had the Cossack failed to see his quarry.

Rainsford's second thought was even more terrible. It sent a shudder of cold horror through his whole being. Why had the general smiled? Why had he turned back?

Rainsford did not want to believe what his reason told him was true, but the truth was as evident as the sun that had by now pushed through the morning mist. The general was playing with him! The general was saving him for another day's sport! The Cossack was the cat; he was the mouse. Then it was that Rainsford knew the full meaning of terror.

"I will not lose my nerve. I will not."

He slid down from the tree, and struck off again into the woods. His face was set and he forced the machinery of his mind to function. Three hundred yards from his hiding place he stopped where a huge dead tree leaned precariously on a smaller, living one. Throwing off his sack of food, Rainsford took his knife from its sheath and began to work with all his energy.

The job was finished at last, and he threw himself down behind a fallen log a hundred feet away. He did not have to wait long. The cat was coming again to play with the mouse.

Following the trail with the sureness of a bloodhound came General Zaroff. Nothing escaped those searching black eyes, no crushed blade of grass, no bent twig, no mark, no matter how faint, in the moss. So intent was the Cossack on his stalking that he was upon the thing Rainsford had made before he saw it. His foot touched the protruding bough that was the trigger. Even as he touched it, the general sensed his danger and leaped back with the agility of an ape. But he was not quite quick enough; the dead tree, delicately adjusted to rest on the cut living one, crashed down and struck the general a glancing blow on the shoulder as it fell; but for his alertness, he would have been smashed beneath it. He staggered, but he did not fall; nor did he drop his revolver. He stood there, rubbing his injured shoulder, and Rainsford, with fear again gripping his heart, heard the general's mocking laugh ring through the jungle.

"Rainsford," called the general, "if you are within sound of my voice, as I suppose you are, let me congratulate you. Not many men know how to make a Malay man-catcher. Luckily for me, I too have hunted in Malaya. You are proving interesting, Mr. Rainsford. I am going now to have my wound dressed; it's only a slight one. But I shall be back. I shall be back."

When the general, nursing his bruised shoulder, had gone, Rainsford took up his flight again. It was flight now, a desperate, hopeless flight that carried him on for some hours. Dusk came, then darkness, and still he pressed on. The ground grew softer under his moccasins; the vegetation grew ranker; denser; insects bit him savagely. Then, as he stepped forward, his foot sank into the ooze. He tried to wrench it back, but the muck sucked viciously at his foot as if it were a giant leech. With a violent effort, he tore his foot loose. He knew where he was now. Death Swamp and its quicksand.

His hands were tight closed as if his nerve were something tangible that someone in the darkness was trying to tear from his grip. The softness of the earth had given him an idea. He stepped back from the quicksand a dozen feet or so and, like some huge prehistoric beaver, he began to dig.

Rainsford had dug himself in in France when a second's delay meant death. That had been a placid pastime compared to his digging now. The pit grew deeper; when it was above his shoulders, he climbed out and from some hard saplings cut stakes and sharpened them to a fine point. These stakes he planted in the bottom of the pit with the points sticking up. With flying fingers he wove a rough carpet of weeds and branches and with it he covered the mouth of the pit. Then, wet with sweat and aching with tiredness, he crouched behind the stump of a lightning-charred tree.

He knew his pursuer was coming; he heard the padding sound of feet on the soft earth, and the night breeze brought him the perfume of the general's cigarette. It seemed to Rainsford that the general was coming with unusual swiftness; he was not feeling his way along, foot by foot. Rainsford, crouching there, could not see the general, nor could he see the pit. He lived a year in a minute. Then he felt an impulse to cry aloud with joy, for he heard the sharp crackle of the breaking branches as the cover of the pit gave way; he heard the sharp scream of pain as the pointed stakes found their mark. He leaped up from his place of concealment. Then he cowered back. Three feet from the pit a man was standing, with an electric torch in his hand.

"You've done well, Rainsford," the voice of the general called. "Your Burmese tiger pit has claimed one of my best dogs. Again you score. I think, Mr. Rainsford, I'll see what you can do against my whole pack. I'm going home for a rest now. Thank you for a most amusing evening."

At daybreak Rainsford, lying near the swamp, was awakened by a sound that made him know that he had new things to learn about fear. It was a distant sound, faint and wavering, but he knew it. It was the baying of a pack of hounds.

Rainsford knew he could do one of two things. He could stay where he was and wait. That was suicide. He could flee. That was postponing the inevitable. For a moment he stood there, thinking. An idea that held a wild chance came to him, and, tightening his belt, he headed away from the swamp.

The baying of the hounds drew nearer, then still nearer, nearer, ever nearer. On a ridge Rainsford climbed a tree. Down a water-course, not a quarter of a mile away, he could see the bush moving. Straining his eyes, he saw the lean figure of General Zaroff; just ahead of him Rainsford made out another figure whose wide shoulders surged through the tall jungle weeds; it was the giant Ivan, and he seemed pulled forward by some unseen force; Rainsford knew that Ivan must be holding the pack in leash.

They would be on him any minute now. His mind worked frantically. He thought of a native trick he had learned in Uganda. He slid down the tree. He caught hold of a springy young sapling and to it he fastened his hunting knife, with the blade pointing down the trail; with a bit of wild grapevine he tied back the sapling. Then he ran for his life. The hounds raised their voices as they hit the fresh scent. Rainsford knew now how an animal at bay feels.

He had to stop to get his breath. The baying of the hounds stopped abruptly, and Rainsford's heart stopped too. They must have reached the knife.

He shinnied excitedly up a tree and looked back. His pursuers had stopped. But the hope that was in Rainsford's brain when he climbed died, for he saw in the shallow valley that General Zaroff was still on his feet. But Ivan was not. The knife, driven by the recoil of the spring tree, had not wholly failed.

Rainsford had hardly tumbled to the ground when the pack took up the cry again.

"Nerve, nerve, nerve!" he panted, as he dashed along. A blue gap showed between the trees dead ahead. Ever nearer drew the hounds. Rainsford forced himself on toward the gap. He reached it. It was the shore of the sea. Across a cove he could see the gloomy gray stone of the château. Twenty feet below him the sea rumbled and hissed. Rainsford hesitated. He heard the hounds. Then he leaped far out into the sea. . . .

When the general and his pack reached the place by the sea, the Cossack stopped. For some minutes he stood regarding the blue-green expanse of water. He shrugged his shoulders. Then he sat down, took a drink of brandy from a silver flask, lit a perfumed cigarette, and hummed a bit from *Madame Butterfly*.

General Zaroff had an exceedingly good dinner in his great paneled dining hall that evening. With it he had a bottle of Pol Roger and half a bottle of Chambertin. Two slight annoyances kept him from perfect enjoyment. One was the thought that it would be difficult to replace Ivan; the other was that his quarry had escaped him; of course, the American hadn't played the game—so thought the general as he tasted his after-dinner liqueur. In his library he read, to soothe himself, from the works of Marcus Aurelius. At ten he went up to his bedroom. He was deliciously tired, he said to himself, as he locked himself in. There was a little moonlight, so, before turning on his light, he went to the window and looked down at the courtyard. He could see the great hounds, and he called, "Better luck another time," to them. Then he switched on the light.

A man, who had been hiding in the curtains of the bed, was standing there.

"Rainsford!" screamed the general. "How in God's name did you get here?"

"Swam," said Rainsford. "I found it quicker than walking through the jungle."

The general sucked in his breath and smiled. "I congratulate you," he said. "You have won the game."

Rainsford did not smile. "I am still a beast at bay," he said, in a low, hoarse voice. "Get ready, General Zaroff."

The general made one of his deepest bows. "I see," he said. "Splendid! One of us is to furnish a repast for the hounds. The other will sleep in this very excellent bed. On guard, Rainsford. . . ."

He had never slept in a better bed, Rainsford decided.

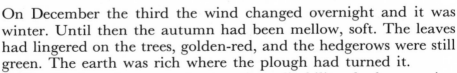

3
The Birds

Daphne du Maurier

On December the third the wind changed overnight and it was winter. Until then the autumn had been mellow, soft. The leaves had lingered on the trees, golden-red, and the hedgerows were still green. The earth was rich where the plough had turned it.

Nat Hocken, because of a wartime disability, had a pension and did not work full time at the farm. He worked three days a week, and they gave him the lighter jobs: hedging, thatching, repairs to the farm buildings.

Although he was married, with children, his was a solitary disposition; he liked best to work alone. It pleased him when he was given a bank to build up, or a gate to mend at the far end of the peninsula, where the sea surrounded the farmland on either side. Then, at midday, he would pause and eat the pasty that his wife had baked for him, and, sitting on the cliff's edge, would watch the birds. Autumn was best for this, better than spring. In spring the birds flew inland, purposeful, intent; they knew where they were bound, the rhythm and ritual of their life brooked no delay. In autumn those that had not migrated overseas but remained to pass the winter were caught up in the same driving urge, but because migration was denied them followed a pattern of their own. Great flocks of them came to the peninsula, restless, uneasy, spending themselves in motion; now wheeling, circling in the sky, now settling to feed on the rich new-turned soil, but even when they fed it was as though they did so without hunger, without desire. Restlessness drove them to the skies again.

Black and white, jackdaw and gull, mingled in strange partnership, seeking some sort of liberation, never satisfied, never still. Flocks of starlings, rustling like silk, flew to fresh pasture, driven by the same necessity of movement, and the smaller birds, the finches and the larks, scattered from tree to hedge as if compelled.

Nat watched them, and he watched the sea birds too. Down in the bay they waited for the tide. They had more patience. Oyster catchers, redshank, sanderling, and curlew watched by the water's edge; as the slow sea sucked at the shore and then withdrew, leaving the strip of seaweed bare and the shingle churned, the sea birds raced and ran upon the beaches. Then that same impulse to flight seized upon them too. Crying, whistling, calling, they skimmed the placid sea and left the shore. Make haste, make speed, hurry and begone; yet where, and to what purpose? The restless urge of autumn, unsatisfying, sad, had put a spell upon them and they must flock, and wheel, and cry; they must spill themselves of motion before winter came.

"Perhaps," thought Nat, munching his pasty by the cliff's edge, "a message comes to the birds in autumn, like a warning. Winter is coming. Many of them perish. And like people who, apprehensive of death before their time, drive themselves to work or folly, the birds do likewise."

The birds had been more restless than ever this fall of the year, the agitation more marked because the days were still. As the tractor traced its path up and down the western hills, the figure of the farmer silhouetted on the driving seat, the whole machine and the man upon it would be lost momentarily in the great cloud of wheeling, crying birds. There were many more than usual, Nat was sure of this. Always, in autumn, they followed the plough, but not in great flocks like these, nor with such clamor.

Nat remarked upon it when hedging was finished for the day. "Yes," said the farmer, "there are more birds about than usual; I've noticed it too. And daring, some of them, taking no notice of the tractor. One or two gulls came so close to my head this afternoon I thought they'd knock my cap off! As it was, I could scarcely see what I was doing when they were overhead and I had the sun in my eyes. I have a notion the weather will change. It will be a hard winter. That's why the birds are restless."

Nat, tramping home across the fields and down the lane to his cottage, saw the birds still flocking over the western hills, in the last glow of the sun. No wind, and the gray sea calm and full. Champion in bloom yet in the hedges, and the air mild. The farmer was right, though, and it was that night the weather turned. Nat's bedroom faced east. He woke just after two and heard the wind in the chimney. Not the storm and bluster of a sou'westerly gale, bringing the rain, but east wind, cold and dry. It sounded hollow in the chimney, and a loose slate rattled on the roof. Nat listened, and he could hear the sea roaring in the bay. Even the air in the small bedroom had turned chill: a draught came under the skirting of the door, blowing upon the bed. Nat drew the blanket around him, leaned closer to the back of his sleeping wife, and stayed wakeful, watchful, aware of misgiving without cause.

Then he heard the tapping on the window. There was no creeper on the cottage walls to break loose and scratch upon the pane. He listened and the tapping continued until, irritated by the sound, Nat got out of bed and went to the window. He opened it, and as he did so something brushed his hand, jabbing at his knuckles, grazing the skin. Then he saw the flutter of the wings and it was gone, over the roof, behind the cottage.

It was a bird; what kind of bird he could not tell. The wind must have driven it to shelter on the sill.

He shut the window and went back to bed but, feeling his knuckles wet, put his mouth to the scratch. The bird had drawn blood. Frightened, he supposed, and bewildered, the bird, seeking shelter, had stabbed at him in the darkness. Once more he settled himself to sleep.

Presently the tapping came again, this time more forceful, more insistent, and now his wife woke at the sound and, turning in the bed, said to him, "See to the window, Nat, it's rattling."

"I've already seen to it," he told her; "there's some bird there trying to get in. Can't you hear the wind? It's blowing from the east, driving the birds to shelter."

"Send them away," she said. "I can't sleep with that noise."

He went to the window for the second time, and now when he opened it there was not one bird upon the sill but half a dozen; they flew straight into his face, attacking him.

He shouted, striking out at them with his arms, scattering them; like the first one, they flew over the roof and disappeared. Quickly he let the window fall and latched it.

"Did you hear that?" he said. "They went for me. Tried to peck my eyes." He stood by the window, peering into the darkness, and could see nothing. His wife, heavy with sleep, murmured from the bed.

"I'm not making it up," he said, angry at her suggestion. "I tell you the birds were on the sill, trying to get into the room."

Suddenly a frightened cry came from the room across the passage where the children slept.

"It's Jill," said his wife, roused at the sound, stitting up in bed. "Go to her, see what's the matter."

Nat lit the candle, but when he opened the bedroom door to cross the passage the draught blew out the flame.

There came a second cry of terror, this time from both children, and stumbling into their room, he felt the beating of wings about him in the darkness. The window was wide open. Through it came the birds, hitting first the ceiling and the walls, then swerving in mid-flight, turning to the children in their beds.

"It's all right, I'm here," shouted Nat, and the children flung themselves, screaming, upon him, while in the darkness the birds rose and dived and came for him again.

"What is it, Nat, what's happened?" his wife called from the farther bedroom, and swiftly he pushed the children through the door to the passage and shut it upon them, so that he was alone now in their bedroom with the birds.

He seized a blanket from the nearest bed and, using it as a weapon, flung it to right and left about him in the air. He felt the thud of bodies, heard the fluttering of wings, but they were not yet defeated, for again and again they returned to the assault, jabbing his hands, his head, the little stabbing beaks sharp as pointed forks. The blanket became a weapon of defence; he wound it about his head, and then in greater darkness beat at the birds with his bare hands. He dared not stumble to the door and open it, lest in doing so the birds should follow him.

How long he fought with them in the darkness he could not tell, but at last the beating of the wings about him lessened and then withdrew, and through the density of the blanket he was aware of light. He waited, listened, there was no sound except the fretful crying of one of the children from the bedroom beyond. The fluttering, the whirring of the wings had ceased.

He took the blanket from his head and stared about him. The cold gray morning light exposed the room. Dawn and the open window had called the living birds; the dead lay on the floor. Nat gazed at the little corpses, shocked and horrified. They were all small birds, none of any size; there must have been fifty of them lying there upon the floor. There were robins, finches, sparrows, blue tits, larks, and bramblings, birds that by nature's law kept to their own flock and their own territory, and now, joining one with another in their urge for battle, had destroyed themselves against the bedroom walls, or in the strife had been destroyed by him. Some had lost feathers in the fight; others had blood, his blood, upon their beaks.

Sickened, Nat went to the window and stared out across his patch of garden to the fields.

It was bitter cold, and the ground had all the hard black look of frost. Not white frost, to shine in the morning sun, but the black frost that the east wind brings. The sea, fiercer now with the turning tide, white-capped and steep, broke harshly in the bay. Of the birds there was no sign. Not a sparrow chattered in the hedge beyond the garden gate, no early missel-thrush or blackbird pecked on the grass for worms. There was no sound at all but the east wind and the sea.

Nat shut the window and the door of the small bedroom, and went back across the passage to his own. His wife sat up in bed, one child asleep beside her, the smaller in her arms, his face bandaged. The curtains were tightly drawn across the window, the candles lit. Her face looked garish in the yellow light. She shook her head for silence.

"He's sleeping now," she whispered, "but only just. Something must have cut him, there was blood at the corner of his eyes. Jill said it was the birds. She said she woke up, and the birds were in the room."

His wife looked up at Nat, searching his face for confirmation. She looked terrified, bewildered, and he did not want her to know that he was also shaken, dazed almost, by the events of the past few hours.

"There are birds in there," he said, "dead birds, nearly fifty of them. Robins, wrens, all the little birds from hereabouts. It's as though a madness seized them with the east wind." He sat down on the bed beside his wife, and held her hand. "It's the weather," he said. "It must be that, it's the hard weather. They aren't the birds, maybe, from here around. They've been driven down from up-country."

"But Nat," whispered his wife, "it's only this night that the weather turned. There's been no snow to drive them. And they can't be hungry yet. There's food for them out there in the fields."

"It's the weather," repeated Nat. "I tell you, it's the weather."

His face, too, was drawn and tired, like hers. They stared at one another for a while without speaking.

"I'll go downstairs and make a cup of tea," he said.

The sight of the kitchen reassured him. The cups and saucers, neatly stacked upon the dresser, the table and chairs, his wife's roll of knitting on her basket chair, the children's toys in a corner cupboard.

He knelt down, raked out the old embers, and relit the fire. The glowing sticks brought normality, the steaming kettle and the brown teapot comfort and security. He drank his tea, carried a cup up to his wife. Then he washed in the scullery, and, putting on his boots, opened the back door.

The sky was hard and leaden, and the brown hills that had gleamed in the sun the day before looked dark and bare. The east wind, like a razor, stripped the trees, and the leaves, crackling and dry, shivered and scattered with the wind's blast. Nat stubbed the earth with his boot. It was frozen hard. He had never known a change so swift and sudden. Black winter had descended in a single night.

The children were awake now. Jill was chattering upstairs and young Johnny crying once again. Nat heard his wife's voice, soothing, comforting. Presently they came down. He had breakfast ready for them, and the routine of the day began.

"Did you drive away the birds?" asked Jill, restored to calm because of the kitchen fire, because of day, because of breakfast.

"Yes, they've all gone now," said Nat. "It was the east wind brought them in. They were frightened and lost, they wanted shelter."

"They tried to peck us," said Jill. "They went for Johnny's eyes."

"Fright made them do that," said Nat. "They didn't know where they were in the dark bedroom."

"I hope they won't come again," said Jill. "Perhaps if we put bread for them outside the window they will eat that and fly away."

She finished her breakfast and then went for her coat and hood, her schoolbooks and her satchel. Nat said nothing, but his wife looked at him across the table. A silent message passed between them.

"I'll walk with her to the bus," he said. "I don't go to the farm today."

And while the child was washing in the scullery he said to his wife, "Keep all the windows closed, and the doors too. Just to be on the safe side. I'll go to the farm. Find out if they heard anything in the night." Then he walked with his small daughter up

the lane. She seemed to have forgotten her experience of the
night before. She danced ahead of him, chasing the leaves, her
face whipped with the cold and rosy under the pixie hood.

"Is it going to snow, Dad?" she said. "It's cold enough."

He glanced up at the bleak sky, felt the wind tear at his
shoulders.

"No," he said, "it's not going to snow. This is a black winter,
not a white one."

All the while he searched the hedgerows for the birds, glanced
over the top of them to the fields beyond, looked to the small
wood above the farm where the rooks and jackdaws gathered. He
saw none.

The other children waited by the bus stop, muffled, hooded
like Jill, the faces white and pinched with cold.

Jill ran to them, waving. "My Dad says it won't snow," she
called. "It's going to be a black winter."

She said nothing of the birds. She began to push and struggle
with another little girl. The bus came ambling up the hill. Nat
saw her on to it, then turned and walked back toward the farm.
It was not his day for work, but he wanted to satisfy himself that
all was well. Jim, the cowman, was clattering in the yard.

"Boss around?" asked Nat.

"Gone to market," said Jim. "It's Tuesday, isn't it?"

He clumped off around the corner of a shed. He had no time
for Nat. Nat was said to be superior. Read books and the like.
Nat had forgotten it was Tuesday. This showed how the events
of the preceding night had shaken him. He went to the back door
of the farmhouse and heard Mrs. Trigg singing in the kitchen, the
wireless making a background to her song.

"Are you there, missus?" called out Nat.

She came to the door, beaming, broad, a good-tempered woman.

"Hullo, Mr. Hocken," she said. "Can you tell me where this
cold is coming from? Is it Russia? I've never seen such a change.
And it's going on, the wireless says. Something to do with the
Arctic Circle."

"We didn't turn on the wireless this morning," said Nat. "Fact
is, we had trouble in the night."

"Kiddies poorly?"

"No . . ." He hardly knew how to explain it. Now, in daylight,
the battle of the birds would sound absurd.

He tried to tell Mrs. Trigg what had happened, but he could
see from her eyes that she thought his story was the result of a
nightmare.

"Sure they were real birds," she said, smiling, "with proper feathers and all? Not the funny-shaped kind that the men see after closing hours on a Saturday night?"

"Mrs. Trigg," he said, "there are fifty dead birds, robins, wrens, and such, lying low on the floor of the children's bedroom. They went for me; they tried to go for young Johnny's eyes."

Mrs. Trigg stared at him doubtfully.

"Well there, now," she answered, "I suppose the weather brought them. Once in the bedroom, they wouldn't know where they were to. Foreign birds maybe, from that Arctic Circle."

"No," said Nat, "they were the birds you see about here every day."

"Funny thing," said Mrs. Trigg, "no explaining it, really. You ought to write up and ask the *Guardian*. They'd have some answer for it. Well, I must be getting on."

She nodded, smiled, and went back into the kitchen.

Nat, dissatisfied, turned to the farm gate. Had it not been for those corpses on the bedroom floor, which he must now collect and bury somewhere, he would have considered the tale exaggeration too.

Jim was standing by the gate.

"Had any trouble with the birds?" asked Nat.

"Birds? What birds?"

"We got them up our place last night. Scores of them, came in the children's bedroom. Quite savage they were."

"Oh?" It took time for anything to penetrate Jim's head. "Never heard of birds acting savage," he said at length. "They get tame-like, sometimes. I've seen them come to the windows for crumbs."

"These birds last night weren't tame."

"No? Cold, maybe. Hungry. You put out some crumbs."

Jim was no more interested than Mrs. Trigg had been. It was, Nat thought, like air raids in the war. None down this end of the country knew what the Plymouth folk had seen and suffered. You had to endure something yourself before it touched you. He walked back along the lane and crossed the stile to his cottage. He found his wife in the kitchen with young Johnny.

"See anyone?" she asked.

"Mrs. Trigg and Jim," he answered. "I don't think they believed me. Anyway, nothing wrong up there."

"You might take the birds away," she said. "I daren't go into the room to make the beds until you do. I'm scared."

"Nothing to scare you now," said Nat. "They're dead, aren't they?"

He went up with a sack and dropped the stiff bodies into it, one by one. Yes, there were fifty of them, all told. Just the ordinary common birds of the hedgerow, nothing as large even as a thrush. It must have been fright that made them act the way they did. Blue tits, wrens—it was incredible to think of the power of their small beaks jabbing at his face and hands the night before. He took the sack out into the garden and was faced now with a fresh problem. The ground was too hard to dig. It was frozen solid, yet no snow had fallen, nothing had happened in the past hours but the coming of the east wind. It was unnatural, queer. The weather prophets must be right. The change was something connected with the Arctic Circle.

The wind seemed to cut him to the bone as he stood there uncertainly, holding the sack. He could see the white-capped seas breaking down under in the bay. He decided to take his birds to the shore and bury them.

When he reached the beach below the headland he could hardly stand, the force of the east wind was so strong. It hurt to draw breath, and his bare hands were blue. Never had he known such cold, not in all the bad winters he could remember. It was low tide. He crunched his way over the shingle to the softer sand and then, his back to the wind, ground a pit in the sand with his heel. He meant to drop the birds into it, but as he opened up the sack the force of the wind carried them, lifted them, as though in flight again, and they were blown away from him along the beach, tossed like feathers, spread and scattered, the bodies of the fifty frozen birds. There was something ugly in the sight. He did not like it. The dead birds were swept away from him by the wind.

"The tide will take them when it turns," he said to himself.

He looked out to sea and watched the crested breakers, combing green. They rose stiffly, curled, and broke again, and because it was ebb tide the roar was distant, more remote, lacking the sound and thunder of the flood.

Then he saw them. The gulls. Out there, riding the seas.

What he had thought at first to be the whitecaps of the waves were gulls. Hundreds, thousands, tens of thousands . . . They rose and fell in the trough of the seas, heads to the wind, like a mighty fleet at anchor, waiting on the tide. To eastward, and to the west, the gulls were there. They stretched as far as his eye could reach, in close formation, line upon line. Had the sea been still they would have covered the bay like a white cloud, head to head, body packed to body. Only the east wind, whipping the sea to breakers, hid them from the shore.

Nat turned and, leaving the beach, climbed the steep path home. Someone should know of this. Someone should be told. Something was happening, because of the wind and the weather, that he did not understand. He wondered if he should go to the call box by the bus stop and ring up the police. Yet what could they do? What could anyone do? Tens and thousands of gulls riding the sea there in the bay because of storm, because of hunger. The police would think him mad, or drunk, or take the statement from him with great calm. "Thank you. Yes, the matter has already been reported. The hard weather is driving the birds inland in great numbers." Nat looked about him. Still no sign of any other bird. Perhaps the cold had sent them all from upcountry? As he drew near to the cottage his wife came to meet him at the door. She called to him, excited. "Nat," she said, "it's on the wireless. They've just read out a special news bulletin. I've written it down."

"What's on the wireless?" he said.

"About the birds," she said. "It's not only here, it's everywhere. In London, all over the country. Something has happened to the birds."

Together they went into the kitchen. He read the piece of paper lying on the table.

"Statement from the Home Office at 11 A.M. today. Reports from all over the country are coming in hourly about the vast quantity of birds flocking above towns, villages, and outlying districts, causing obstruction and damage and even attacking individuals. It is thought that the Arctic air stream, at present covering the British Isles, is causing birds to migrate south in immense numbers, and that intense hunger may drive these birds to attack human beings. Householders are warned to see to their windows, doors, and chimneys, and to take reasonable precautions for the safety of their children. A further statement will be issued later."

A kind of excitement seized Nat; he looked at his wife in triumph.

"There you are," he said. "Let's hope they'll hear that at the farm. Mrs. Trigg will know it wasn't any story. It's true. All over the country. I've been telling myself all morning there's something wrong. And just now, down on the beach, I looked out to sea and there are gulls, thousands of them, tens of thousands—you couldn't put a pin between their heads—and they're all out there, riding on the sea, waiting."

"What are they waiting for, Nat?" she asked.

He stared at her, then looked down again at the piece of paper.

"I don't know," he said slowly. "It says here the birds are hungry."

He went over to the drawer where he kept his hammer and tools.

"What are you going to do, Nat?"

"See to the windows and the chimneys too, like they tell you."

"You think they would break in, with the windows shut? Those sparrows and robins and such? Why, how could they?"

He did not answer. He was not thinking of the robins and the sparrows. He was thinking of the gulls. . . .

He went upstairs and worked there the rest of the morning, boarding the windows of the bedrooms, filling up the chimney bases. Good thing it was his free day and he was not working at the farm. It reminded him of the old days, at the beginning of the war. He was not married then, and he had made all the black-out boards for his mother's house in Plymouth. Made the shelter too. Not that it had been of any use when the moment came. He wondered if they would take these precautions up at the farm. He doubted it. Too easygoing, Harry Trigg and his missus. Maybe they'd laugh at the whole thing. Go off to a dance or a whist drive.

"Dinner's ready." She called him, from the kitchen.

"All right. Coming down."

He was pleased with his handiwork. The frames fitted nicely over the little panes and at the bases of the chimneys.

When dinner was over and his wife was washing up, Nat switched on the one o'clock news. The same announcement was repeated, the one which she had taken down during the morning, but the news bulletin enlarged upon it. "The flocks of birds have caused dislocation in all areas," read the announcer, "and in London the sky was so dense at ten o'clock this morning that it seemed as if the city was covered by a vast black cloud.

"The birds settled on rooftops, on window ledges, and on chimneys. The species included blackbirds, thrush, the common house sparrow, and, as might be expected in the metropolis, a vast quantity of pigeons and starlings, and that frequenter of the London river, the black-headed gull. The sight has been so unusual that traffic came to a standstill in many thoroughfares, work was abandoned in shops and offices, and the streets and pavements were crowded with people standing about to watch the birds."

Various incidents were recounted, the suspected reason of cold and hunger started again, and warnings to householders repeated. The announcer's voice was smooth and suave. Nat had the impression that this man, in particular, treated the whole business as he would an elaborate joke. There would be others like him, hundreds of them, who did not know what it was to struggle in darkness with a flock of birds. There would be parties tonight in London, like the ones they gave on election nights. People standing about, shouting and laughing. "Come and watch the birds!"

Nat switched off the wireless. He got up and started work on the kitchen windows. His wife watched him, young Johnny at her heels.

"What, boards for down here too?" she said. "Why, I'll have to light up before three o'clock. I see no call for boards down here."

"Better be sure than sorry," answered Nat. "I'm not going to take any chances."

"What they ought to do," she said, "is to call the Army out and shoot the birds. That would soon scare them off."

"Let them try," said Nat. "How'd they set about it?"

"They have the Army to the docks," she answered, "when the dockers strike. The soldiers go down and unload the ships."

"Yes," said Nat, "and the population of London is eight million or more. Think of all the buildings, all the flats and houses. Do you think they've enough soldiers to go round shooting birds from every roof?"

"I don't know. But something should be done. They ought to do something."

Nat thought to himself that "they" were no doubt considering the problem at that very moment, but whatever "they" decided to do in London and the big cities would not help the people here, three hundred miles away. Each householder must look after his own.

"How are we off for food?" he said.

"Now, Nat, whatever next?"

"Never mind. What have you got in the larder?"

"It's shopping day tomorrow, you know that. I don't keep uncooked food hanging about, it goes off. Butcher doesn't call till the day after. But I can bring back something when I go in tomorrow."

Nat did not want to scare her. He thought it possible that she might not go to town tomorrow. He looked in the larder for himself, and in the cupboard where she kept her tins. They would do for a couple of days. Bread was low.

"What about the baker?"

"He comes tomorrow too."

He saw she had flour. If the baker did not call she had enough to bake one loaf.

"We'd be better off in old days," he said, "when the women baked twice a week, and had pilchards salted, and there was food for a family to last a siege, if need be."

"I've tried the children with tinned fish, they don't like it," she said.

Nat went on hammering the boards across the kitchen windows. Candles. They were low on candles too. That must be another thing she meant to buy tomorrow. Well, it could not be helped. They must go to bed early tonight. That was, if . . .

He got up and went out of the back door and stood in the garden, looking down toward the sea. There had been no sun all day, and now, at barely three o'clock, a kind of darkness had already come, the sky sullen, heavy, colorless like salt. He could hear the vicious sea drumming on the rocks. He walked down the path, halfway to the beach. And then he stopped. He could see the tide had turned. The rock that had shown in midmorning was now covered, but it was not the sea that held his eyes. The gulls had risen. They were circling, hundreds of them, thousands of them, lifting their wings against the wind. It was the gulls that made the darkening of the sky. And they were silent. They made not a sound. They just went on soaring and circling, rising, falling, trying their strength against the wind.

Nat turned. He ran up the path, back to the cottage.

"I'm going for Jill," he said. "I'll wait for her at the bus stop."

"What's the matter?" asked his wife. "You've gone quite white."

"Keep Johnny inside," he said. "Keep the door shut. Light up now, and draw the curtains."

"It's only just gone three," she said.

"Never mind. Do what I tell you."

He looked inside the tool shed outside the back door. Nothing there of much use. A spade was too heavy, and a fork no good. He took the hoe. It was the only possible tool, and light enough to carry.

He started walking up the lane to the bus stop, and now and again glanced back over his shoulder.

The gulls had risen higher now, their circles were broader, wider, they were spreading out in huge formation across the sky.

He hurried on; although he knew the bus would not come to

the top of the hill before four o'clock he had to hurry. He passed no one on the way. He was glad of this. No time to stop and chatter.

At the top of the hill he waited. He was much too soon. There was half an hour still to go. The east wind came whipping across the fields from the higher ground. He stamped his feet and blew upon his hands. In the distance he could see the clay hills, white and clean, against the heavy pallor of the sky. Something black rose from behind them, like a smudge at first, then widening, becoming deeper, and the smudge became a cloud, and the cloud divided again into five other clouds, spreading north, east, south, and west, and they were not clouds at all; they were birds. He watched them travel across the sky, and as one section passed overhead, within two or three hundred feet of him, he knew, from their speed, they were bound inland, upcountry; they had no business with the people here on the peninsula. They were rooks, crows, jackdaws, magpies, jays, all birds that usually preyed upon the smaller species; but this afternoon they were bound on some other mission.

"They've been given the towns," thought Nat; "they know what they have to do. We don't matter so much here. The gulls will serve for us. The others go to the towns."

He went to the call box, stepped inside, and lifted the receiver. The exchange would do. They would pass the message on.

"I'm speaking from Highway," he said, "by the bus stop. I want to report large formations of birds traveling upcountry. The gulls are also forming in the bay."

"All right," answered the voice, laconic, weary.

"You'll be sure and pass the message on to the proper quarter?"

"Yes . . . yes . . ." Impatient now, fed-up. The buzzing note resumed.

"She's another," thought Nat, "she doesn't care. Maybe she's had to answer calls all day. She hopes to go to the pictures to-night. She'll squeeze some fellow's hand, and point up at the sky, and 'Look at all them birds!' She doesn't care."

The bus came lumbering up the hill. Jill climbed out, and three or four other children. The bus went on toward the town.

"What's the hoe for, Dad?"

They crowded around him, laughing, pointing.

"I just brought it along," he said. "Come on now, let's get home. It's cold, no hanging about. Here, you. I'll watch you across the fields, see how fast you can run."

He was speaking to Jill's companions, who came from different

families, living in the council houses. A short cut would take them
to the cottages.

"We want to play a bit in the lane," said one of them.

"No you don't. You go off home or I'll tell your Mammy."

They whispered to one another, round-eyed, then scuttled off
across the fields. Jill stared at her father, her mouth sullen.

"We always play in the lane," she said.

"Not tonight you don't," he said. "Come on now, no dawdling."

He could see the gulls now, circling the fields, coming in toward
the land. Still silent. Still no sound.

"Look, Dad, look over there, look at all the gulls."

"Yes. Hurry, now."

"Where are they flying to? Where are they going?"

"Upcountry, I dare say. Where it's warmer."

He seized her hand and dragged her after him along the lane.

"Don't go so fast. I can't keep up."

The gulls were copying the rooks and crows. They were spreading out in formation across the sky. They headed, in bands of
thousands, to the four compass points.

"Dad, what is it? What are the gulls doing?"

They were not intent upon their flight, as the crows, as the
jackdaws had been. They still circled overhead. Nor did they fly
so high. It was as though they waited upon some signal. As though
some decision had yet to be given. The order was not clear.

"Do you want me to carry you, Jill? Here, come pick-a-back."

This way he might put on speed; but he was wrong. Jill was
heavy. She kept slipping. And she was crying too. His sense of
urgency, of fear, had communicated itself to the child.

"I wish the gulls would go away. I don't like them. They're
coming closer to the lane."

He put her down again. He started running, swinging Jill after
him. As they went past the farm turning he saw the farmer back-
ing his car out of the garage. Nat called to him.

"Can you give us a lift?" he said.

"What's that?"

Mr. Trigg turned in the driving seat and stared at them. Then
a smile came to his cheerful, rubicund face.

"It looks as though we're in for some fun," he said. "Have you
seen the gulls? Jim and I are going to take a crack at them. Everyone's gone bird-crazy, talking of nothing else. I hear you were
troubled in the night. Want a gun?"

Nat shook his head.

The small car was packed. There was just room for Jill, if she crouched on top of the petrol tins on the back seat.

"I don't want a gun," said Nat, "but I'd be obliged if you'd run Jill home. She's scared of the birds."

He spoke briefly. He did not want to talk in front of Jill.

"O.K.," said the farmer, "I'll take her home. Why don't you stop behind and join the shooting match? We'll make the feathers fly."

Jill climbed in, and turning the car, the driver sped up the lane. Nat followed after. Trigg must be crazy. What use was a gun against a sky of birds?

Now that Nat was not responsible for Jill, he had time to look about him. The birds were still circling above the fields. Mostly herring gull, but the black-backed gull among them. Usually they kept apart. Now they were united. Some bond had brought them together. It was the black-backed gull that attacked the smaller birds, and even newborn lambs, so he'd heard. He'd never seen it done. He remembered this now, though, looking above him in the sky. They were coming in toward the farm. They were circling lower in the sky, and the black-backed gulls were to the front, the black-backed gulls were leading. The farm, then, was their target. They were making for the farm.

Nat increased his pace toward his own cottage. He saw the farmer's car turn and come back along the lane. It drew up beside him with a jerk.

"The kid has run inside," said the farmer. "Your wife was watching for her. Well, what do you make of it? They're saying in town the Russians have done it. The Russians have poisoned the birds."

"How could they do that?" asked Nat.

"Don't ask me. You know how stories get around. Will you join my shooting match?"

"No, I'll get along home. The wife will be worried."

"My missus says if you could eat gull there'd be some sense in it," said Trigg. "We'd have roast gull, baked gull, and pickle 'em into the bargain. You wait until I let off a few barrels into the brutes. That'll scare 'em."

"Have you boarded your windows?" asked Nat.

"No. Lot of nonsense. They like to scare you on the wireless. I've had more to do today than to go round boarding up my windows."

"I'd board them now, if I were you."

"Garn. You're windy. Like to come to our place to sleep?"

"No, thanks all the same."

"All right. See you in the morning. Give you a gull breakfast."

The farmer grinned and turned his car to the farm entrance.

Nat hurried on. Past the little wood, past the old barn, and then across the stile to the remaining field.

As he jumped the stile he heard the whir of wings. A black-backed gull dived down at him from the sky, missed, swerved in flight, and rose to dive again. In a moment it was joined by others, six, seven, a dozen, black-backed and herring mixed. Nat dropped his hoe. The hoe was useless. Covering his head with his arms, he ran toward the cottage. They kept coming at him from the air, silent save for the beating wings. The terrible, fluttering wings. He would feel the blood on his hands, his wrists, his neck. Each stab of a swooping beak tore his flesh. If only he could keep them from his eyes. Nothing else mattered. He must keep them from his eyes. They had not learned yet how to cling to a shoulder, how to rip clothing, how to dive in mass upon the head, upon the body. But with each dive, with each attack, they became bolder. And they had no thought for themselves. When they dived low and missed, they crashed, bruised and broken, on the ground. As Nat ran he stumbled, kicking their spent bodies in front of him.

He found the door; he hammered upon it with his bleeding hands. Because of the boarded windows no light shone. Everything was dark.

"Let me in," he shouted. "I'ts Nat. Let me in."

He shouted loud to make himself heard above the whir of the gulls' wings.

Then he saw the gannet, poised for the dive, above him in the sky. The gulls circled, retired, soared, one after another, against the wind. Only the gannet remained. One single gannet above him in the sky. The wings folded suddenly to its body. It dropped like a stone. Nat screamed, and the door opened. He stumbled across the threshold, and his wife threw her weight against the door.

They heard the thud of the gannet as it fell.

His wife dressed his wounds. They were not deep. The backs of his hands had suffered most, and his wrists. Had he not worn a cap they would have reached his head. As to the gannet . . . the gannet could have split his skull.

The children were crying, of course. They had seen the blood on their father's hands.

"It's all right now," he told them. "I'm not hurt. Just a few scratches. You play with Johnny, Jill. Mammy will wash these cuts."

He half shut the door to the scullery so that they could not see. His wife was ashen. She began running water from the sink.

"I saw them overhead," she whispered. "They began collecting just as Jill ran in with Mr. Trigg. I shut the door fast, and it jammed. That's why I couldn't open it at once when you came."

"Thank God they waited for me," he said. "Jill would have fallen at once. One bird alone would have done it."

Furtively, so as not to alarm the children, they whispered together as she bandaged his hands and the back of his neck.

"They're flying inland," he said, "thousands of them. Rooks, crows, all the bigger birds. I saw them from the bus stop. They're making for the towns."

"But what can they do, Nat?"

"They'll attack. Go for everyone out in the streets. Then they'll try the windows, the chimneys."

"Why don't the authorities do something? Why don't they get the Army, get machine guns, anything?"

"There's been no time. Nobody's prepared. We'll hear what they have to say on the six o'clock news."

Nat went back into the kitchen, followed by his wife. Johnny was playing quietly on the floor. Only Jill looked anxious.

"I can hear the birds," she said. "Listen, Dad."

Nat listened. Muffled sounds came from the windows, from the door. Wings brushing the surface, sliding, scraping, seeking a way of entry. The sound of many bodies, pressed together, shuffling on the sills. Now and again came a thud, a crash, as some bird dived and fell. "Some of them will kill themselves that way," he thought, "but not enough. Never enough."

"All right," he said aloud, "I've got boards over the windows, Jill. The birds can't get in."

He went and examined all the windows. His work had been thorough. Every gap was closed. He would make extra certain, however. He found wedges, pieces of old tin, strips of wood and metal, and fastened them at the sides to reinforce the boards. His hammering helped to deafen the sound of the birds, the shuffling, the tapping, and more ominous—he did not want his wife or the children to hear it—the splinter of cracked glass.

"Turn on the wireless," he said. "Let's have the wireless."

This would drown the sound also. He went upstairs to the bedrooms and reinforced the windows there. Now he could hear the birds on the roof, the scraping of claws, a sliding, jostling sound.

He decided they must sleep in the kitchen, keep up the fire, bring down the mattresses, and lay them out on the floor. He was afraid of the bedroom chimneys. The boards he had placed at the chimney bases might give way. In the kitchen they would be safe because of the fire. He would have to make a joke of it. Pretend to the children they were playing at camp. If the worst happened, and the birds forced an entry down the bedroom chimneys, it would be hours, days perhaps, before they could break down the doors. The birds would be imprisoned in the bedrooms. They could do no harm there. Crowded together, they would stifle and die.

He began to bring the mattresses downstairs. At sight of them his wife's eyes widened in apprehension. She thought the birds had already broken in upstairs.

"All right," he said cheerfully, "we'll all sleep together in the kitchen tonight. More cozy here by the fire. Then we shan't be worried by those silly old birds tapping at the windows."

He made the children help him rearrange the furniture, and he took the precaution of moving the dresser, with his wife's help, across the window. It fitted well. It was an added safeguard. The mattresses could now be lain, one beside the other, against the wall where the dresser had stood.

"We're safe enough now," he thought. "We're snug and tight, like an air-raid shelter. We can hold out. It's just the food that worries me. Food, and coal for the fire. We've enough for two or three days, not more. By that time . . ."

No use thinking ahead as far as that. And they'd be giving directions on the wireless. People would be told what to do. And now, in the midst of many problems, he realized that it was dance music only coming over the air. Not Children's Hour, as it should have been. He glanced at the dial. Yes, they were on the Home Service all right. Dance records. He switched to the Light program. He knew the reason. The usual programs had been abandoned. This only happened at exceptional times. Elections and such. He tried to remember if it had happened in the war, during the heavy raids on London. But of course. The B.B.C. was not stationed in London during the war. The programs were broadcast from other, temporary quarters. "We're better off here," he thought; "we're better off here in the kitchen, with the windows and the doors boarded, than they are up in the towns. Thank God we're not in the towns."

At six o'clock the records ceased. The time signal was given. No matter if it scared the children, he must hear the news. There was a pause after the pips. Then the announcer spoke. His voice was solemn, grave. Quite different from midday.

"This is London," he said. "A National Emergency was proclaimed at four o'clock this afternoon. Measures are being taken to safeguard the lives and property of the population, but it must be understood that these are not easy to effect immediately, owing to the unforeseen and unparalleled nature of the present crisis. Every householder must take precautions to his own building, and where several people live together, as in flats and apartments, they must unite to do the utmost they can to prevent entry. It is absolutely imperative that every individual stay indoors tonight and that no one at all remain on the streets, or roads, or anywhere without doors. The birds, in vast numbers, are attacking anyone on sight, and have already begun an assault upon buildings; but these, with due care, should be impenetrable. The population is asked to remain calm and not to panic. Owing to the exceptional nature of the emergency, there will be no further transmission from any broadcasting station until 7 A.M. tomorrow."

They played the National Anthem. Nothing more happened. Nat switched off the set. He looked at his wife. She stared back at him.

"What's it mean?" said Jill. "What did the news say?"

"There won't be any more programs tonight," said Nat. "There's been a breakdown at the B.B.C."

"Is it the birds?" asked Jill. "Have the birds done it?"

"No," said Nat, "it's just that everyone's very busy, and then of course they have to get rid of the birds, messing everything up, in the towns. Well, we can manage without the wireless for one evening."

"I wish we had a gramophone," said Jill. "That would be better than nothing."

She had her face turned to the dresser backed against the windows. Try as they did to ignore it, they were all aware of the shuffling, the stabbing, the persistent beating and sweeping of wings.

"We'll have supper early," suggested Nat. "Something for a treat. Ask Mammy. Toasted cheese, eh? Something we all like?"

He winked and nodded at his wife. He wanted the look of dread, of apprehension, to go from Jill's face.

He helped with the supper, whistling, singing, making as much clatter as he could, and it seemed to him that the shuffling and the tapping were not so intense as they had been at first. Presently he went up to the bedrooms and listened, and he no longer heard the jostling for place upon the roof.

"They've got reasoning powers," he thought; "they know it's

hard to break in here. They'll try elsewhere. They won't waste their time with us."

Supper passed without incident, and then, when they were clearing away, they heard a new sound, droning, familiar, a sound they all knew and understood.

His wife looked up at him, her face alight. "It's planes," she said. "They're sending out planes after the birds. That's what I said they ought to do all along. That will get them. Isn't that gunfire? Can't you hear guns?"

It might be gunfire out at sea. Nat could not tell. Big naval guns might have an effect upon the gulls out at sea, but the gulls were inland now. The guns couldn't shell the shore because of the population.

"It's good, isn't it," said his wife, "to hear the planes?" And Jill, catching her enthusiasm, jumped up and down with Johnny. "The planes will get the birds. The planes will shoot them."

Just then they heard a crash about two miles distant, followed by a second, then a third. The droning became more distant, passed away out to sea.

"What was that?" asked his wife. "Were they dropping bombs on the birds?"

"I don't know," answered Nat. "I don't think so."

He did not want to tell her that the sound they had heard was the crashing of aircraft. It was, he had no doubt, a venture on the part of the authorities to send out reconnaissance forces, but they might have known the venture was suicidal. What could aircraft do against birds that flung themselves to death against propeller and fuselage, but hurtle to the ground themselves? This was being tried now, he supposed, over the whole country. And at a cost. Someone high up had lost his head.

"Where have the planes gone, Dad?" asked Jill.

"Back to base," he said. "Come on, now, time to truck down for bed."

It kept his wife occupied, undressing the children before the fire, seeing to the bedding, one thing and another, while he went around the cottage again, making sure that nothing had worked loose. There was no further drone of aircraft, and the naval guns had ceased. "Waste of life and effort," Nat said to himself. "We can't destroy enough of them that way. Cost too heavy. There's always gas. Maybe they'll try spraying with gas, mustard gas. We'll be warned first, of course, if they do. There's one thing, the best brains of the country will be on to it tonight."

Somehow the thought reassured him. He had a picture of scientists, naturalists, technicians, and all those chaps they called the back-room boys, summoned to a council; they'd be working on the problem now. This was not a job for the government, for the chiefs of staff—they would merely carry out the orders of the scientists.

"They'll have to be ruthless," he thought. "Where the trouble's worst they'll have to risk more lives, if they use gas. All the livestock, too, and the soil—all contaminated. As long as everyone doesn't panic. That's the trouble. People panicking, losing their heads. The B.B.C. was right to warn us of that."

Upstairs in the bedrooms all was quiet. No further scraping and stabbing at the windows. A lull in battle. Forces regrouping. Wasn't that what they called it in the old wartime bulletins? The wind hadn't dropped, though. He could still hear it roaring in the chimneys. And the sea breaking down on the shore. Then he remembered the tide. The tide would be on the turn. Maybe the lull in battle was because of the tide. There was some law the birds obeyed, and it was all to do with the east wind and the tide.

He glanced at his watch. Nearly eight o'clock. It must have gone high water an hour ago. That explained the lull: the birds attacked with the flood tide. It might not work that way inland, upcountry, but it seemed as if it was so this way on the coast. He reckoned the time limit in his head. They had six hours to go without attack. When the tide turned again, around one-twenty in the morning, the birds would come back. . . .

There were two things he could do. The first was to rest, with his wife and the children, and all of them snatch what sleep they could, until the small hours. The second was to go out, see how they were faring at the farm, see if the telephone was still working there, so that they might get news from the exchange.

He called softly to his wife, who had just settled the children. She came halfway up the stairs and he whispered to her.

"You're not to go," she said at once. "You're not to go and leave me alone with the children. I can't stand it."

Her voice rose hysterically. He hushed her, calmed her.

"All right," he said, "all right. I'll wait till morning. And we'll get the wireless bulletin then too, at seven. But in the morning, when the tide ebbs again, I'll try for the farm, and they may let us have bread and potatoes, and milk too."

His mind was busy again, planning against emergency. They would not have milked, of course, this evening. The cows would be standing by the gate, waiting in the yard, with the household inside, battened behind boards, as they were here at the cottage. That is, if they had time to take precautions. He thought of the farmer,

Trigg, smiling at him from the car. There would have been no shooting party, not tonight.

The children were asleep. His wife, still clothed, was sitting on her mattress. She watched him, her eyes nervous.

"What are you going to do?" she whispered.

He shook his head for silence. Softly, stealthily, he opened the back door and looked outside.

It was pitch dark. The wind was blowing harder than ever, coming in steady gusts, icy, from the sea. He kicked at the step outside the door. It was heaped with birds. There were dead birds everywhere. Under the windows, against the walls. These were the suicides, the divers, the ones with broken necks. Wherever he looked he saw dead birds. No trace of the living. The living had flown seaward with the turn of the tide. The gulls would be riding the seas now, as they had done in the forenoon.

In the far distance, on the hill where the tractor had been two days before, something was burning. One of the aircraft that had crashed; the fire, fanned by the wind, had set light to a stack.

He looked at the bodies of the birds, and he had a notion that if he heaped them, one upon the other, on the windows sills they would make added protection for the next attack. Not much, perhaps, but something. The bodies would have to be clawed at, pecked, and dragged aside before the living birds could gain purchase on the sills and attack the panes. He set to work in the darkness. It was queer, he hated touching them. The bodies were still warm and bloody. The blood matted their feathers. He felt his stomach turn, but he went on with his work. He noticed grimly that every windowpane was shattered. Only the boards had kept the birds from breaking in. He stuffed the cracked panes with the bleeding bodies of the birds.

When he had finished he went back into the cottage. He barricaded the kitchen door, made it doubly secure. He took off his bandages, sticky with the birds' blood, not with his own cuts, and put on fresh plaster.

His wife had made him cocoa and he drank it thirstily. He was very tired.

"All right," he said, smiling, "don't worry. We'll get through."

He lay down on his mattress and closed his eyes. He slept at once. He dreamt uneasily, because through his dreams there ran a thread of something forgotten. Some piece of work, neglected, that he should have done. Some precaution that he had known well but had not taken, and he could not put a name to it in his dreams. It was connected in some way with the burning aircraft and the stack upon the hill. He went on sleeping, though; he did not awake. It was his wife shaking his shoulder that awoke him finally.

"They've begun," she sobbed. "They've started this last hour. I can't listen to it any longer alone. There's something smelling bad too, something burning."

Then he remembered. He had forgotten to make up the fire. It was smoldering, nearly out. He got up swiftly and lit the lamp. The hammering had started at the windows and the doors, but it was not that he minded now. It was the smell of singed feathers. The smell filled the kitchen. He knew at once what it was. The birds were coming down the chimney, squeezing their way down to the kitchen range.

He got sticks and paper and put them on the embers, then reached for the can of paraffin.

"Stand back," he shouted to his wife. "We've got to risk this."

He threw the paraffin on to the fire. The flame roared up the pipe, and down upon the fire fell the scorched, blackened bodies of the birds.

The children woke, crying, "What is it?" asked Jill. "What's happened?"

Nat had no time to answer. He was raking the bodies from the chimney, clawing them out onto the floor. The flames still roared, and the danger of the chimney catching fire was one he had to take. The flames would send away the living birds from the chimney top. The lower joint was the difficulty, though. This was choked with the smoldering, helpless bodies of the birds caught by fire. He scarcely heeded the attack on the windows and the door: let them beat their wings, break their beaks, lose their lives, in the attempt to force an entry into his home. They would not break in. He thanked God he had one of the old cottages, with small windows, stout walls. Not like the new council houses. Heaven help them up the lane in the new council houses.

"Stop crying," he called to the children. "There's nothing to be afraid of, stop crying."

He went on raking at the burning, smoldering bodies as they fell into the fire.

"This'll fetch them," he said to himself, "the draught and the flames together. We're all right, as long as the chimney doesn't catch. I ought to be shot for this. It's all my fault. Last thing, I should have made up the fire. I knew there was something."

Amid the scratching and tearing at the window boards came the sudden homely striking of the kitchen clock. Three A.M. A little more than four hours yet to go. He could not be sure of the exact time of high water. He reckoned it would not turn much before half-past seven, twenty to eight.

"Light up the primus," he said to his wife. "Make us some tea, and the kids some cocoa. No use sitting around doing nothing."

That was the line. Keep her busy, and the children too. Move about, eat, drink; always best to be on the go.

He waited by the range. The flames were dying. But no more blackened bodies fell from the chimney. He thrust his poker up as far as it could go and found nothing. It was clear. The chimney was clear. He wiped the sweat from his forehead.

"Come on now, Jill," he said, "bring me some more sticks. We'll have a good fire going directly." She wouldn't come near him, though. She was staring at the heaped singed bodies of the birds.

"Never mind them," he said. "We'll put those in the passage when I've got the fire steady."

The danger of the chimney was over. It could not happen again, not if the fire was kept burning day and night.

"I'll have to get more fuel from the farm tomorrow," he thought. "This will never last. I'll manage, though. I can do all that with the ebb tide. It can be worked, fetching what we need, when the tide's turned. We've just got to adapt ourselves, that's all."

They drank tea and cocoa and ate slices of bread. Only half a loaf left, Nat noticed. Never mind, though, they'd get by.

"Stop it," said young Johnny, pointing to the window with his spoon. "Stop it, you old birds."

"That's right," said Nat, smiling, "we don't want the old beggars, do we? Had enough of 'em."

They began to cheer when they heard the thud of the suicide birds.

"There's another, Dad," cried Jill. "He's done for."

"He's had it," said Nat. "There he goes, the blighter."

This was the way to face up to it. This was the spirit. If they could keep this up, hang on like this until seven, when the first news bulletin came through, they would not have done too badly.

"Give us a fag," he said to his wife. "A bit of a smoke will clear away the smell of the scorched feathers."

"There's only two left in the packet," she said. "I was going to buy you some from the Co-op."

"I'll have one," he said. "T'other will keep for a rainy day."

No sense trying to make the children rest. There was no rest to be got while the tapping and the scratching went on at the windows. He sat with one arm around his wife and the other around

Jill, with Johnny on his mother's lap and the blankets heaped about them on the mattress.

"You can't help admiring the beggars," he said; "they've got persistence. You'd think they'd tire of the game, but not a bit of it."

Admiration was hard to sustain. The tapping went on and on and a new rasping note struck. Nat's ear, as though a sharper beak than any hitherto had come to take over from its fellows. He tried to remember the names of birds; he tried to think which species would go for this particular job. It was not the tap of the woodpecker. That would be light and frequent. This was more serious, because if it continued long the wood would splinter as the glass had done. Then he remembered the hawks. Could the hawks have taken over from the gulls? Were there buzzards now upon the sills, using talons as well as beaks? Hawks, buzzards, kestrels, falcons—he had forgotten the birds of prey. He had forgotten the gripping power of the birds of prey. Three hours to go, and while they waited, the sound of the splintering wood, the talons tearing at the wood.

Nat looked about him, seeing what furniture he could destroy to fortify the door. The windows were safe because of the dresser. He was not certain of the door. He went upstairs, but when he reached the landing he paused and listened. There was a soft patter on the floor of the children's bedroom. The birds had broken through. . . . He put his ear to the door. No mistake. He could hear the rustle of wings and the light patter as they searched the floor. The other bedroom was still clear. He went into it and began bringing out the furniture, to pile at the head of the stairs should the door of the children's bedroom go. It was a preparation. It might never be needed. He could not stack the furniture against the door, because it opened inward. The only possible thing was to have it at the top of the stairs.

"Come down, Nat, what are you doing?" called his wife.

"I won't be long," he shouted. "Just making everything shipshape up here."

He did not want her to come, he did not want her to hear the pattering of the feet in the children's bedroom, the brushing of those wings against the door.

At five-thirty he suggested breakfast, bacon and fried bread, if only to stop the growing look of panic in his wife's eyes and to calm the fretful children. She did not know about the birds upstairs. The bedroom, luckily, was not over the kitchen. Had it been so, she could not have failed to hear the sound of them up there, tapping the boards. And the silly, senseless thud of the suicide birds, the death and glory boys, who flew into the bedroom, smashing their heads against the walls. He knew them of old, the herring gulls. They had no brains. The black-backs were different; they knew what they were doing. So did the buzzards, the hawks. . . .

He found himself watching the clock, gazing at the hands that went so slowly around the dial. If his theory was not correct, if the attack did not cease with the turn of the tide, he knew they were beaten. They could not continue through the long day without air, without rest, without more fuel, without. . . . His mind raced. He knew there were so many things they needed to withstand siege. They were not fully prepared. They were not ready. It might be that it would be safer in the towns after all. If he could get a message through on the farm telephone to his cousin, only a short journey by train upcountry, they might be able to hire a car. That would be quicker—hire a car between tides. . . .

His wife's voice, calling his name, drove away the sudden, desperate desire for sleep.

"What is it? What now?" he said sharply.

"The wireless," said his wife. "I've been watching the clock. It's nearly seven."

"Don't twist the knob," he said, impatient for the first time. "It's on the Home where it is. They'll speak from the Home."

They waited. The kitchen clock struck seven. There was no sound. No chimes, no music. They waited until a quarter past, switching to the Light. The result was the same. No news bulletin came through.

"We've heard wrong," he said. "They won't be broadcasting until eight o'clock."

They left it switched on, and Nat thought of the battery, wondered how much power was left in it. It was generally recharged when his wife went shopping in the town. If the battery failed they would not hear the instructions.

"It's getting light," whispered his wife. "I can't see it but I can feel it. And the birds aren't hammering so loud."

She was right. The rasping, tearing sound grew fainter every moment. So did the shuffling, the jostling for place upon the step, upon the sills. The tide was on the turn. By eight there was no sound at all. Only the wind. The children, lulled at last by the stillness, fell asleep. At half-past eight Nat switched the wireless off.

"What are you doing? We'll miss the news," said his wife.

"There isn't going to be any news," said Nat. "We've got to depend upon ourselves."

He went to the door and slowly pulled away the barricades. He drew the bolts and, kicking the bodies from the step outside the door, breathed the cold air. He had six working hours before him, and he knew he must reserve his strength for the right things, not waste it in any way. Food, and light, and fuel; these were the necessary things. If he could get them in sufficiency, they could endure another night.

He stepped into the garden, and as he did so he saw the living birds. The gulls had gone to ride the sea, as they had done before; they sought sea food, and the buoyancy of the tide, before they returned to the attack. Not so the land birds. They waited and watched. Nat saw them, on the hedgerows, on the soil, crowded in the trees, outside in the field, line upon line of birds, all still, doing nothing.

He went to the end of his small garden. The birds did not move. They went on watching him.

"I've got to get food," said Nat to himself. "I've got to go to the farm to find food."

He went back to the cottage. He saw to the windows and the doors. He went upstairs and opened the children's bedroom. It was empty, except for the dead birds on the floor. The living were out there, in the garden, in the fields. He went downstairs.

"I'm going to the farm," he said.

His wife clung to him. She had seen the living birds from the open door.

"Take us with you," she begged. "We can't stay here alone. I'd rather die than stay here alone."

He considered the matter. He nodded.

"Come on, then," he said. "Bring baskets, and Johnny's pram. We can load up the pram."

They dressed against the biting wind, wore gloves and scarves. His wife put Johnny in the pram. Nat took Jill's hand.

"The birds," she whimpered. "They're all out there in the fields."

"They won't hurt us," he said, "not in the light."

They started walking across the field toward the stile, and the birds did not move. They waited, their heads turned to the wind.

When they reached the turning to the farm, Nat stopped and told his wife to wait in the shelter of the hedge with the two children.

"But I want to see Mrs. Trigg," she protested. "There are lots of things we can borrow if they went to market yesterday; not only bread and . . ."

"Wait here," Nat interrupted. "I'll be back in a moment."

The cows were lowing, moving restlessly in the yard, and he could see a gap in the fence where the sheep had knocked their way through, to roam unchecked in the front garden before the farmhouse. No smoke came from the chimneys. He was filled with misgiving. He did not want his wife or the children to go down to the farm.

"Don't gib now," said Nat, harshly, "do what I say."

She withdrew with the pram into the hedge, screening herself and the children from the wind.

He went down alone to the farm. He pushed his way through the herd of bellowing cows, which turned this way and that, distressed, their udders full. He saw the car standing by the gate, not put away in the garage. The windows of the farmhouse were smashed. There were many dead gulls lying in the yard and around the house. The living birds perched on the group of trees behind the farm and on the roof of the house. They were quite still. They watched him.

Jim's body lay in the yard . . . what was left of it. When the birds had finished, the cows had trampled him. His gun was beside him. The door of the house was shut and bolted, but as the windows were smashed it was easy to lift them and climb through. Trigg's body was close to the telephone. He must have been trying to get through to the exchange when the birds came for him. The receiver was hanging loose, the instrument torn from the wall. No sign of Mrs. Trigg. She would be upstairs. Was it any use going up? Sickened, Nat knew what he would find.

"Thank God," he said to himself, "there were no children."

He forced himself to climb the stairs, but halfway he turned and descended again. He could see her legs protruding from the open bedroom door. Beside her were the bodies of the black-backed gulls, and an umbrella, broken.

"It's no use," thought Nat, "doing anything. I've only got five hours, less than that. The Triggs would understand. I must load up with what I can find."

He tramped back to his wife and children.

"I'm going to fill up the car with stuff," he said. "I'll put coal in it, and paraffin for the primus. We'll take it home and return for a fresh load."

"What about the Triggs?" asked his wife.

"They must have gone to friends," he said.

"Shall I come and help you, then?"

"No; there's a mess down there. Cows and sheep all over the place. Wait, I'll get the car. You can sit in it."

Clumsily he backed the car out of the yard and into the lane. His wife and the children could not see Jim's body from there.

"Stay here," he said. "Never mind the pram. The pram can be fetched later. I'm going to load the car."

Her eyes watched his all the time. He believed she understood, otherwise she would have suggested helping him to find the bread and groceries.

They made three journeys altogether, backward and forward between their cottage and the farm, before he was satisfied they had everything they needed. It was surprising, once he started thinking, how many things were necessary. Almost the most important of all was planking for the windows. He had to go around searching for timber. He wanted to renew the boards on all the windows at the cottage. Candles, paraffin, nails, tinned stuff; the list was endless. Besides all that, he milked three of the cows. The rest, poor brutes, would have to go on bellowing.

On the final journey he drove the car to the bus stop, got out, and went to the telephone box. He waited a few minutes, jangling the receiver. No good, though. The line was dead. He climbed onto a bank and looked over the countryside, but there was no sign of life at all, nothing in the fields but the waiting watching birds. Some of them slept—he could see the beaks tucked into the feathers.

"You'd think they'd be feeding," he said to himself, "not just standing in that way."

Then he remembered. They were gorged with food. They had eaten their fill during the night. That was why they did not move this morning. . . .

No smoke came from the chimneys of the council house. He thought of the children who had run across the fields the night before.

"I should have known," he thought; "I ought to have taken them home with me."

He lifted his face to the sky. It was colorless and gray. The bare trees on the landscape looked bent and blackened by the east wind. The cold did not affect the living birds waiting out there in the fields.

"This is the time they ought to get them," said Nat; "they're a sitting target now. They must be doing this all over the country. Why don't our aircraft take off now and spray them with mustard gas? What are all our chaps doing? They must know, they must see for themselves."

He went back to the car and got into the driver's seat.

"Go quickly past that second gate," whispered his wife. "The postman lying there. I don't want Jill to see."

He accelerated. The little Morris bumped and rattled along the lane. The children shrieked with laughter.

"Up-a-down, up-a-down," shouted young Johnny.

It was a quarter to one by the time they reached the cottage. Only an hour to go.

"Better have cold dinner," said Nat. "Hot up something for yourself and the children, some of that soup. I've no time to eat now. I've got to unload all this stuff."

He got everything inside the cottage. It could be sorted later. Give them all something to do during the long hours ahead. First he must see to the windows and the doors.

He went around the cottage methodically, testing every window, every door. He climbed onto the roof also, and fixed boards across every chimney, except the kitchen. The cold was so intense he could hardly bear it, but the job had to be done. Now and again he would look up, searching the sky for aircraft. None came. As he worked he cursed the inefficiency of the authorities.

"It's always the same," he muttered, "they always let us down. Muddle, muddle, from the start. No plan, no real organization. And we don't matter down here. That's what it is. The people upcountry have priority. They're using gas up there, no doubt, and all the aircraft. We've got to wait and take what comes."

He paused, his work on the bedroom chimney finished, and looked out to sea. Something was moving out there. Something gray and white among the breakers.

"Good old Navy," he said, "they never let us down. They're coming down-channel, they're turning in the bay."

He waited, straining his eyes, watering in the wind, toward the sea. He was wrong, though. It was not ships. The Navy was not there. The gulls were rising from the sea. The massed flocks in the fields, with ruffled feathers, rose in formation from the ground and, wing to wing, soared upward to the sky.

The tide had turned again.

Nat climbed down the ladder and went inside the kitchen. The family were at dinner. It was a little after two. He bolted the door, put up the barricade, and lit the lamp.

"It's nighttime," said young Johnny.

His wife had switched on the wireless once again, but no sound came from it.

"I've been all around the dial," she said, "foreign stations, and that lot. I can't get anything."

"Maybe they have the same trouble," he said. "Maybe it's the same right through Europe."

She poured out a plateful of the Triggs' soup, cut him a large slice of the Triggs' bread, and spread their dripping upon it.

They ate in silence. A piece of the dripping ran down young Johnny's chin and fell onto the table.

"Manners, Johnny," said Jill. "You should learn to wipe your mouth."

The tapping began at the windows, at the door. The rustling, the jostling, the pushing for position on the sills. The first thud of the suicide gulls upon the step.

"Won't America do something?" said his wife. "They've always been our allies, haven't they? Surely America will do something?"

Nat did not answer. The boards were strong against the windows, and on the chimneys too. The cottage was filled with stores, with fuel, with all they needed for the next few days. When he had finished dinner he would put the stuff away, stack it neatly, get everything shipshape, handy-like. His wife could help him, and the children too. They'd tire themselves out, between now and a quarter to nine, when the tide would ebb; then he'd tuck them down on their mattresses, see that they slept good and sound until three in the morning.

He had a new scheme for the windows, which was to fix barbed wire in front of the boards. He had brought a great roll of it from the farm. The nuisance was, he'd have to work at this in the dark, when the lull came between nine and three. Pity he had not thought of it before. Still, as long as the wife slept, and the kids, that was the main thing.

The smaller birds were at the windows now. He recognized the light tap-tapping of their beaks and the soft brush of their wings. The hawks ignored the windows. They concentrated their attack upon the door. Nat listened to the tearing sound of splintering wood, and wondered how many million years of memory were stored in those little brains, behind the stabbing beaks, the piercing eyes, now giving them this instinct to destroy mankind with all the deft precision of machines.

"I'll smoke that last fag," he said to his wife. "Stupid of me, it was the one thing I forgot to bring back from the farm."

He reached for it, switched on the silent wireless. He threw the empty packet on the fire, and watched it burn.

4

Puzzle for Poppy

Patrick Quentin

"Yes, Miss Crump," snapped Iris into the phone. "No. Miss Crump. Oh, nuts, Miss Crump."

My wife flung down the receiver.

"Well?" I asked.

"She won't let us use the patio. It's that dog, that great fat St. Bernard. It mustn't be disturbed."

"Why?"

"It has to be alone with its beautiful thoughts. It's going to become a mother. Peter, it's revolting. There must be something in the lease."

"There isn't," I said.

When I'd rented our half of this La Jolla hacienda for my shore leave, the lease specified that all rights to the enclosed patio belonged to our eccentric co-tenant. It oughtn't to have mattered, but it did because Iris had recently skyrocketed to fame as a movie star and it was impossible for us to appear on the streets without being mobbed. For the last couple of days we have been virtually beleaguered in our apartment. We were crazy about being beleaguered together, but even Héloise and Abelard needed a little fresh air once in a while.

That's why the patio was so important.

Iris was staring through the locked French windows at the forbidden delights of the patio. Suddenly she turned.

"Peter, I'll die if I don't get things into my lungs—ozone and things. We'll just have to go to the beach."

"And be torn limb from limb by your public again?"

"I'm sorry, darling. I'm terrible sorry." Iris unzippered herself from her housecoat and scrambled into slacks and a shirtwaist. She tossed me my naval hat. "Come, Lieutenant—to the slaughter."

When we emerged on the street, we collided head-on with a man carrying groceries into the house. As we disentangled ourselves from celery stalks, there was a click and a squeal of delight followed by a powerful whistle. I turned to see a small girl who had been lying in wait with a camera. She was an unsightly little girl with sandy pigtails and a brace on her teeth.

"Gee," she announced. "I can get two buckth for thith thnap from Barney Thtone. He'th thappy about you, Mith Duluth."

Other children, materializing in response to her whistle, were galloping toward us. The grocery man came out of the house. Passers-by stopped, stared and closed in—a woman in scarlet slacks, two sailors, a flurry of bobby-soxers, a policeman.

"This," said Iris grimly, "is the end."

She escaped from her fans and marched back to the two front doors of our hacienda. She rang the buzzer on the door that wasn't ours. She rang persistently. At length there was the clatter of a chain sliding into place and the door opened wide enough to reveal the face of Miss Crump. It was a small, faded face with a most uncordial expression.

"Yes?" asked Miss Crump.

"We're the Duluths," said Iris. "I just called you. I know about your dog, but . . ."

"Not *my* dog," corrected Miss Crump. "Mrs. Wilberframe's dog. The late Mrs. Wilberframe of Glendale who has a nephew and a niece-in-law of whom I know a great deal in Ogden Bluffs, Utah. At least, they *ought* to be in Ogden Bluffs."

This unnecessary information was flung at us like a challenge. Then Miss Crump's face flushed into sudden dimpled pleasure.

"Duluth! Iris Duluth. You're *the* Iris Duluth of the movies?"

"Yes," said Iris.

"Oh, why didn't you tell me over the phone? My favorite actress! How exciting! Poor thing—mobbed by your fans. Of course you may use the patio. I will give you the key to open your French windows. Any time."

Miraculously the chain was off the door. It opened halfway and then stopped. Miss Crump was staring at me with a return of suspicion.

"You *are* Miss Duluth's husband?"

"Mrs. Duluth's husband," I corrected her. "Lieutenant Duluth."

She still peered. "I mean, you have proof?"

I was beyond being surprised by Miss Crump. I fumbled from my wallet a dog-eared snapshot of Iris and me in full wedding regalia outside the church. Miss Crump studied it carefully and then returned it.

"You must please excuse me. What a sweet bride! It's just that I can't be too careful—for Poppy."

"Poppy?" queried Iris. "The St. Bernard?"

Miss Crump nodded. "It is Poppy's house, you see. Poppy pays the rent."

"The dog," said Iris faintly, "pays the rent?"

"Yes, my dear. Poppy is very well-to-do. She is hardly more than a puppy, but she is one of the richest dogs, I suppose, in the whole world."

Although we entertained grave doubts as to Miss Crump's sanity, we were soon in swimming suits and stepping through our open French windows into the sunshine of the patio. Miss Crump introduced us to Poppy.

In spite of our former prejudices, Poppy disarmed us immediately. She was just a big, bouncing, natural girl unspoiled by wealth. She greeted us with great thumps of her tail. She leaped up at Iris, dabbing at her cheek with a long, pink tongue. Later, when we had settled on striped mattresses under orange trees, she curled into a big clumsy ball at my side and laid her vast muzzle on my stomach.

"Look, she likes you." Miss Crump was glowing. "Oh, I knew she would!"

Iris, luxuriating in the sunshine, asked the polite question. "Tell us about Poppy. How did she makes her money?"

"Oh, she did not make it. She inherited it." Miss Crump sat down on a white iron chair. "Mrs. Wilberframe was a very wealthy woman. She was devoted to Poppy."

"And left her all her money?" I asked.

"Not quite all. There was a little nest egg for me. I was her companion, you see, for many years. But I am to look after Poppy. That is why I received the nest egg. Poppy pays me a generous salary too." She fingered nondescript beads at her throat. "Mrs. Wilberframe was anxious for Poppy to have only the best and I

am sure I try to do the right thing. Poppy has the master bedroom, of course. I take the little one in front. And then if Poppy
has steak for dinner, I have hamburger." She stared intensely. "I
would not have an easy moment if I felt that Poppy did not get the
best."

Poppy, her head on my stomach, coughed. She banged her tail
against the flagstones apologetically.

Iris reached across me to pat her. "Has she been rich for long?"

"Oh, no, Mrs. Wilberframe passed on only a few weeks ago."
Miss Crump paused. "And it has been a great responsibility for
me." She paused again and then blurted: "You're my friends,
aren't you? Oh, I am sure you are. Please, please, won't you help
me? I am all alone and I am so frightened."

"Frightened?" I looked up and, sure enough, her little bird face
was peaked with fear.

"For Poppy." Miss Crump leaned forward. "Oh, Lieutenant, it
is like a nightmare. Because I know. I just know they are trying
to murder her!"

"They?" Iris sat up straight.

"Mrs. Wilberframe's nephew and his wife. From Ogden Bluffs,
Utah."

"You mentioned them when you opened the door."

"I mention them to everyone who comes to the house. You see,
I do not know what they look like and I do not want them to
think I am not on my guard."

I watched her. She might have looked like a silly spinster with
a bee in her bonnet. She didn't. She looked nice and quite sane,
only scared.

"Oh, they are not good people. Not at all. There is nothing
they would not stoop to. Back in Glendale, I found pieces of meat
in the front yard. Poisoned meat, I know. And on a lonely road,
they shot at Poppy. Oh, the police laughed at me. A car back-
firing, they said. But I know differently. I know they won't stop
till Poppy is dead." She threw her little hands up to her face. "I
ran away from them in Glendale. That is why I came to La Jolla.
But they have caught up with us. I know. Oh dear, poor Poppy
who is so sweet without a nasty thought in her head."

Poppy, hearing her name mentioned, smiled and panted.

"But this nephew and his wife from Ogden Bluffs, why should
they want to murder her?" My wife's eyes were gleaming with a
detective enthusiasm I knew of old. "Are they after her money?"

"Of course," said Miss Crump passionately. "It's the will. The
nephew is Mrs. Wilberframe's only living relative, but she de-

liberately cut him off and I am sure I do not blame her. All the money goes to Poppy and—er—Poppy's little ones."

"Isn't the nephew contesting a screwy will like that?" I asked.

"Not yet. To contest a will takes a great deal of money—lawyer fees and things. It would be much, much cheaper for him to kill Poppy. You see, one thing is not covered by the will. If Poppy were to die before she became a mother, the nephew would in- herit the whole estate. Oh, I have done everything in my power. The moment the—er—suitable season arrived, I found a husband for Poppy. In a few weeks now,—the little ones are expected. But these next few weeks . . ."

Miss Crump dabbed at her eyes with a small handkerchief. "Oh, the Glendale police were most unsympathetic. They even men- tioned the fact that the sentence for shooting or killing a dog in this state is shockingly light—a small fine at most. I called the police here and asked for protection. They said they'd send a man around sometime but they were hardly civil. So you see, there is no protection from the law and no redress. There is no one to help me."

"You've got us," said Iris in a burst of sympathy.

"Oh . . . oh . . ." The handkerchief fluttered from Miss Crump's face. "I knew you were my friends. You dear, dear things. Oh, Poppy, they are going to help us."

Poppy, busy licking my stomach, did not reply. Somewhat ap- palled by Iris' hasty promise but ready to stand by her, I said:

"Sure, we'll help, Miss Crump. First, what's the nephew's name?"

"Henry. Henry Blodgett. But he won't use that name. Oh, no, he will be too clever for that."

"And you don't know what he looks like?"

"Mrs. Wilberframe destroyed his photograph many years ago when he bit her as a small boy. With yellow curls, I understand. That is when the trouble between them started."

"At least you know what age he is?"

"He should be about thirty."

"And the wife?" asked Iris.

"I know nothing about her," said Miss Crump coldly, "except that she is supposed to be a red-headed person, a former actress."

"And what makes you so sure one or both of them have come to La Jolla?"

Miss Crump folded her arms in her lap. "Last night. A telephone call."

"A telephone call?"

"A voice asking if I was Miss Crump, and then—silence. Miss

Crump leaned toward me. "Oh, now they know I am here. They know I never let Poppy out. They know every morning I search the patio for meat, traps. They must realize that the only possible way to reach her is to enter the house."

"Break in?"

Miss Crump shook her tight curls. "It is possible. But I believe they will rely on guile rather than violence. It is against that we must be on our guard. You are the only people who have come to the door since that telephone call. Now anyone else that comes to your apartment or mine, whatever their excuse . . ." She lowered her voice. "Anyone may be Henry Blodgett or his wife and we will have to outwit them."

A fly settled on one of Poppy's valuable ears. She did not seem to notice it. Miss Crump watched us earnestly and then gave a self-scolding cluck.

"Dear me, here I have been burdening you with Poppy's problems and you must be hungry. How about a little salad for luncheon? I always feel guilty about eating in the middle of the day when Poppy has her one meal at night. But with guests—yes, and allies—I am sure Mrs. Wilberframe would not have grudged the expense."

With a smile that was half-shy, half-conspiratorial, she fluttered away.

I looked at Iris. "Well," I said, "is she a nut or do we believe her?"

"I rather think," said my wife, "that we believe her."

"Why?"

"Just because." Iris' face wore the entranced expression which had won her so many fans in her last picture. "Oh, Peter, don't you see what fun it will be? A beautiful St. Bernard in peril. A wicked villain with golden curls who bit his aunt."

"He won't have golden curls any more," I said. "He's a big boy now."

Iris, her body warm from the sun, leaned over me and put both arms around Poppy's massive neck.

"Poor Poppy," she said. "Really, this shouldn't happen to a dog!"

The first thing happened some hours after Miss Crump's little salad luncheon while Iris and I were sunning ourselves. Miss Crump, who had been preparing Poppy's dinner and her own in her apartment, came running to announce:

"There is a man at the door! He claims he is from the electric light company to read the meter. Oh, dear, if he is legitimate and we do not let him in, there will be trouble with the electric light company and if . . ." She wrung her hands. "Oh, what shall we do?"

I reached for a bathrobe. "You and Iris stay here. And for Mrs. Wilberframe's sake, hang onto Poppy."

I found the man outside the locked front door. He was about thirty with thinning hair and wore an army discharge button. He showed me his credentials. They seemed in perfect order. There was nothing for it but to let him in. I took him into the kitchen where Poppy's luscious steak and Miss Crump's modest hamburger were lying where Miss Crump had left them on the table. I hovered over the man while he located the meter. I never let him out of my sight until he had departed. In answer to Miss Crump's anxious questioning, I could only say that if the man had been Henry Blodgett he knew how much electricity she'd used in the past month—but that was all.

The next caller showed up a few minutes later. Leaving Iris, indignant at being out of things, to stand by Poppy, Miss Crump and I handled the visitor. This time it was a slim, brash girl with bright auburn hair and a navy-blue slack suit. She was, she said, the sister of the woman who owned the hacienda. She wanted a photograph for the newspapers—a photograph of her Uncle William who had just been promoted to Rear Admiral in the Pacific. The photograph was in a trunk in the attic.

Miss Crump, reacting to the unlikeliness of the request, refused entry. The red-head wasn't the type that wilted. When she started talking darkly of eviction, I overrode Miss Crump and offered to conduct her to the attic. The girl gave me one quick experienced look and flounced into the hall.

The attic was reached by the back stairs through the kitchen. I conducted the red-head directly to her claimed destination. There were trunks. She searched through them. At length she produced a photograph of a limp young man in a raccoon coat.

"My Uncle William," she snapped, "as a youth."

"Pretty," I said.

I took her back to the front door and she left. If she had been Mrs. Blodgett, she knew how to take care of herself, she knew how many trunks there were in the attic—and that was all.

Iris and I dressed and were drinking Daiquiris under a green-and-white-striped umbrella when Miss Crump appeared followed by a young policeman. She was very pleased about the policeman. He had come, she said, in answer to her complaint. She showed him Poppy; she babbled out her story of the Blodgetts. He obviously thought she was a harmless lunatic, but she didn't seem to realize it. After she had let him out, she settled beamingly down with us.

"I suppose," said Iris, "you asked him for his credentials?"

"I . . ." Miss Crump's face clouded. "My dear, you don't think that perhaps he wasn't a real police . . . ?"

"To me," said Iris, "everyone's a Blodgett until proved to the contrary."

"Oh, dear," said Miss Crump.

Nothing else happened. By evening Iris and I were back in our part of the house. Poppy had hated to see us go. We had hated to leave her. A mutual crush had developed between us.

But now that we were alone again, the sinister Blodgetts did not seem very substantial. Iris made a creditable *Bœuf Stroganov* from yesterday's leftovers and changed into a lime-green negligée. I was busy being a sailor on leave with his girl when the phone rang. I reached over Iris for the receiver, said "Hello," and then sat rigid listening.

It was Miss Crump's voice. But something was horribly wrong with it. It came across hoarse and gasping.

"Come," it said. "Oh, come. The French windows. Oh, please . . ."

The voice faded. I heard the clatter of a dropped receiver.

"It must be Poppy," I said to Iris. "Quick."

We ran out into the dark patio. Across it, I could see the French windows of Miss Crump's apartment. They were half open, and as I looked Poppy squirmed through to the patio. She bounded toward us, whining.

"Poppy's all right," said Iris. "Quick!"

We ran to Miss Crump's windows. Poppy barged past us into the living room. We followed. All the lights were on. Poppy had galloped around a high-backed davenport. We went to it and looked over it.

Poppy was crouching on the carpet, her huge muzzle dropped on her paws. She was howling and staring straight at Miss Crump.

Poppy's paid companion was on the floor too. She lay motionless on her back, her legs twisted under her, her small, gray face distorted, her lips stretched in a dreadful smile.

I knelt down by Poppy. I picked up Miss Crump's thin wrist and felt for the pulse. Poppy was still howling. Iris stood, straight and white.

"Peter, tell me. Is she dead?"

"Not quite. But only just not quite. Poison. It looks like strychnine . . ."

We called a doctor. We called the police. The doctor came, muttered a shocked diagnosis of strychnine poisoning and rushed Miss Crump to the hospital. I asked if she had a chance. He didn't answer. I knew what that meant. Soon the police came and there was so much to say and do and think that I hadn't time to brood about poor Miss Crump.

We told Inspector Green the Blodgett story. It was obvious to us that somehow Miss Crump had been poisoned by them in mistake for Poppy. Since no one had entered the house that day except three callers, one of them, we said, must have been a Blodgett. All the Inspector had to do, we said, was to locate those three people and find out which was a Blodgett.

Inspector Green watched us pokerfaced and made no comment. After he'd left, we took the companionless Poppy back to our part of the house. She climbed on the bed and stretched out between us, her tail thumping, her head flopped on the pillows. We didn't have the heart to evict her. It was not one of our better nights.

Early next morning, a policeman took us to Miss Crump's apartment. Inspector Green was waiting in the living room. I didn't like his stare.

"We've analyzed the hamburger she was eating last night," he said. "There was enough strychnine in it to kill an elephant."

"Hamburger!" exclaimed Iris. "Then that proves she was poisoned by the Blodgetts!"

"Why?" asked Inspector Green.

"They didn't know how conscientious Miss Crump was. They didn't know she always bought steak for Poppy and hamburger for herself. They saw the steak and the hamburger and they naturally assumed the hamburger was for Poppy, so they poisoned that."

"That's right," I cut in. "The steak and the hamburger were lying right on the kitchen table when all three of those people came in yesterday."

"I see," said the Inspector.

He nodded to a policeman who left the room and returned with three people—the balding young man from the electric light company, the red-headed vixen, and the young policeman. None of them looked happy.

"You're willing to swear," the Inspector asked us, "that these were the only three people who entered this house yesterday."

"Yes," said Iris.

"And you think one of them is either Blodgett or his wife?"

"They've got to be."

Inspector Green smiled faintly. "Mr. Burns here has been with the electric light company for five years except for a year when he was in the army. The electric light company is willing to vouch for that. Miss Curtis has been identified as the sister of the lady who owns this house and the niece of Rear Admiral Moss. She has no connection with any Blodgetts and has never been in Utah." He paused. "As for Officer Patterson, he has been a member of the police force here for eight years. I personally sent him around yesterday to follow up Miss Crump's complaint."

The Inspector produced an envelope from his pocket and tossed it to me. "I've had these photographs of Mr. and Mrs. Henry Blodgett flown from the files of the Ogden Bluffs *Tribune.*"

I pulled the photographs out of the envelope. We stared at them. Neither Mr. or Mrs. Blodgett looked at all the sort of person you would like to know. But neither of them bore the slightest resemblance to any of the three suspects in front of us.

"It might also interest you," said the Inspector quietly, "that I've checked with the Ogden Bluffs police. Mr. Blodgett has been sick in bed for over a week and his wife has been nursing him. There is a doctor's certificate to that effect."

Inspector Green gazed down at his hands. They were competent hands. "It looks to me that the whole Blodgett story was built up in Miss Crump's mind—or yours." His gray eyes stared right through us. "If we have to eliminate the Blodgetts and these three people from suspicion, that leaves only two others who had the slightest chance of poisoning the hamburger."

Iris blinked. "Us?"

"You," said Inspector Green almost sadly.

They didn't arrest us, of course. We had no conceivable motive. But Inspector Green questioned us minutely and when he left there was a policeman lounging outside the door.

We spent a harried afternoon racking our brains and getting nowhere. Iris was the one who had the inspiration. Suddenly, just after she had fed Poppy the remains of the *Stroganov,* she exclaimed:

"Good heavens above, of course!"

"Of course what?"

She spun to me, her eyes shining. "Barney Thtone," she lisped. "Why didn't we realize? Come on!"

She ran out of the house into the street. She grabbed the lounging policeman by the arm.

"You live here," she said. "Who's Barney Stone?"

"Barney Stone?" The policeman stared. "He's the son of the druggist on the corner."

Iris raced me to the drugstore. She was attracting quite a crowd. The policeman followed, too.

In the drugstore, a thin young man with spectacles stood behind the prescription counter.

"Mr. Stone?" asked Iris.

His mouth dropped open. "Gee, Miss Duluth. I never dreamed. . . . Gee, Miss Duluth, what can I do for you? Cigarettes? An alarm clock?"

"A little girl," said Iris. "A little girl with sandy pigtails and a brace on her teeth. What's her name? Where does she live?"

Barney Stone said promptly: "You mean Daisy Kornfeld. Kind of homely. Just down the block. 712. Miss Duluth, I certainly . . ."

"Thanks," cut in Iris and we were off again with our ever growing escort.

Daisy was sitting in the Kornfeld parlor, glumly thumping the piano. Ushered in by an excited, cooing Mrs. Kornfeld, Iris interrupted Daisy's rendition of *The Jolly Farmer.*

"Daisy, that picture you took of me yesterday to sell to Mr. Stone, is it developed yet?"

"Gee, no, Mith Duluth. I ain't got the developing money yet. Theventy-five thenth. Ma don't give me but a nickel an hour for practithing thith piano."

"Here." Iris thrust a ten-dollar bill into her hand. "I'll buy the whole roll. Run get the camera. We'll have it developed right away."

"Gee." The mercenary Daisy stared with blank incredulity at the ten-dollar bill.

I stared just as blankly myself. I wasn't being bright at all.

I wasn't much brighter an hour later. We were back in our apartment, waiting for Inspector Green. Poppy, all for love, was trying to climb into my lap. Iris, who had charmed Barney Stone into developing Daisy's films, clutched the yellow envelope of snaps in her hand. She had sent our policeman away on a secret mission, but an infuriating passion for the dramatic had kept her from telling or showing me anything. I had to wait for Inspector Green.

Eventually Iris' policeman returned and whispered with her in the hall. Then Inspector Green came. He looked cold and hostile. Poppy didn't like him. She growled. Sometimes Poppy was smart.

Inspector Green said, "You've been running all over town. I told you to stay here."

"I know." Iris' voice was meek. "It's just that I wanted to solve poor Miss Crump's poisoning."

"Solve it?" Inspector Green's query was skeptical.

"Yes. It's awfully simple really. I can't imagine why we didn't think of it from the start."

"You mean you know who poisoned her?"

"Of course." Iris smiled, a maddening smile. "Henry Blodgett."

"But . . ."

"Check with the airlines. I think you'll find that Blodgett flew in from Ogden Bluffs a few days ago and flew back today. As for his being sick in bed under his wife's care, I guess that'll make Mrs. Blodgett an accessory before the fact, won't it?"

Inspector Green was pop-eyed.

"Oh, it's my fault really," continued Iris. "I said no one came to the house yesterday except those three people. There was someone else, but he was so ordinary, so run-of-the-mill, that I forgot him completely."

I was beginning to see then. Inspector Greene snapped, "And this run-of-the-mill character?"

"The man," said Iris sweetly, "who had the best chance of all to poison the hamburger, *the man who delivered it*—the man from the Supermarket.

"We don't have to guess. We have proof." Iris fumbled in the yellow envelope. "Yesterday morning as we were going out, we bumped into the man delivering Miss Crump's groceries. Just at that moment, a sweet little girl took a snap of us. This snap."

She selected a print and handed it to Inspector Green. I moved to look at it over his shoulder.

"I'm afraid Daisy is an impressionistic photographer," murmured Iris. "That hip on the right is me. The buttocks are my husband. But the figure in the middle—quite a masterly likeness of Henry Blodgett, isn't it? Of course, there's the grocery apron, the unshaven chin . . ."

She was right. Daisy had only winged Iris and me but with the grocery man she had scored a direct hit. And the grocery man was unquestionably Henry Blodgett.

Iris nodded to her policeman. "Sergeant Blair took a copy of the snap around the neighborhood groceries. They recognized Blodgett at the Supermarket. They hired him day before yesterday. He made a few deliveries this morning, including Miss Crump's, and took a powder without his pay."

"Well . . ." stammered Inspector Green. "Well . . ."

"Just how many charges can you get him on?" asked my wife hopefully. "Attempted homicide, conspiracy to defraud, illegal possession of poisonous drugs. . . . I hope you give him the works when you get him."

"We'll get him, all right," said Inspector Green.

Iris leaned over and patted Poppy's head affectionately.

"Don't worry, darling. I'm sure Miss Crump will get well and we'll throw a lovely christening party for your little strangers . . ."

Iris was right about the Blodgetts. Henry got the works. And his wife was held as an accessory. Iris was right about Miss Crump too. She is still in the hospital but improving steadily and will almost certainly be well enough to attend the christening party.

Meanwhile, at her request, Poppy is staying with us, awaiting maternity with rollicking unconcern.

It's nice having a dog who pays the rent.

5
Eyewitness

Robert Arthur

Los Angeles, 1940

Outside it was raining—raining in hard black lines of water that slanted down out of the sky the way they had the night the girl vanished.

She was out there now, out there somewhere in the black wet night, just as she had been every night now for the last four weeks. Out there where her husband had left her, cold, crumpled, dead, all the warmth and love gone out of her, all the color gone from her cheeks, all the light from her eyes. Out there in the night that had hidden her murder under a pall of blackness, and the rain that had been pouring down from the heavens when her husband hid her body.

Davis knew she had been murdered—knew it as well as he knew the alphabet, or his name, or the day of the week, all those things so familiar a man never has to think of them. Davis knew it, but he couldn't prove it; and desperately, doggedly, he wanted to prove it, as he had never wanted a prove anything before in fourteen years on the Force.

He parked his car and trudged through the acute angle of the falling rain, water dripping down his shapeless felt hat, down his square rugged face, down his old ulster, down his legs, over his shoes. Trudged through the alley and turned in the stage door of the theater, where he slapped the rain from his hat and from his ulster before he asked to speak to Master.

With his hat off, his forehead gleamed where the hair was going back, and gray showed up in the hair that was left. He wasn't old, not even middle-aged, but his face looked old and tired to-night, like the face of a man who has been too long trying to do doing something he desperately wants to do and cannot.

The doorman showed Davis into the little dressing room where Master sat, quietly smoking, while his Negro dresser bustled about. Master was a big man, broad-shouldered, with a mane of blond hair and bright blue eyes that stared unwinkingly—stared as if they never blinked, so that a man might become nervous merely from the impact of their moveless gaze.

It was almost an hour before the evening curtain rose on Master's act. Davis took a gingerly seat on the edge of a chair, the water running across the floor below him from his shoes, and began, choosing his words with great care, like a man anxious to hew exactly to the line of fact and err not a hair on either side.

"There's a lot of talk about perfect murders going around," Davis said harshly. "And if such a thing is possible, this may be it."

Master nodded, as if he understood all that had not been said— understood that Davis had heard of him somehow, somewhere, had heard of some murder he had brought his efforts to bear upon in the past, had come to him now for help and was trying desperately to interest him in the case he had brought; under- stood that Davis desperately, fiercely wanted help, but would not ask for it.

"We think she's dead, but we don't know," Davis went on. "We think he killed her; but we don't know that either. If she's dead, we can't find the body. If we could find the body, we might not be able to prove it was murder. If we could prove it was murder, still we might have trouble proving *he* did it. And yet we're sure she's dead, it's murder, and he did it. That's the only explanation that fits the facts."

Master nodded again, understanding that it was Davis who was sure it was murder, and Davis was sure *he,* whoever *he* might be, had done it.

Master helped himself to a cigar from a box at hand, and passed one to the detective. Davis took it, but forgot to light it; merely put it in his mouth and chewed on it as he spoke.

"She died in the darkness," Davis went on, still speaking carefully. "Died in the complete blackness of a city without lights. It was the night of the big flood—Wednesday, the second of March —and all the lights went out for more than half an hour. There were no lights at all, except candles indoors and automobile headlights out, and the headlights cut only thin, pale paths of light through the rain and the darkness."

He paused, as if suddenly feeling the words coming out too fast, too expressively for a Headquarters detective ten years in plainclothes.

But Master still nodded, still understanding the emotion behind what Davis was telling him, and after a moment of sucking hard on the unlighted cigar to collect his thoughts, Davis continued:

"She was young, she was pretty, she was loving. She was always laughing, always gay. She had been married three years, and her husband was an actor—a young leading man in pictures. But he had been only a car-hop at a drive-and-eat before the movies, and she had been the same, making twelve dollars a week and living on it. They met, they got married—and then the movies found him and he began to make money and still more money.

"Began to see a big future ahead of him."

Davis paused long enough to light the cigar with a hand that trembled a bit.

"You see, he's tall and smooth—that's the only word to describe him. Inside he's yellow, rotten; but outside he's big, tanned, with even white teeth and eyes that seem to promise something to every woman he meets. And he's been rising in pictures because of women—stars who have taken an interest in him. Lately there's been one in particular. She's getting old, but she's still powerful and can do a lot for him. But won't as long as he's married.

"So you see, he wants to get rid of his wife. He can't get a divorce. He has no grounds. But he feels that she's holding him back, keeping him from rising to the top, keeping him from becoming a big star; she's dead weight around his neck. He does not love her; he's too selfish to love anyone but himself. Now all he thinks of is getting rid of her. He even thinks of murder; or if somehow she would only disappear.

"Well, a month ago the lights went out, and she disappeared."

The detective stopped again; his voice was becoming hoarse.

"They lived in Hollywood, off Beachwood Drive, in the hills above Hollywood Boulevard. Not as fashionable a place as he wanted, but the best he could afford yet. Besides, it kept her and her mother, who stayed with them, out of sight, behind the scenes.

"She kept house while he worked; she stayed at home while he was out, sometimes all night, making 'contacts' and being seen in fashionable places. Many of his associates didn't know he was married.

"She never complained, never chided him. She never even guessed he was sorry he had ever married her. She was loyal—loyal all the way through."

Davis stopped, then went on more calmly.

"To amuse herself, she went for long walks in the hills or went to the movies alone. On this night, this Wednesday night, she went to an early show at the Pantages Theater. Her mother was out playing bridge, and he was working.

"He came home around eight, just after her mother. A few minutes later she phoned him. It was raining. It had been raining for days. There were floods all through the San Fernando Valley. A bridge in Long Beach washed out, drowning a dozen or more. But Hollywood saw only the rain. The floods scarcely touched Hollywood.

"So she phoned him that because of the rain she couldn't get a taxi. Would he come for her and pick her up in front of the theater?

"He said he would. His mind was full of hot, bright, ambitious schemes that night. She—the movie star—had been talking to him that day, we've learned. She'd promised him the lead in her next picture. If—well, you know what that *if* was.

"No doubt he'd often thought of killing her before that night. But that night the opportunity came. Ten minutes after he left the house, every light in the city went out."

Davis let his words sink in. He leaned forward and tapped the big blond man on the knee for extra emphasis.

"Every light in the city went out. It's a strange feeling when that happens, when the power fails, when the lights go off and the radios go silent, and all the street corners are as dark as the inside of a grave. A candle flickers here, a match there, and they only make the darkness darker. Well, that's what happened that night.

"He wasn't gone long. He came back to the house within forty-five minutes, before the lights came on again. And she wasn't with him.

"He said he couldn't find her. That he had parked the car and searched for her in front of the Pantages. He thought she must have gotten panicky when the lights went out, and found a taxi, or started walking, or something. He thought she'd be home ahead of him. But she wasn't. She never came home. So presently he called us. Called us and told us his story. That he had missed her in the darkness, and now she had vanished.

"Well, we took down his story and promised to broadcast an alarm. A lot of people vanished that night, in the flood, and we had our hands full. Some of them are still missing too. Possibly he figured on that.

"After taking down his story, we left; of course our investigation that night was only the sketchiest. It was several days before we got around to making any thorough investigation. And then it was too late.

"So there it was. She had vanished. Where? God knows. What can happen on the streets of a darkened city? Anything.

"Around midnight her husband went out in the car again. He was gone for hours, until almost morning, in the pouring rain. The lights were on again, but because of the weather the streets were deserted. No one could be found who had seen him or his car. Where had he gone? What had he done? He said he had been driving around in a half-crazy condition, hunting for her, calling her name, driving aimlessly, hoping to find her wandering in a daze, perhaps, but unhurt.

"Well, perhaps. But you know what we think?"

Davis tapped Master's knee again.

"We think that he found her in the darkness in front of the Pantages and she got in the car with him. In the darkness, no one would notice what car stopped, or who got in. No one saw her get in. He drove part way home, and still the lights didn't come on. He was burning with resentment of her.

"And suddenly, impulsively, there on a side street, unseen in the night, the windows of the car fogged by the driving rain, he throttled her. Throttled her and hid her body in the baggage trunk of the car, where it was when he returned home and called us.

"Where it was until he went out on that long drive, in which he claimed he was searching for her. But when he was really hiding her body—hiding it so well we've never found it."

There was bitterness in the detective's voice, and Master understood that this case meant something personal to him; not just a routine assignment.

"Do you know Los Angeles?" the detective asked, and Master

shook his head. "Well," Davis told him, "Los Angeles is a big
place. There are arroyos and caves in the hills, old quarries, parks,
lakes, rivers, abandoned mine workings—places a man might hide
a body, right inside the county limits.

"Suppose he had previously picked a place, had had it in mind
all along. Suppose he had done that, you can see how difficult it
would be for us to find her. In the end, we might never find her,
unless chance stepped in."

Davis sagged suddenly, like a tired man.

"If we could only find her," he said quietly. "That's all I hope
to do. There's almost no chance to prove guilt against him under
the circumstances. Though I'd like to. God knows how I'd like to!"

For the first time, though the fact had escaped the detective's
attention, Master spoke.

"I think we will find her," he said.

"But he'll go free!" Davis said harshly.

Master shook his head slowly.

"Perhaps not," he said somberly. "You forget the eyewitness."

"The eyewitness!" the detective exclaimed. "There was no eyewitness!"

"To every murder there is an eyewitness," the big blond man
rumbled.

"Poppycock!" the detective snapped irritably. "It would be a
big help if there were. Don't you suppose more murderers would
go to the chair if such a thing were true? Unless you mean God,
who can't help us any."

"There is always an eyewitness," Master said quietly, but his
words carried force and conviction. "Sometimes it is hard to make
him speak."

He seemed to withdraw from the room for a moment into some
inward meditation. Then:

"But tonight, I think, from what you have told me, we will
be able to make him speak. We will find the body. And I think
the one who saw the murder will give you the evidence needed
to convict."

Davis opened his mouth, to protest, to argue; then he shut
it again. He did not know what the big man meant, but he was
at the end of his own rope. And somehow Master's words carried
conviction.

"First," Master instructed, "call the husband and tell him you
are going to come tonight to take him to his wife's body. Say
that an eyewitness to her disappearance knows where she is. Say
that she was murdered, and her murder was seen, her murderer

followed when he hid the body. Tell him nothing more. Let him think over your words until we come. Now I have a show to do. I will be with you later."

Davis did as the big man told him. Then, with a growing sense of awe and wonder, he watched Master's performance. After that, just before midnight, when Master had changed into rough tweeds and an ulster, they took Davis's car and drove out toward Hollywood.

His name was Harold Murney, and at midnight they found him waiting for them, alone in a small house in the Hollywood hills, where from his living-room window the blue and red neons of Hollywood gleamed faintly through the pouring rain.

He was tall and broad shouldered, as Davis had described him, and hard. Amazingly hard. It was in his voice, in his eyes. Hard and evil.

But Davis was hard too. His square face, dripping water from the rain blown into their faces as he and Master came up the long footpath from the drive to the house, glistened in the light. His eyes gleamed too, a peculiar blue gleam of hope and hatred. Murney was the man he wanted to convict, and Murney knew it. But he knew, the detective did, that there was no shadow of evidence against the younger man, and so did the actor.

So, whether guilty or innocent, Murney could easily stare back insolently at Davis without flinching, without showing any alarm.

"You said you'd found my wife?" Murney asked suspiciously, glancing from Master to Davis and back to the big blond man, whose presence the detective had not bothered to explain.

"I said we'd take you to her," Davis replied dully.

Murney stared at him suspiciously, his eyes green beneath half lowered lids.

"Where?" he asked.

"Where her murderer hid her," Davis told him evenly.

"Murderer?"

Murney's voice indicated only what it should have—shock and surprise. If he was guilty, as a murderer he was a good actor too.

"Are you sure you're not mistaken?" the young man asked then, coolly, and Davis shook his head. "No," the actor answered himself, after a moment, "I suppose it's your business to be sure. All right, you say you've found her and she was murdered. Have you got her murderer?"

Davis shook his head again, his eyes fixed unwinkingly on Murney.

"We'll have him shortly after we've taken you to the body," he answered. "The murder, as well as the concealment of the body, was seen by an eyewitness, fortunately."

This time Murney's breath did suck in perceptibly.

"It seems incredible," he said, and now he let amusement creep into his voice. "Frankly, I don't believe you've found my wife, that she was murdered, or that there is any such eyewitness. If there is, why didn't he speak up sooner?"

"He had his reasons," Davis said, and his voice was suddenly harsh. "But he will speak now. I suppose, Murney, you've no objection to coming with us to identify your wife and help us nab her killer?"

Murney hesitated for an instant. Some of the ruddy color had gone from his cheeks. But when he spoke his voice was still easy, still confident.

"Of course not," he said loudly. "You know how much I want to help you."

All this time Master had not spoken, had only stood there, his face wet with rain because he had worn no hat, his bright blue eyes staring unwinkingly at Murney. The actor took his eyes off Master now with an effort.

"I'll get my coat and be right with you," he said roughly. "Though I'm convinced it's a wild goose chase."

He got dressed for the weather, and Davis led the way down the footpath.

"We'll take my car," he said. "Too bad it's a coupé. We'll be a bit crowded."

His words were regretful, but his voice was not. He slid in behind the wheel and Harold Murney, after a moment's hesitation, got in beside him. Last of all Master squeezed himself in and closed the car door.

Davis started the motor and let in the clutch. They were jammed tightly together, but none of the men commented on the fact. Davis and Master stared straight ahead, the detective seeming intent on his driving. Murney glanced quickly from one face to the other, but could read nothing in them. Jammed between the two, he sat stiffly, as if he found the space too small in which to relax.

"We are going to retrace the murderer's path," Davis said quietly, as the car rolled silently downhill and into Beachwood Drive, the only direction in which it could go.

Murney started to speak, and then thought better of it. But he shifted a little uneasily as they coasted downward toward Franklin Avenue, and he almost jumped when Master, for the first time, spoke.

"Turn here," he said suddenly. "Right."

Davis braked and turned into Scenic Drive, after almost overrunning the narrow entrance of the street. Momentary surprise showed on Harold Murney's face; then his lips tightened, and he said nothing as they crossed Gower and came to Vista Del Mar, a crooked, hilly street lined with houses almost European in their picturesqueness.

"Left," Master said abruptly.

They turned left, drifted down Vista Del Mar, and came out on Franklin. At Master's order they turned right on Franklin, crossed Argyle, Vine, and Ivar, climbed the hill, dropped down a steep slope, and pulled up at broad Cahuenga Boulevard.

"Right," Master said here, as Harold Murney stirred again, and an instant later ordered them sharply left at the traffic light onto Wilcox, and then quickly right again on the continuation of Franklin.

From time to time Murney had shifted uneasily, wedged between the two men, at all this maneuvering. When presently they pulled up for the stop light at Highland Avenue, and Master ordered them left, he burst out in a voice gone a little shrill:

"Where are we going with all this nonsensical driving?" he demanded. "What kind of a game are you playing? There's no police station in this direction, no hospital, no morgue. I demand to know where you are taking me!"

"Along the path of a murderer," Master told him, deeply, "and that route is always twisted."

They swung left, then right at the next light, and straight ahead until they came to a dead end. Then left, and drifted downward a hundred yards or so to stop where La Brea and Hollywood crossed, having reached the point by a devious and twisting route for whose choosing there seemed little reason.

Harold Murney seemed to be losing his self-control.

"I demand you let me out!" he said shrilly, his voice higher still. "This is fantastic. This is some sort of plot. You haven't found my wife and you don't know where she is. I think you're trying to shake me down!"

"We are showing you the route a murderer took," Master told him quietly. "The devious, back-street route he took in the rainy night that was like this night, the winding route he took to obviate every possible chance of being seen and noticed."

Murney gulped and swallowed hard.

"That's nonsense!" he cried. "That's ridiculous! How do you know my wife's murderer came this way—if she was murdered? You don't. You couldn't."

But his voice held a note that seemed to indicate he was trying to convince himself, not them. Davis did not even turn to look at him, merely guided the car straight ahead down La Brea Boulevard, past Sunset and past Santa Monica.

But as they swung right on Melrose at Master's orders, Murney tried to reach across the big blond man and open the car door.

"I demand that you let me out!" he gasped, almost sobbingly. "You've no legal right to keep me if I want to get out."

Master stretched out an arm and pinned him into his seat. Biting his lips and seeming to shake a little, as if from rage, Murney sat back.

Then they were turning northward again, the windshield wiper clicking busily, sweeping aside the water that filmed the glass between each downward swing of the arm. The rain beat down on the steel top of the coupé, and the motor purred with a soft, even beat.

They rolled along for block after block and then, in response to a quiet word from Master, their course changed. They turned, and presently they were climbing a long slope that led them away from Hollywood and its rain-haloed lights, toward the darkness of the valley beyond.

Murney was sitting rigidly between the two men. But he jumped when Master's voice rang out, almost accusingly.

"Right!"

Davis swung them into a side street, dark, deserted. They idled along, and no house lights showed, only dim street lights at long intervals. Presently their lights reflected from the rain-wet boards of a high fence. Master turned his head a little, from right to left. Between them Murney sat in wire-tight tenseness.

"Stop!" The word was like a pistol shot. Even Davis jumped a bit. Then he pulled to the curb and cut the motor. It expired with a little cough, and for a moment they sat there in complete silence, broken only by the persistent beating of the rain.

"Apex Pictures' storage lot," Davis said aloud, though as if to himself. "Where they store all their old scenery and sets, stuff that hasn't any value."

Master nodded.

"Let us get out here," he suggested, and, opening the car door, descended.

He stood on the pavement until Murney reluctantly, it seemed, descended, though only a few minutes before he had been anxious to get out of the car. The actor tried to light a cigarette, cupping the match in his hand and bending over; but the flame wavered and shook and went out. With a curse he flung the wet cigarette into the gutter.

"I don't know why you've brought me here," he said wildly. "But I'm going home, do you hear? You can't keep me! You can't!"

Master linked an arm through his and held him.

"What are you afraid of?" Davis sneered. "You haven't done anything, have you? You didn't murder her, did you?"

"No, no, you know well enough I didn't!" Harold Murney cried.

"Then come on," Davis said, "before you make us think different."

"I think we will go inside," Master said evenly, and beaten, shaking, the actor fell into step with him.

With Davis on the other side, they walked slowly along the high fence. The rain still fell, wetly and insistently, and there was no one to see them. They could have been taking the actor to murder him, and no one would have noticed.

After fifty yards they came to a high gate, and Master stopped.

"Gate," Davis said. "It's locked. I'll get tools."

He went back to the car, returned with a flashlight and a tire iron. A twist of the tire iron burst the staples that held the padlock; the gate creaked open.

"Now we will go in," Master said.

"No!" Murney cried, squirming but unable to break free. "I won't go in with you! You have no right to bring me here! What do you want, anyway, what do you want?"

"Only for you to identify your wife," Davis said. "Come along. We're almost there."

With the flashlight cutting a wedge out of the darkness in front of them they entered, their feet crunching loud on graveled paths. Davis fanned the flashlight about, and the rays glinted off the peeling surface of a plaster mosque, off a Norman castle made of wood and paper, off the squat shape of an Egyptian pyramid.

Master led them down one of the dark paths, moving slowly, slowly, as if on the verge of stopping at any moment. They passed mouldering scenery flats, and the wreck of an entire Western town that consisted only of false building fronts, ragged and tattered. The path curved; they came back toward the Egyptian pyramid. Abruptly Master halted.

"Shine your light about," he said to Davis. The detective did so.

"A pyramid made out of wood and plaster," he said aloud. "A model of the Sphinx with the head fallen off. A big, imitation Egyptian sarcophagus. Some artificial rocks. A——"

"The sarcophagus," Master interrupted. "Yes, the sarcophagus —an imitation of an ancient burial place; a fitting spot to find the body of a murder victim. Open it, and let us see if our eye-witness spoke the truth."

"No!" Murney screamed now, and his lunge to break free was maddened, desperate. "She's not here! You must be crazy, think-ing she is. How could she be here? This is a trick, a trick!"

The two men held him until his struggles ceased and he stood, shaken by dry, gasping sobs. They did not speak. When the actor was quiet again, Davis released his arm. He strode forward, played his flashlight briefly over the scaling paint of the wooden sarcophagus. Then he thrust in the tire iron. A push, and the lid of the sarcophagus lifted. Davis let it crash to the ground. He turned his flashlight into the interior.

She was there. She lay stretched out, one arm flung up across her face as if to shut out the light. But no light would trouble her eyes again. She had been there for a month, and she was no longer beautiful.

"She's here," Davis said, and the words could hardly be heard about the soft sound of the rain.

"I know," Master answered. "I know. Our eyewitness told us the truth. Look at her, Murney. Look at her and identify her."

"No!" the actor cried. "No! You knew! You knew all along! You had to know. You couldn't have brought me here, couldn't have retraced the exact route I drove to get here that night, if you didn't know. Someone told you. Someone saw me and told you. Oh God, why did they have to see me?"

Davis had a pair of handcuffs. As the actor fell to his knees in the gravel path, breathing heavily, his mouth and eyes and face all loose, slack, twisted, Davis used them.

He pulled and Harold Murney rose shudderingly to his feet.

"But I couldn't have been followed!" he screamed. "Couldn't have! I'd have known if I had been. Nobody could have followed me through all those twists and turns without my seeing them.

Tell me! Tell me! How did you bring me here over the same route I used? How? How?"

He beat with his handcuffed wrists on the detective's chest, and Davis caught his arms and held them. Master moved over and fastened his bright gaze on the actor's face.

"You brought us here," he said. "Your guilty conscience brought us here. It was a trick, if you will. Nevertheless, it was you who guided us every inch of the way to this spot."

"No! I didn't! I didn't!"

"You brought us here just as anyone who has hidden something, and has that hidden thing much on his mind, will inevitably lead one who knows the secret to the hiding place.

"I said it was your conscience. Call it, if you want to be more technical, your involuntary muscular responses to mental commands that were not quite given. We passed a corner where you had turned that night. You did not want us to know you had turned there. Your brain thought of the turn, thought that we must not know of it. So you twitched. You jerked slightly in that direction. As your mind thought, your body moved—not much, but enough for me.

"For I was wedged tightly beside you, remember, and I knew how to read these little movements your body could not keep from making. I learned the trick from Harry Houdini, who was the master of us all. At your leisure you can learn more about it, for it is written in one of his books.

"It is always easy when the subject is nervous, and you were nervous. That is why we called you earlier in the evening, told you we would lead you to her body. To make you nervous."

"Who—who are you?" Harold Murney whispered. "You're not a detective. Who——"

"His name is Master." Davis answered the question. "He is a professional stage magician and prestidigitator. Too bad you'll never see him work. His act is a sensation. Especially when he has a member of the audience take something and hide it, and then, walking beside the hider, finds the hidden object without fail, every time."

"Then who're you?" Murney screamed at Davis. "You're not a detective either! No detective would have hounded me like this. No detective would have thought of it. Who're you?"

"I'm a detective," Davis told him, "but I'm also the fellow she was going to marry until you came along. That's who I am."

"Oh—you—then you—you——"

The breath gasped and bubbled in Harold Murney's throat.

"Then you lied!" he choked out. "You lied. There was no eye-witness. There was no one to give evidence. There was no witness and you couldn't have convicted me!"

Davis shook his head.

"No," he said, "I didn't lie. There was an eyewitness. He led us here and he gave us the evidence we needed. The eyewitness who is always present at every murder. The one who always sees the crime—the one who commits it. In this case you, Murney, you —you were the eyewitness we meant!"

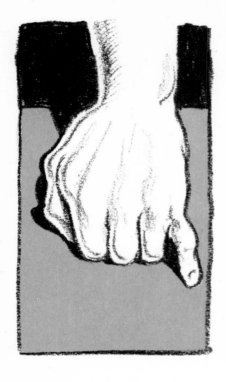

6

Man from the South

Roald Dahl

It was getting on toward six o'clock so I thought I'd buy myself a beer and go out and sit in a deck chair by the swimming pool and have a little evening sun.

I went to the bar and got the beer and carried it outside and wandered down the garden toward the pool.

It was a fine garden with lawns and beds of azaleas and tall coconut palms, and the wind was blowing strongly through the tops of the palm trees, making the leaves hiss and crackle as though they were on fire. I could see the clusters of big brown nuts hanging down underneath the leaves.

There were plenty of deck chairs around the swimming pool and there were white tables and huge brightly colored umbrellas and sunburned men and women sitting around in bathing suits. In the pool itself there were three or four girls and about a dozen boys, all splashing about and making a lot of noise and throwing a large rubber ball at one another.

I stood watching them. The girls were English girls from the hotel. The boys I didn't know about, but they sounded American and I thought they were probably naval cadets who'd come ashore from the U.S. naval training vessel which had arrived in harbor that morning.

I went over and sat under a yellow umbrella where there were four empty seats, and I poured my beer and settled back comfortably with a cigarette.

It was very pleasant sitting there in the sunshine with beer and a cigarette. It was pleasant to sit and watch the bathers splashing about in the green water.

The American sailors were getting on nicely with the English girls. They'd reached the stage where they were diving under the water and tipping them up by their legs.

Just then I noticed a small, oldish man walking briskly around the edge of the pool. He was immaculately dressed in a white suit and he walked very quickly with little bouncing strides, pushing himself high up onto his toes with each step. He had on a large creamy Panama hat, and he came bouncing along the side of the pool, looking at the people and the chairs.

He stopped beside me and smiled, showing two rows of very small, uneven teeth, slightly tarnished. I smiled back.

"Excuse pleess, but may I sit here?"

"Certainly," I said. "Go ahead."

He bobbed around to the back of the chair and inspected it for safety, then he sat down and crossed his legs. His white buckskin shoes had little holes punched all over them for ventilation.

"A fine evening," he said. "They are all evenings fine here in Jamaica." I couldn't tell if the accent were Italian or Spanish, but I felt fairly sure he was some sort of a South American. And old too, when you saw him close. Probably around sixty-eight or seventy.

"Yes," I said. "It is wonderful here, isn't it."

"And who, might I ask, are all dese? Dese is no hotel people." He was pointing at the bathers in the pool.

"I think they're American sailors," I told him. "They're Americans who are learning to be sailors."

"Of course dey are Americans. Who else in de world is going to make as much noise at dat? You are not American, no?"

"No," I said. "I am not."

Suddenly one of the American cadets was standing in front of us. He was dripping wet from the pool and one of the English girls was standing there with him.

"Are these chairs taken?" he said.

"No," I answered.

"Mind if I sit down?"

"Go ahead."

"Thanks," he said. He had a towel in his hand and when he sat down he unrolled it and produced a pack of cigarettes and a lighter. He offered the cigarettes to the girl and she refused; then he offered them to me and I took one. The little man said, "Tank you, no, but I tink I have a cigar." He pulled out a crocodile case and got himself a cigar, then he produced a knife which had a small scissors in it and he snipped the end off the cigar.

"Here, let me give you a light." The American boy held up his lighter.

"Dat will not work in dis wind."

"Sure, it'll work. It always works."

The little man removed his unlighted cigar from his mouth, cocked his head on one side and looked at the boy.

*"All-*ways?" he said slowly.

"Sure, it never fails. Not with me, anyway."

The little man's head was still cocked over on one side and he was still watching the boy. "Well, well. So you say dis famous lighter it never fails. Iss dat what you say?"

"Sure," the boy said. "That's right." He was about nineteen or twenty with a long freckled face and a rather sharp birdlike nose. His chest was not very sunburned and there were freckles there too, and a few wisps of pale-reddish hair. He was holding the lighter in his right hand, ready to flip the wheel. "It never fails," he said, smiling now because he was purposely exaggerating his little boast. "I promise you it never fails."

"One momint, pleess." The hand that held the cigar came up high, palm outward, as though it were stopping traffic. "Now juss one momint." He had a curiously soft, toneless voice and he kept looking at the boy all the time.

"Shall we not perhaps make a little bet on dat?" He smiled at the boy. "Shall we not make a little bet on whether your lighter lights?"

"Sure, I'll bet," the boy said. "Why not?"

"You like to bet?"

"Sure, I'll always bet."

The man paused and examined his cigar, and I must say I didn't much like the way he was behaving. It seemed he was already trying to make something out of this, and to embarrass the boy, and at the same time I had the feeling he was relishing a private little secret all his own.

He looked up again at the boy and said slowly, "I like to bet, too. Why we don't have a good bet on dis ting? A good big bet."

"Now wait a minute," the boy said. "I can't do that. But I'll bet you a quarter. I'll even bet you a dollar, or whatever it is over here—some shillings, I guess."

The little man waved his hand again. "Listen to me. Now we have some fun. We make a bet. Den we go up to my room here in de hotel where iss no wind and I bet you you cannot light dis famous lighter of yours ten times running without missing once."

"I'll bet I can," the boy said.

"All right. Good. We make a bet, yes?"

"Sure. I'll bet you a buck."

"No, no. I make you a very good bet. I am rich man and I am sporting man also. Listen to me. Outside de hotel iss my car. Iss very fine car. American car from your country. Cadillac—"

"Hey, now. Wait a minute." The boy leaned back in his deck chair and he laughed. "I can't put up that sort of property. This is crazy."

"Not crazy at all. You strike lighter successfully ten times running and Cadillac is yours. You like to have dis Cadillac, yes?"

"Sure, I'd like to have a Cadillac." The boy was still grinning.

"All right. Fine. We make a bet and I put up my Cadillac."

"And what do I put up?"

The little man carefully removed the red band from his still unlighted cigar. "I never ask you, my friend, to bet something you cannot afford. You understand?"

"Then what do I bet?"

"I make it very easy for you, yes?"

"Okay. You make it easy."

"Some small ting you can afford to give away, and if you did happen to lose it you would not feel too bad. Right?"

"Such as what?"

"Such as, perhaps, de little finger of your left hand."

"My *what!*" The boy stopped grinning.

"Yes. Why not? You win, you take de car. You looss, I take de finger."

"I don't get it. How d'you mean, you take the finger?"

"I chop it off."

"Jumping jeepers! That's a crazy bet. I think I'll just make it a dollar."

The little man leaned back, spread out his hands palms upward and gave a tiny contemptuous shrug of the shoulders. "Well, well, well," he said. "I do not understand. You say it lights but you will not bet. Den we forget it, yes?"

The boy sat quite still, staring at the bathers in the pool. Then he remembered suddenly he hadn't lighted his cigarette. He put it between his lips, cupped his hands around the lighter and flipped the wheel. The wick lighted and burned with a small, steady, yellow flame and the way he held his hands the wind didn't get to it at all.

"Could I have a light, too?" I said.

"Gee, I'm sorry. I forgot you didn't have one."

I held out my hand for the lighter, but he stood up and came over to do it for me.

"Thank you," I said, and he returned to his seat.

"You having a good time?" I asked.

"Fine," he answered. "It's pretty nice here."

There was a silence then, and I could see that the little man had succeeded in disturbing the boy with his absurd proposal. He was sitting there very still, and it was obvious that a small tension was beginning to build up inside him. Then he started shifting about in his seat, and rubbing his chest, and stroking the back of his neck, and finally he placed both hands on his knees and began tap-tapping with his fingers against the kneecaps. Soon he was tapping with one of his feet as well.

"Now just let me check up on this bet of yours," he said at last. "You say we go up to your room and if I make this lighter light ten times running I win a Cadillac. If it misses just once then I forfeit the little finger of my left hand. Is that right?"

"Certainly. Dat is de bet. But I tink you are afraid."

"What do we do if I lose? Do I have to hold my finger out while you chop it off?"

"Oh, no! Dat would be no good. And you might be tempted to refuse to hold it out. What I should do I should tie one of your hands to de table before we started and I should stand dere with a knife ready to go *chop* de momint your lighter missed."

"What year is the Cadillac?" the boy asked.

"Excuse. I not understand."

"What year—how old is the Cadillac?"

"Ah! How old? Yes. It is last year. Quite new car. But I see you are not betting man. Americans never are." The boy paused for just a moment and he glanced first at the English girl, then at me. "Yes," he said sharply. "I'll bet you."

"Good!" The little man clapped his hands together quietly, once. "Fine," he said. "We do it now. And you, sir," he turned to me, "you would perhaps be good enough to, what you call it, to—to referee." He had pale, almost colorless eyes with tiny bright black pupils.

"Well," I said. "I think it's a crazy bet. I don't think I like it very much."

"Nor do I," said the English girl. It was the first time she'd spoken. "I think it's a stupid, ridiculous bet."

"Are you serious about cutting off this boy's finger if he loses?" I said.

"Certainly I am. Also about giving him Cadillac if he win. Come now. We go to my room."

He stood up. "You like to put on some clothes first?" he said.

"No," the boy answered. "I'll come like this." Then he turned to me. "I'd consider it a favor if you'd come along and referee."

"All right," I said. "I'll come along, but I don't like the bet."

"You come too," he said to the girl. "You come and watch."

The little man led the way back through the garden to the hotel. He was animated now, and excited, and that seemed to make him bounce up higher than ever on his toes as he walked along.

"I live in annex," he said. "You like to see car first? Iss just here."

He took us to where we could see the front driveway of the hotel and he stopped and pointed to a sleek pale green Cadillac parked close by.

"Dere she iss. De green one. You like?"

"Say, that's a nice car," the boy said.

"All right. Now we go up and see if you can win her."

We followed him into the annex and up one flight of stairs. He unlocked his door and we all trooped into what was a large pleasant double bedroom. There was a woman's dressing gown lying across the bottom of one of the beds.

"First," he said, "we 'ave a little Martini."

The drinks were on a small table in the far corner, all ready to be mixed, and there was a shaker and ice and plenty of glasses. He began to make the Martini, but meanwhile he'd rung the bell and now there was a knock on the door and a maid came in.

"Ah!" he said, putting down the bottle of gin, taking a wallet from his pocket and pulling out a pound note. "You will do something for me now, pleess." He gave the maid the pound.

"You keep dat," he said. "And now we are going to play a little game in here and I want you to go off and find for me two—no tree tings. I want some nails; I want a hammer, and I want a chopping knife, a butcher's chopping knife which you can borrow from de kitchen. You can get, yes?"

"A *chopping knife!*" The maid opened her eyes wide and clasped her hands in front of her. "You mean a *real* chopping knife?"

"Yes, yes, of course. Come on now, pleess. You can find those tings surely for me."

"Yes, sir, I'll try, sir. Surely I'll try to get them." And she went.

The little man handed round the Martinis. We stood there and sipped them, the boy with the long freckled face and the pointed nose, bare-bodied except for a pair of faded brown bathing shorts; the English girl, a large-boned, fair-haired girl wearing a pale blue bathing suit, who watched the boy over the top of her glass all the time; the little man with the colorless eyes standing there in his immaculate white suit drinking his Martini and looking at the girl in her pale blue bathing dress. I didn't know what to make of it all. The man seemed serious about the bet and he seemed serious about the business of cutting off the finger. But what if the boy lost? Then we'd have to rush him to the hospital in the Cadillac that he hadn't won. That would be a fine thing. Now wouldn't that be a really fine thing? It would be a silly unnecessary thing so far as I could see.

"Don't you think this is rather a silly bet?" I said.

"I think it's a fine bet," the boy answered.

"I think it's a stupid, ridiculous bet," the girl said. "What'll happen if you lose?"

"It won't matter. Come to think of it, I can't remember ever in my life having had any use for the little finger on my left hand. Here he is." The boy took hold of the finger. "Here he is and he hasn't ever done a thing for me yet. So why shouldn't I bet him. I think it's a fine bet."

The little man smiled and picked up the shaker and refilled our glasses.

"Before we begin," he said, "I will present to de—to de referee de key of de car." He produced a car key from his pocket and gave it to me. "De papers," he said, "de owning papers and insurance are in de pocket of de car."

Then the maid came in again. In one hand she carried a small chopper, the kind used by butchers for chopping meat bones, and in the other a hammer and a bag of nails.

"Good! You get dem all. Tank you, tank you. Now you can go." He waited until the maid had closed the door, then he put the implements on one of the beds and said, "Now we prepare ourselves, yes?" And to the boy, "Help me, pleess, with dis table. We carry it out a little."

It was the usual kind of hotel writing desk, just a plain rectan-

gular table about four feet by three with a blotting pad, ink, pens
and paper. They carried it out into the room away from the wall,
and removed the writing things.

"And now," he said, "a chair." He picked up a chair and placed
it beside the table. He was very brisk and very animated, like a
person organizing games at a children's party. "And now de nails.
I must put in de nails." He fetched the nails and he began to
hammer them into the top of the table.

We stood there, the boy, the girl, and I, watching the little man
at work. We watched him hammer two nails into the table, about
six inches apart. He didn't hammer them right home; he allowed
a small part of each one to stick up. Then he tested them for firm-
ness with his fingers.

Anyone would think he had done this before, I told myself. He
never hesitates. Table, nails, hammer, kitchen chopper. He knows
exactly what he needs and how to arrange it.

"And now," he said, "all we want is some string." He found
some string. "All right, at last we are ready. Will you please to sit
here at de table," he said to the boy.

The boy put his glass away and sat down.

"Now place de left hand between dese two nails. De nails are
only so I can tie your hand in place. All right, good. Now I tie
your hand secure to de table—so."

He wound the string around the boy's wrist, then several times
around the wide part of the hand, then he fastened it tight to the
nails. He made a good job of it and when he'd finished there wasn't
any question about the boy being able to draw his hand away.
But he could move his fingers.

"Now pleess, clench de fist, all except for de little finger. You
must leave de little finger sticking out, lying on de table."

"*Ex*-cellent! *Ex*-cellent! Now we are ready. Wid your right hand
you manipulate de lighter. But one momint, pleess."

He skipped over to the bed and picked up the chopper. He came
back and stood beside the table with the chopper in his hand.

"We are all ready?" he said. "Mister referee, you must say to
begin."

The English girl was standing there in her pale blue bathing
costume right behind the boy's chair. She was just standing there,
not saying anything. The boy was sitting quite still, holding the
lighter in his right hand, looking at the chopper. The little man
was looking at me.

"Are you ready?" I asked the boy.

"I'm ready."

"And you?" to the little man.

"Quite ready," he said and he lifted the chopper up in the air and held it there about two feet above the boy's finger, ready to chop. The boy watched it, but he didn't flinch and his mouth didn't move at all. He merely raised his eyebrows and frowned.

"All right," I said. "Go ahead."

The boy said, "Will you please count aloud the number of times I light it?"

"Yes," I said. "I'll do that."

With his thumb he raised the top of the lighter, and again with the thumb he gave the wheel a sharp flick. The flint sparked and the wick caught fire and burned with a small yellow flame.

"One!" I called.

He didn't blow the flame out; he closed the top of the lighter on it and he waited for perhaps five seconds before opening it again.

He flicked the wheel very strongly and once more there was a small flame burning on the wick.

"Two!"

No one else said anything. The boy kept his eyes on the lighter. The little man held the chopper up in the air and he too was watching the lighter.

"Three!"

"Four!"

"Five!"

"Six!"

"Seven!" Obviously it was one of those lighters that worked. The flint gave a big spark and the wick was the right length. I watched the thumb snapping the top down onto the flame. Then a pause. Then the thumb raising the top once more. This was an all-thumb operation. The thumb did everything. I took a breath, ready to say eight. The thumb flicked the wheel. The flint sparked. The little flame appeared.

"Eight!" I said, and as I said it the door opened. We all turned and we saw a woman standing in the doorway, a small, black-haired woman, rather old, who stood there for about two seconds, then rushed forward shouting, "Carlos! Carlos!" She grabbed his wrist, took the chopper from him, threw it on the bed, took hold of the little man by the lapels of his white suit and began shaking him very vigorously, talking to him fast and loud and fiercely all the time in some Spanish-sounding language. She shook him so fast you couldn't see him any more. He became a faint, misty, quickly moving outline, like the spokes of a turning wheel.

Then she slowed down and the little man came into view again and she hauled him across the room and pushed him backward onto one of the beds. He sat on the edge of it blinking his eyes and testing his head to see if it would still turn on his neck.

"I am so sorry," the woman said. "I am so terribly sorry that this should happen." She spoke almost perfect English.

"It is too bad," she went on. "I suppose it is really my fault. For ten minutes I leave him alone to go and have my hair washed and I come back and he is at it again." She looked sorry and deeply concerned.

The boy was untying his hand from the table. The English girl and I stood there and said nothing.

"He is a menace," the woman said. "Down where we live at home he has taken altogether forty-seven fingers from different people, and he has lost eleven cars. In the end they threatened to have him put away somewhere. That's why I brought him up here."

"We were only having a little bet," mumbled the little man from the bed.

"I suppose he bet you a car," the woman said.

"Yes," the boy answered. "A Cadillac."

"He has no car. It's mine. And that makes it worse," she said. "that he should bet you when he has nothing to bet with. I am ashamed and very sorry about it all." She seemed an awfully nice woman.

"Well," I said, "then here's the key of your car." I put it on the table.

"We were only having a little bet," mumbled the little man.

"He hasn't anything left to bet with," the woman said. "He hasn't a thing in the world. Not a thing. As a matter of fact I myself won it all from him a long while ago. It took time, a lot of time, and it was hard work, but I won it all in the end." She looked up at the boy and she smiled, a slow sad smile, and she came over and put out a hand to take the key from the table.

I can see it now, that hand of hers; it had only one finger on it and a thumb.

7

Black Magic

Sax Rohmer

"He is one of the most cunning criminals alive," said Bazarada tensely; "that's all."

From the open window at which I stood, I could se a flowery headland and the blue sea of Funchal Harbor.

"I asked you to come out and meet me here, Maurice—I've sent Laroo and all the rest on back to England—because quite by accident I picked up certain information on the ship. I decided that the man known as Dr. Sarafan, highly respected resident of Madeira, and the notorious Servius Jerome, were one and the same! I had had a long radiogram from my old friend Ned. W. Regan in New York, asking me to look out for Jerome."

"So the man is up to his old tricks?"

"With a difference this time, Maurice! You say that the facts of the case had not been made public up to the time you left London, but briefly this man Jerome succeeded in getting Mary Coppinger, only daughter of Mark Coppinger, the drugstore millionaire, completely under his thumb. Mary was staying in London with her aunt, Mrs. Burton Dugan. Jerome was a regular visitor. He has some extraordinary power over women—and no one, it seems, knew of his foul reputation. Three weeks ago Mary disappeared—so did

Jerome! Now, her father, back in New York, has been invited to pay a hundred thousand dollars—"

"Yes!" I turned and stared at him. "It's the most unique form of blackmail I ever heard of."

"A hundred thousand dollars *not* to marry the girl. It's certainly original! You see, the blackguard figures, once they are married, old Coppinger will pay anything to secure a divorce. He has him both ways."

"But you say he refused?"

"He instructed Ned Regan right away and started for Europe. I radioed Regan to come here and I expect him and Mark Coppinger at almost any time. But the colossal impudence of Dr. Sarafan, as he is known in this town, amazes me."

I was glad to know that Regan was coming. The most famous detective in the world is a sound ally, and Buzzy, who had no concrete evidence to support his case, had met with a cold reception from the authorities. Dr. Sarafan had a large *quinta* within easy distance of Funchal, which he occupied from time to time, and the civil governor had frankly laughed at Bazarada. The American consul had proved little more helpful. This, particularly, had irritated Buzzy. Then Dr. Sarafan in person had been announced; at that moment was ascending the stairs.

His card lay on the table: "Dr. Emmanuel Sarafan."

Now the owner of the card was approaching the door, and both Buzzy and I were watching that door—for one of the most evil men alive was about to enter.

A peremptory knock sounded.

"Come in," said Bazarada.

The door opened slowly and Servius Jerome walked into the room.

The mere act of writing the man's name fills me with something of the loathing which I had experienced when first I saw him. Scotland Yard has a stout dossier in its files respecting this unfrocked priest who had become a practicing black magician. Cunningly he had avoided criminal prosecution, but had been expelled from England, then from France.

The man had deep knowledge allied to the instincts of Satan, and, in return for substantial sums, initiated his victims into strange rites. Ruin—in three cases, death—marked his footsteps through Europe. His notorious Temple of Adonis in Sicily had been secretly visited by Bazarada at the request of the parents of a girl whom Jerome had robbed of most of her possessions and then driven mad. Bazarada had succeeded in breaking up the unsavory organization.

And now Servius Jerome stood before us.

He was a man of no more than medium height, but of powerful frame, with massive, intellectual features and piercing dark eyes shadowed by craggy brows. He was rather bald in front but his graying dark hair grew long at the back. He was dressed in black and wore an unusual caped overcoat. In one slender white hand, upon which a conspicuous talismanic ring glittered, he held a wide-brimmed black hat.

He ignored my existence and stared across the room at Bazarada.

Words failed to convey the aura which surrounded him.

His face might have had the dignity of profound scholarship but for subtle lines that had scarred its beauty. Jerome was not a man to be ignored. He radiated evil. He was a figure of power. I doubt if any man living today has studied the dark mysteries of nature more deeply than Servius Jerome. If there be such a man I do not envy him.

Bazarada's fixed regard met the challenge of those strange eyes. Two powerful wills clashed.

"Well?" said Servius Jerome. "Have you anything to say to me, Bazarada?"

"Not yet," Buzzy replied quietly.

Jerome continued to watch him. Although it may sound a queer confession, I was glad he was not watching *me*. Frankly, there was something in this man's presence that I found terrifying.

"You crossed my path a year ago," he said, "thrusting yourself into my private affairs. The greatest experiment of my life you ruined, when you caused me to be expelled from Sicily. Bazarada, I never forgot. You are a conjurer—a vaudeville artist. You work with traps and mirrors and other mechanical devices. You call yourself a magician! What do you know of magic?"

Bazarada continued to watch him but did not speak.

"Magic is the power to control others, Bazarada. As Dr. Sarafan I have been known and respected in Madeira for many years. You have tried to tell the authorities that Dr. Sarafan is Servius Jerome. They laugh. Why? Because I have asserted my control. My magic above yours.

"You suspect that a certain lady wishes to marry me. You cannot understand—therefore you come here to interfere with me. You will be good enough to give your assurance that you will remain outside my affairs. Or, if you prefer, you will bear the consequences of your refusal."

Then Bazarada spoke. He did not stir; his heavy-lidded eyes scarcely flickered.

"You have the impudence to suppose," he said, "that you can abduct the daughter of a prominent United States citizen, and by means of your *magic* escape the consequences. You expose yourself, Jerome, to a form of retaliation which undoubtedly would do you good. In other words"—he suddenly stood up, and I saw Jerome's delicate fingers tighten upon the brim of the black hat—"unless you are out of this room in exactly fifteen seconds I am going to kick you downstairs!"

The almost unnatural composure of this master of the black arts did not for a moment desert him.

Servius Jerome slightly inclined his head, turned and went out. I heard his slow, retreating footsteps in the corridor.

"Tonight," said Bazarada, "we are going to visit the Quinta de Santa Lucia. I have been there once but I want to see Mary Coppinger. . . ."

Around us was moonlight and woodland. Look as far as I would at straight, upstanding pines, nothing stirred in the mystic blue light. Left of the mountain road was sheer rock. Above and beyond, the forest climbed to some peak we could not see.

Higher we mounted and higher. There were awkward corners where we seemed to overhang tree-clad slopes, hairpin bends above dizzy pine tops. For a long time Bazarada drove in silence, then:

"We are nearly there, Maurice," he said. "We have to walk the last lap. The sound of the car would ruin our plans."

There came a sort of moon-bathed clearing in the woodland and Buzzy drove into a shadowy bay. We got out.

We set out along a mere forest track, Bazarada using a flashlight to guide us. This path mounted very steeply. And I stumbled in his wake.

"There must be some other way to the place," I said.

"There is," he replied curtly. "But we dare not use it."

A few paces farther and shadow gave place to bright moonlight. Bazarada snapped off the light.

"Look," he said, "there is the Quinta de Santa Lucia."

I stood beside him looking in the direction he indicated. A low, rambling building, obviously of great age, overhung a deep ravine. Moonlight poured down upon it like molten silver.

"It was on what used to be a main road, but a road now barely used; and it was formerly a guest house connected with a monastery of which no trace remains. Look! There's a car driving up now."

I watched. The headlights of the car came slowly around a precipitous road and disappeared into the shadows of the building.

"A visitor for Servius Jerome."

"Probably the priest. Mary Coppinger was under age, and an heiress, when Jerome induced her to go away. Therefore he laid himself open to prosecution for *abduction!* But tomorrow is her twenty-first birthday. If he succeeds in marrying her, the case will become complicated. This way."

He extended his hand and led me, otherwise I could never have followed the crazy path which we pursued, and which I divined he had explored earlier. It led to a sort of outbuilding, formerly, as I saw, a stable, and here we pulled up.

"Stand by, Maurice," said Buzzy.

I listened to a familiar fumbling. We were hidden by a belt of black shadow cast by the full moon; then:

"Inside! Quick!" I heard.

I found myself in a place, illuminated by Bazarada's flashlight, which, as I had assumed, had at one time afforded accommodation for quite a dozen horses.

"Follow on," Buzzy instructed; "walk softly."

At the end of the place there was more fumbling—and another door had magically been opened.

"Stairs!" Bazarada whispered.

We mounted a number of stairs.

"Take the torch. I am uncertain of this lock."

I directed the ray upon the lock of a great iron-studded door which no man but Bazarada would have dreamed of attempting to force. About us all was silent; but I was apprehensive of the very silence. I watched him at work as so often I had watched, and suddenly the door was open.

"Sorry for the delay," he murmured. "An old-fashioned Portuguese lock for which I was not looking. Go easy now—we are in the house of Servius Jerome."

In the torchlight I saw a corridor, the floor covered with coarse matting; heavy beams and rough plaster work took me back to the age in which this corridor had been planned.

"Step softly! If there is anyone in the room we are going to, the success or failure of our visit turns upon silencing him."

He opened an unlocked door and started into a small room. There was a lighted opening on the farther side. It resembled an opera box and I saw that it was empty.

"I had come provided," Buzzy whispered, "but it is unnecessary. Close the door. Don't bolt it."

I did as he directed, turned and looked in the direction of the light.

Below me was a small chapel.

"I anticipated a chapel," said Bazarada. "It is characteristic. Servius Jerome, as you know, poses as a high priest of some religion purely of his own invention. I assume that it is here, tomorrow, that the wedding is planned to take place. I wonder if the priest will be a real priest? This we must find out. I deduce that he will be. A legal marriage would suit Jerome's purpose."

I was about to move when Bazarada gripped my arm tightly.

Servius Jerome, wearing a cassock and a purple biretta, walked silently in at the back of the altar.

With all the reverence of a priest performing his duties, he attended to the flame, rearranged the flowers, knelt for a moment, and went out again.

"I am tempted to suppose," Bazarada whispered, "that this man has begun to believe his own religion. A brilliant madman is a most dangerous opponent."

We retired without let or hindrance.

Bazarada, who in times of urgency had a swift, silent, Indianlike walk, seized my hand and led me around the south angle of the building. Sometimes I was tempted to believe that Buzzy could see in the dark. We moved at great speed through impenetrable shadow. From time to time he would mutter: "Duck your head—over hanging branch," and then—"Three steps up—be careful."

It was a queer experience. For if I could not see where we were going, how could Buzzy see?

I presently recognized that we stood upon a tree-clad bank from which, over the top of a high wall, one could command a view of beautiful moonlit gardens.

There was a terraced garden, graced by flowering trees. There were beds of roses. Somewhere, a fountain was playing. I had just begun to speak, when:

"Quiet!" Buzzy said urgently. "Look!"

A girl was approaching us, coming up the steps from a lower terrace to one immediately below the wall. She wore a soft, robe-like dress, and the moonlight glittered on her fair hair.

Suddenly, Buzzy was no longer at my side.

I stared right and left into shadow. I could see nothing, hear nothing. Then I saw him, a crouching silhouette on top of the old wall, and heard his quiet voice:

"Mary."

The girl stopped. I saw her look up. She was pretty, but her beauty was of the kind which has no strength of character behind it. She had large childish eyes and a petulant, full-lipped mouth. Her expression was that of a sleepwalker.

"Yes?" she said in a dreamy voice, which contained no note of alarm.

"Your father has sent me to look for you, Mary."

Mary Coppinger continued to look up.

"Why?" she asked. "I am very happy. Tell Father that I am very happy."

She disappeared from my view, but presently I could hear the sound of footsteps walking along the path directly under the wall. Buzzy's silhouette vanished. A moment later he was beside me.

"You see, Maurice," he said, speaking a little breathlessly, "she is completely in the man's power. And she is not the first. Tomorrow is her twenty-first birthday, but at the time of her abduction she was a minor. Ned Regan has a warrant for Jerome's arrest. It looks as though we are helpless until Ned arrives."

Another of those blind marches led by my friend, who could see in the dark, and we were back where the car was hidden. We had just climbed in and Buzzy was about to start when a man came racing up the road toward us.

"Sit tight," said Bazarada. "I don't think we can be seen here."

I saw now that a second man followed the first. One glimpse I had in the moonlight of the two runners. Both were swarthy fellows. Suddenly the first runner stooped, picked up a big stone and turned swiftly. The second man carried a knife. I saw its flash as he threw it . . . but he was too late.

The stone, hurled with terrific force, struck him squarely between the eyes. He staggered back, seemed to crumple up, and slumped face downward on the path. The stone thrower, with never another glance, turned and ran on up a narrow lane.

"Good God!" I muttered.

"Although it's none of our business," said Buzzy, "I think we should see if there's anything we can do."

We jumped out. He held my arm for a moment, listening. Receding footsteps grew faint in the distance.

A very brief examination was sufficient. The man was dead.

"This is a ghastly business!" I spoke in a low voice. "What do we do?"

"In the circumstances," said Bazarada, "I think this is where we beat it. Since there is no other house to my knowledge within two miles, I assume that the murderer and the murdered were servants of Jerome. Remembering that he formerly had a temple in Sicily, I suspect that they were Sicilians. I am not without sympathy for the stone-thrower."

We set out for Funchal. It was a roundabout and, at night an exciting route.

Perhaps in my many experiences with Bazarada I never had quite such a shock as that which awaited me when we arrived at the hotel. Two policemen in Offenbach uniforms, and a plain-clothes officer, were standing in the lobby when we entered. The manager, much perturbed, asked us all to step into his office.

"I am sure," he exclaimed, "that there is some terrible mistake."

"No mistake, I think," said the plain-clothes officer, speaking very good English. "Is your name Bazarada?"

"It is."

"I hold a warrant for your arrest."

"You must be mad!" I said.

"Upon what charge?" Bazarada asked quietly.

"Upon the charge of having murdered, tonight, Pietro Ascani, a servant of Dr. Sarafan."

I experienced a sudden chill.

"Of course there is some terrible error," the manager cried, "some frightful misunderstanding."

"On what evidence has this warrant been issued?" Bazarada asked.

"Dr. Sarafan lodged the information. He is at headquarters now."

Bazarada looked at me.

"Be silent, Maurice," he said smiling—but his eyes flashed an urgent message. "Do nothing. Say nothing. Try nothing. Wait for Ned Regán . . . I am at your service, Officer."

On the way to police headquarters I reviewed the situation. It was appalling enough. I realized that one of those occurrences which are fate's practical jokes had been instantly turned to advantage by Servius Jerome. Perhaps the murderer had seen us after all—or perhaps, secretly, Jerome himself had been watching. Whichever the true explanation might be, the plain fact remained that Buzzy's freedom depended upon my word being accepted against that of Jerome—probably reinforced by other lying witnesses!

The officer on duty in the ancient and gloomy building in which presently I found myself had exactly that air of smug self-sufficiency and absence of common sense which infuriates me. Dr. Sarafan had been unable to wait, but had made a written deposition. Throughout, Bazarada remained perfectly calm.

"But," I shouted at one stage of the proceedings, "the statement of Dr. Sarafan as recorded is an absolute fabrication!"

"Maurice!" Buzzy said sternly.

"It appears," the official went on, ignoring my outburst, "that the dead man detected the accused on the premises of Dr. Sarafan, and,. endeavoring to detain him, met his death at the accused's hands. He was struck down with a stone, picked up on the roadside. Police officers are now investigating the scene of the murder. In the meantime—"

He banged a bell that stood upon his desk.

The two police who had called at the hotel stepped into the office. There followed a rapid order in Portuguese, a language of which I understood very little. I saw Bazarada smile. In response to a tap on the shoulder he nodded to me, turned and walked out between the two policemen. The door closed.

A third policeman, whom I strongly suspected of representing the remainder of the force on duty, appeared at my elbow. He tapped me on the shoulder.

I was boiling with indignation when I reached the British consul. I dragged him out from a dinner party remorselessly, and he listened to the story I had to tell.

"It's a remarkable story, Mr. Roder," he admitted, incredulity in his frank blue eyes. "Dr. Sarafan, who spends, I suppose, some three or four months of the year in his villa here, is admittedly a mysterious figure. He is carrying out, I understand, certain important experiments. He is well thought of and much respected in Funchal. You must realize that in a murder charge bail is not allowed. And, as I see the matter, it is your word—which, believe me, I don't doubt—against Dr. Sarafan. What can I do?"

It was my first experience of that curious apathy which claims residents in these lotus eaters' islands. In this emergency, I realized, I stood quite alone.

My attempt to obtain an interview with the governor of the island resulted in an unmistakable rebuff.

On my way back from this in a state of furious irritation, I feverishly reviewed the facts. The wretched Mary Coppinger was obviously in the power of Servius Jerome. Short of kidnaping her, I could see no hope of saving her from the man. The charge of abduction, upon which Ned Regan had succeeded in obtaining a warrant for Jerome's arrest, might possibly have prevented the marriage had Regan arrived in time. But that it would result in any action being taken against Jerome, I doubted. In some way, Coppinger, or his representatives, had managed to suppress the story of Mary's disappearance. In the circumstances this did not help matters. I was still puzzling over these things and the plight of Bazarada when I stepped into the lobby of the hotel.

Servius Jerome stood up to meet me!

"Mr. Roder," he said, and I found myself falling under the spell of his strange eyes, "I have waited for you for a purpose."

There was no one else in the lobby—and clearly he read my thoughts, for:

"What could it avail?" he asked quietly. "I am no weakling. Even supposing that you knocked me out, in what way would this benefit Mary Coppinger or Bazarada?"

In the empty lobby I stood silent, watching him.

"You have presumed to come between me and the woman I intend to marry—"

It was on the tip of my tongue to say: "The woman you love so well that you offered to accept a hundred thousand dollars *not* to marry her"—but, in the nick of time, wiser counsel checked me.

"I am a stickler for the letter of the law. My fiancée comes of age tomorrow. The wedding takes place at the somewhat unusual hour of eight o'clock in the morning. Be good enough to respect my wishes in the matter, and to refrain from interfering with my personal affairs. Your friend Bazarada is in an unhappy position. I have influence here. I might withdraw the charge against him if he, on his part, agreed to leave Madeira without causing me further trouble. Are you disposed, Mr. Roder, to make this promise on his behalf?"

"I am not."

"In the circumstances, then, I have no alternative but to proceed to the prison and to interview Bazarada in person."

"You are welcome."

"Perhaps you would care to accompany me?"

"I would accompany you nowhere, unless possibly to your execution. You are a scoundrel whose name stinks throughout Europe. A kidnaper, a blackmailer. Yet here you stand before me, and I am helpless."

I suppose I was taunting him, trying to tempt him to attack me; for I was fighting mad. But, slightly inclining his head, he walked out of the lobby—a sinister, black-cloaked figure.

I fell into a troubled sleep with Bazarada's strange injunction, "Do nothing. Say nothing. Try nothing—wait for Ned Regan," going round and round in my brain like a refrain. A loud banging on the door awakened me.

Springing up, I glanced at my watch. The hour was 4 A.M.

The banging on the door continued. I got out of bed, crossed and opened the door.

The burly form of Ned W. Regan confronted me.

"Hello, Mr. Roder!" he exclaimed, and grasped my hand in a

mighty grip. "What's this I hear? We anchored forty-five minutes back. Passengers don't come ashore earlier than nine. But ship's orders don't apply to Ned Regan. Mr. Coppinger's here with me and the American consul's right downstairs. He didn't want to come—but he's here!"

Now I was wide awake.

"Mr. Regan! Thank God you've arrived! Bazarada's in jail."

"So I'm told."

Ned Regan thoughtfully flicked a lighter into action and rekindled a fragment of cigar.

"We must get him out."

"Buzzy can wait," Regan replied, returning the lighter to his pocket. "What we must do is this: You know this hideaway in the hills, where the man Jerome, or Sarafan as he calls himself, has smuggled the girl? That's our objective, sir. And we're going to send up blue fireworks in this little island!"

The presence of the big man was inspiring. When I got down to the lobby I found the manager, hastily dressed, standing there. Mr. Coppinger, a quiet, gray-haired New Englander, whose glance told the whole story of the agony he had suffered, met me. Thurston—the American consul with whom Bazarada had come to loggerheads—greeted me rather coldly.

"I've stirred everybody up," Ned Regan bellowed, "but we won't wait for 'em. Come along. We're off for the hideout in the hills."

In two cars, which the restless energy of Ned W. Regan had conjured up at that hour of the morning in a sleepy town, we set out for the Quinta de Santa Lucia. I traveled in the leading car, Ned Regan beside me.

At the point where, on my previous visit, Bazarada had parked the car, I indicated a narrow lane which led to the proper entrance.

Knocking and ringing for a time produced no result. Then the door was opened.

I beheld the yellow face of the Sicilian who had murdered his fellow countryman before my eyes! He was obviously frightened.

"Please, what is it?" he inquired.

The American consul replied in fluent Portuguese. The man answered him with much waving of hands.

"He says," Thurston explained, "that something terrible has happened. His master, Dr. Sarafan, is missing."

"That's not terrible," bellowed Regan, "it's just normal—what I expected! He's got wind I'm here!"

"But the doctor's fiancée, so he describes her, is also missing," Thurston continued.

"What!"

"They were to be married in the chapel at eight o'clock. The priest is already in the house."

He spoke again in Portuguese, and the man excitedly replied.

"Dr. Sarafan returned home late last night. He admitted himself with his key and went straight up to his study. This man saw him on the stairs. He turned all lights out and went to bed."

"What then?"

"He was awakened by a scream. You must know, Mr. Regan, that one of the servants was murdered here last night. The household is naturally restless. They thought it came from the room occupied by—"

"My daughter!" Mark Coppinger whispered—"It was Mary! Good God! This is awful. Please go on, Mr. Thurston. What does the man say?"

"He says, Mr. Coppinger, that they rushed to her room. The room was empty, although the bed had been slept in. They then hurried to Dr. Sarafan's room. There was no one there!"

"What time was that?"

"Just after three A.M."

Two windows opened somewhere above. I saw heads peeping out.

"A likely story!" Ned Regan roared. "Come on, Roder—we'll search the place!"

"I warn you that you have no powers," Thurston exclaimed.

"Powers or not, I'm doing it!" said Ned Regan.

He, myself, Mark Coppinger and one of the two drivers searched the house.

Neither Dr. Sarafan nor Mary Coppinger was in the Quinta da Santa Lucia.

Funchal was coming to life when we regained its outskirts. Ned Regan was furious.

I told him all I knew of the murder charge upon which Bazarada lay in jail.

"Two canary birds fighting out their private quarrels!" Ned Regan shouted above the roar of the motor. "This scoundrel saw his chance and took it quick! He used it as a frame-up to get rid of Buzzy, that's clear enough. It worked. We know where Buzzy is. What's bothering me is this: Where's the man Jerome? Where's Mary?"

By the time we reached the jail, Ned Regan's early activities had borne fruit. A representative of the governor awaited us, and we were admitted immediately. Mr. Coppinger was reduced to a pitiable state.

"Wait here, Mr. Coppinger," said Regan as we entered. "Just sit quiet. She's somewhere on the island and we'll get her."

"It is next to impossible that she should have left," Thurston murmured. "The American freighter *Dahomey* sailed at half past four this morning—but she carries no passengers."

"Then forget it," said Reagan.

We walked along a gloomy stone corridor, Regan following the man who held the keys. I came next with Thurston. The police officer and the governor's representatives brought up the rear. Our footsteps echoed hollowly as we descended stone steps. Before a forbidding door we paused. A key was inserted in the lock. The door swung open.

I saw a gloomy dungeon. One high, barred window admitted scanty light.

Ned Regan rushed in. "Buzzy!" he shouted. "Buzzy!"

There was no reply.

"Let's have more light! I can't see a thing in here!"

The man with the keys flashed a light upon the bed. A man was lying there, inert, face to the wall. I recognized Bazarada's white linen suit.

Then Regan turned him over. His wrists were lashed together—so were his ankles. A cloth was bound over his mouth.

"But what is this?" the governor's deputy asked.

"It's an outrage!" Ned Regan cut the lashings and removed the gag.

Eyes bloodshot, glaring, Servius Jerome struggled upright and confronted us!

He was beyond speech himself, and he was greeted by a silence of stupefaction. It was broken by a loud, harsh voice—the voice of one who, however astounding the circumstances, keeps his head and keeps his job clearly in view.

"I have a warrant for your arrest, Servius Jerome, otherwise Emmanuel Sarafan! My name is Ned W. Regan!"

In upon the bable that ensued broke a call from outside the cell:

"Radio message for Mr. Roder."

I turned. One of the Offenbach policemen was holding up an envelope. I sprang rather than walked into the gloomy corridor and opened the message. This is what I read:

FROM S. S. DAHOMEY

TO MAURICE RODER, REID'S HOTEL OR FUNCHAL JAIL. BOUND FOR LAS PALMAS. WILL WAIT THERE. HAVE MARY COPPINGER WITH ME.

BAZARADA

8

Treasure Trove

F. Tennyson Jesse

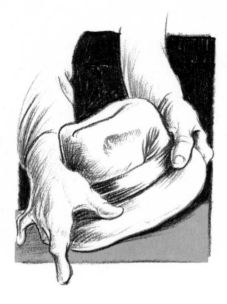

Summer stayed late that year, and it was not until the last day of October that Brandon realized it had gone. Then a storm sprang up which went sweeping over the marshes, ruffling the still, gray waters of the meres and inlets, and rending the leaves from the twisted trees. After it had passed, the warmth had gone from the air and only a pale, wintry sunshine lay pure and chill over the fen land. A few leaves still clung to the elms that grew about the farm place, and, as he pushed open the gate of the farmyard, he heard the cawing of the rooks about their nests, which showed black amid the bare branches.

Brandon felt for the moment the classic melancholy appropriate to the dying year, annual reminder of the Autumn that approaches to every man. But the next moment, turning his head to look back the way he had come, he saw that between the pale brown masses of the reeds the waters were a cold, bright blue, and the crystalline notes of the robin, practicing for its winter song, came to his ear. Beauty still lived in this fenny country and his heart responded gratefully.

He went across the muddy yard and met his friend Miles in the doorway of the farmhouse. Dear, good Miles—sun or rain, summer

or winter, held very little message for him that was not strictly
utilitarian. But Mile's ruddy, outdoor face seemed somehow to have
lost its usual cheerfulness of outlook, though it would certainly not
be because of anything to do with some allegorical message of the
dying summer.

"Have you seen Tom and Jack?" asked Miles. "They were supposed to be ploughing in the five-acre today, and they're not to be
found. They're so dependable as a rule."

"Tom and Jack? No. It doesn't matter, does it? I suppose they're
harrowing or mulching or marling or sowing or some other of the
many processes that you indulge in."

The strange expression on his host's face had not lightened.

"They've been queer," he said, "darn queer, for two days now,
ever since they found that cursed treasure while ploughing the
reclaimed piece of wasteland over by the big dyke. This morning
they looked so queerly at each other I didn't quite like them going
out together. There's something odd about it, Bill. I don't like it."

Brandon smiled and began to stuff his pipe.

"Nonsense, what could be wrong with your men?" he said. "It
won't be the first time a little bit of money has gone to a man's
head. They'll get over it, you'll see."

But to himself he was thinking that it was a bit queer all the
same. Everyone knew Tom and Jack, they were the famous friends
of the village. Damon and Pythias weren't in it when it came to
friendship. They had been to the same Council school as boys, been
in the same footer team in the winter, same cricket team in the
summer, skated together, gone duck-shooting together, gone fishing
together, fought in the same regiment through the war and had
even married twin sisters, and as far as anyone knew there had
never been a wry word between them. They were not men of any
special ability which would have caused them to grow away from
the class of life into which they had been born, but in that class
they were easily first in their district. Honest, decent, intelligent
men, a little slow in the process of their thoughts, perhaps, but none
the less shrewd and sound for that. Tom a year younger, slightly
built and active, Jack heavy compared with his friend, but strong
as a bull. Tom might be quick in his temper, but it was soon over.
Jack had the serenity that often goes with men of his large build.
It seemed sad and a little odd that a few dirty antique coins should
have been able to come between them.

"Why don't you tell them," he suggested to Miles, "that their
old coins are probably worth very little?"

"I have," said Miles. "But you know what these people are, they

always imagine anything they dig up must be of immense value
and that the British Museum would buy it for a large sum. I can
understand that part of it, what I can't understand is that they
should begin to quarrel over it. I should have thought they'd have
been only too glad to share it, however much or little it's worth.
Besides, their working hours are not over yet, and I've never known
them to down tools until the right hour, generally not till after it.
They're the real old-fashioned kind that doesn't like to leave a job
half done."

Scarcely had he said this when one of the maid-servants came
running from the passage at his back, calling to him in a loud and
frightened voice:

"Come quick, sir, Tom and Jack be fighting in the barn, they're
killing each other. . . ."

Miles turned and ran through the house, out into the front
garden and across it, Brandon at his heels.

The big barn stood on the slope of the field beyond, a wooden
building, black with pitch, with a red fluted roof. Beside it the
straw ricks gleamed golden in the late sunshine. The two men ran
up the slope of the field where the trodden turf was heavy and
greasy to their feet and Brandon, outstepping his more elderly host,
burst through the door into the barn.

For the first moment it all seemed very dark to him, a darkness
filled with dust motes that wreathed like steam in the rays shining
through the doorway. The smell of cattle and trodden earth, and
of the sweet stored hay, filled the dimness; rafters and rough wooden
pillars stood out in the gloom. Then, as sight grew clear, his ears
became aware of a horrible sound of sobbing that rose and fell, and
the thud of blows. Two men were fighting, backward and forward,
on the earthy floor. As Miles and Brandon sprang forward, the
bigger man, who was winning, rained blows upon either side of
his opponent's head, and the smaller man, from whom came the
noise of sobbing, suddenly crumpled up and fell to the floor, where
he lay still.

"Good God, man!" cried Miles, hanging onto the big fellow's
arm. "You must be mad, you might kill him."

The man turned a ravaged face to his master.

"I shouldn't care if I had, the dirty hound!" he said. "He's a
thief, that's what he is."

"Tom a thief! Nonsense. Why, you'd have fought anybody else
who said as much."

"Aye, I *would* have," said the man. "But not now. . . . He's
stolen all the money we dug up in the new field. He's hidden it

away somewhere and won't say where. He's just lying and saying
he hasn't got it."

Brandon had knelt down beside the unconscious Tom, whose
face was running with blood; now he looked up and said:

"Well, you've nearly killed him. Even if it's true, you ought to
be ashamed of yourself, and I don't believe it *is* true. Tom wouldn't
do a thing like that. By God, Miles, look at his fists. Open your
fists."

And he got up and advanced on Jack, who stood staring sullenly
at him, his clenched fists still held before him. Jack offered no
resistance as his master and Brandon pulled his fingers apart and
discovered, clenched in each hand, a ragged flint stone, their ends
dripping with Tom's blood. Brandon, looking at Jack's glazed eyes,
said nothing; it would be little use saying anything, he felt, to a
man as changed from the self they all knew, as this man was.
Instead, he said to Miles:

"We must get Tom out of this. You and Jack pick him up while
I have a look around."

With surprising docility Jack bent down and picked up gently
the head he had ill-treated, and he and Miles between them carried the unconscious man out through the ray of sunlight into the
air.

Brandon sat down on an upturned bucket near at hand. He felt
sick and ill at the sight of the blood, an idiosyncrasy of his so
unconquerable that he had ceased to be ashamed of it. It seemed
to him that the dim air of the barn was laden still with the violent
passions that had been released there, that the element of strange-
ness in this sudden hatred sickened the very sunlight that slanted
in upon the spot trodden by the men's struggling feet.

Brandon was not normally a super-sensitive man, but all his life
he had been the prey of moments which had taken and shaken
him oddly, moments when he had seemed not through any superior
gifts of his own, but because of some outer compulsion, to be aware
of more than most men, of more than, ordinarily, he would have
been aware of himself. Usually these strange spaces of clarity were
prefaced by an unaccountable aspect of external things; a familiar
tree or bookshelf would take on a look that he could only describe
himself as "tilted," as though the angle of the visible world had
started off in a new direction, pointing toward an unknown dimen-
sion; as though the tree or bookshelf had lost, all of a sudden, its
treeness or furniturehood, and become a wedge thrust into space.
At the time this would seem all right to him; only afterwards,
looking back, his senses still giddy, he would realize the different

tilt. And, cutting across this new space, there would come a wedge of light, tilted at the same new angle, which for the moment was the right angle, and in it he would be aware of, rather than see, a new and more complete aspect of something he had only imperfectly known before. A friend's motive for doing what had to him previously seemed inexplicable; the solution to some riddle in the history lecture he was working out; of sometimes even a fresh light upon a matter which had no earthly connection, as far as he knew, with himself.

He was almost hypnotized into this feeling now, as he sat there in the barn, but he shook off the dizzying sensations, like the familiar pins and needles of the children, that were stealing over him, and told himself it was due to the upset of his nerves and to the angle of the shaft of light that streamed in at the door. He got to his feet and as he did so he caught sight of a battered felt hat lying against the wall of the barn. He went over to it to take it up. He recognized it as Tom's by its peculiar light-gray color and by the blue jay's feather stuck in the band. He bent to pick it up, but to his surprise it was so unexpectedly heavy in his hand that he almost dropped it. He ran his fingers behind the head lining of the crown; wrapped in a thin piece of stuff he felt the uneven surfaces of coins. So Tom had lied after all . . . he had concealed the coins. Brandon felt as when he had seen the flints concealed in Jack's fists.

He picked up the hat, and went heavily out of the barn with the hat carried between his two hands. He crossed the garden and went into the little room outside the front door which Miles used as his office.

Brandon closed the door and sat down at the table, pushing away papers and ledgers to make a clear space in front of him. Then he turned the hat up, and pulled out the pack of coins which lay, snakelike, curled around the crown. He unfolded the strip of soiled silk handkerchief and poured the coins out on the table before him. There they lay, the source of all the trouble between Tom and Jack, a mere handful of dirty, almost shapeless coins. Brandon looked at them curiously. They were so old and battered he could only just make out the head of a Caesar—which, he knew not, but the Roman look of it was unmistakable. It seemed incredible that through these coins, the passion of envy, mounting murder high, had come into being. . . . He scraped the coins together in his two hands.

And then, as he sat there, the strange sensation came flooding over him, drenching him, as it were, to the tips of his fingers and toes, so that he felt he could not move if the house caught fire about him. He felt very cold, in spite of the tingling that pervaded him, and he knew—how, he could not have told—that he was holding in his palms things so evil that his very flesh revolted, things so evil that whenever they were discovered and rediscovered by men they brought evil in their train. He knew, with a dreadful clearness in the midst of this dark red mist, that these things had been turned up by the ploughshare, or dragged from the sea, or cast upon beaches throughout the years, and whosoever found them knew desolation and decay of everything that had been his until then. There beat at him persistently the knowledge that he must take these things out and throw them away in the place where it' was least likely they would be found for generations to come. He must weight them heavily and cast them out to sea, or throw them into the still waters of some disused pit.

He struggled violently against the feeling of horror that held him, because he wished to see about this business as soon as might be, and by a violent effort of the will he pulled himself back into the present. The evening sun was still shining into the little room. Shaking, but with the tingling slowly growing less all over his body, he drew his hands away from the clustering coins and let them fall upon the table. He passed his palm across his wet forehead and told himself that in another moment or so he would be able to do what he had to do, and quite soon he stood up, his steady self again, although not denying he had been shaken.

It was suddenly that the dreadful idea took him. Putting out his hands he began to count the coins; he counted three times, always hoping that in his hurry he might have erred, but count as he would, the battered pieces of silver numbered thirty. Brandon leaped up, and drew away from the table, his hands shaking. He found himself saying in a dreadful whisper: "Thirty pieces of silver . . . thirty pieces . . . of silver."

9

Yours Truly,
Jack the Ripper

Robert Bloch

I looked at the stage Englishman. He looked at me.

"Sir Guy Hollis?" I asked.

"Indeed. Have I the pleasure of addressing John Carmody, the psychiatrist?"

I nodded. My eyes swept over the figure of my distinguished visitor. Tall, lean, sandy-haired—with the traditional tufted mustache. And the tweeds. I suspected a monocle concealed in a vest pocket, and wondered if he'd left his umbrella in the outer office.

But more than that, I wondered what the devil had impelled Sir Guy Hollis of the British Embassy to seek out a total stranger here in Chicago.

Sir Guy didn't help matters any as he sat down. He cleared his throat, glanced around nervously, tapped his pipe against the side of the desk. Then he opened his mouth.

"What do you think of London?" he said.

"Why—"

"I'd like to discuss London with you, Mr. Carmody."

I meet all kinds. So I merely smiled, sat back, and gave him his head.

"Have you ever noticed anything strange about that city?" he asked.

"Well, the fog is famous."

"Yes, the fog. That's important. It usually provides the perfect setting."

"Setting for what?"

Sir Guy Hollis gave me an enigmatic grin.

"Murder," he murmured.

"Murder?"

"Yes. Hasn't it struck you that London, of all cities, has a peculiar affinity for those who contemplate homicide?"

They don't talk that way, except in books. Still, it was an interesting thought. London as an ideal spot for a murder!

"As you mentioned," said Sir Guy, "there is a natural reason for this. The fog is an ideal background. And then too the British have a peculiar attitude in such matters. You might call it their sporting instinct. They regard murder as sort of a game."

I sat up straight. Here was a theory.

"Yes, I needn't bore you with homicide statistics. The record is there. Aesthetically, temperamentally, the Englishman is interested in crimes of violence.

"A man commits murder. Then the excitement begins. The game starts. Will the criminal outwit the police? You can read between the lines in their newspaper stories. Everybody is waiting to see who will score.

"British law regards a prisoner as guilty until proven innocent. That's *their* advantage. But first they must catch their prisoner. And London bobbies are not allowed to carry firearms. That's a point for the fugitive. You see? All part of the rules of the game."

I wondered what Sir Guy was driving at. Either a point or a strait jacket. But I kept my mouth shut and let him continue.

"The logical result of this British attitude toward murder is—Sherlock Holmes," he said.

"Have you ever noticed how popular the theme of murder is in British fiction and drama?"

I smiled. I was back on familiar ground.

"*Angel Street,*" I suggested.

"*Ladies in Retirement,*" he continued. "*Night Must Fall.*"

"*Payment Deferred,*" I added. "*Laburnum Grove. Kind Lady. Love from a Stranger. Portrait of a Man with Red Hair. Black Limelight.*"

He nodded. "Think of the motion pictures of Alfred Hitchcock and Emlyn Williams. The actors—Wilfred Lawson and Leslie Banks."

"Charles Laughton," I continued for him. "Edmund Gwenn. Basil Rathbone. Raymond Massey. Sir Cedric Hardwicke."

"You're quite an expert on this sort of thing yourself," he told me.

"Not at all." I smiled. "I'm a psychiatrist."

Then I leaned forward. I didn't change my tone of voice. "All I know," I said sweetly, "is why you come up to my office and discuss murder melodramas with me."

It stung him. He sat back and blinked a little.

"That isn't my intention," he murmured. "No. Not at all. I was just advancing a theory—"

"Stalling," I said. "Stalling. Come on, Sir Guy—spit it out."

Talking like a gangster is all part of the applied psychiatric technique. At least, it worked for me.

It worked this time.

Sir Guy stopped bleating. His eyes narrowed. When he leaned forward again he meant business.

"Mr. Carmody," he said, "have you ever heard of—Jack the Ripper?"

"The murderer?" I asked.

"Exactly. The greatest monster of them all. Worse than Spring-heel Jack or Crippen. Jack the Ripper. Red Jack."

"I've heard of him," I said.

"Do you know his history?"

I got tough again. "Listen, Sir Guy," I muttered. "I don't think we'll get any place swapping old wives' tales about famous crimes of history."

Another bull's-eye. He took a deep breath.

"This is no old wives' tale. It's a matter of life or death."

He was so wrapped up in his obsession he even talked that way. Well—I was willing to listen. We psychiatrists get paid for listening.

"Go ahead," I told him. "Let's have the story."

Sir Guy lit a cigarette and began to talk.

"London, 1888," he began. "Late summer and early fall. That was the time. Out of nowhere came the shadowy figure of Jack the Ripper—a stalking shadow with a knife, prowling through London's East End. Haunting the squalid dives of Whitechapel, Spitalfields. Where he came from no one knew. But he brought death. Death in a knife.

"Six times that knife descended to slash the throats and bodies of London's women. Drabs and alley sluts. August 7th was the date of the first butchery. They found her body lying there with 39 stab wounds. A ghastly murder. On August 31st, another victim. The press became interested. The slum inhabitants were more deeply interested still.

"Who was this unknown killer who prowled in their midst and struck at will in the deserted alleyways of night-town? And what was more important—when would he strike again?

"September 8th was the date. Scotland Yard assigned special deputies. Rumors ran rampant. The atrocious nature of the slayings was the subject for shocking speculation.

"The killer used a knife—expertly. He cut throats. He chose victims and settings with a fiendish deliberation. No one saw him or heard him. But watchmen making their gray rounds in the dawn would stumble across the hacked and horrid thing that was the Ripper's handiwork.

"Who was he? What was he? A mad surgeon? A butcher? An insane scientist? A pathological degenerate escaped from an asylum? A deranged nobleman? A member of the London police?

"Then the poem appeared in the newspapers. The anonymous poem, designed to put a stop to speculations—but which only aroused public interest to a further frenzy. A mocking little stanza:

> I'm not a butcher, I'm not a kid
> Nor yet a foreign skipper,
> But I'm your own true loving friend,
> Yours truly—Jack the Ripper.

"And on September 30th, two more throats were slashed open."
I interrupted Sir Guy for a moment.
"Very interesting," I commented. I'm afraid a faint hint of sarcasm crept into my voice.
He winced, but didn't falter in his narrative.
"There was silence, then, in London for a time. Silence, and a nameless fear. When would Red Jack strike again? They waited through October. Every figment of fog concealed his phantom presence. Concealed it well—for nothing was learned of the Ripper's identity, or his purpose. The drabs of London shivered in the raw wind of early November. Shivered, and were thankful for the coming of each morning's sun.

"November 9th. They found her in her room. She lay there very quietly, limbs neatly arranged. And beside her, with equal neatness, were laid her head and heart. The Ripper had outdone himself in execution.

"Then, panic. But needless panic. For though press, police, and populace alike waited in sick dread, Jack the Ripper did not strike again.

"Months passed. A year. The immediate interest died, but not the memory. They said Jack had skipped to America. That he had committed suicide. They said—and they wrote. They've written ever since. Theories, hypotheses, arguments, treatises. But to this day no one knows who Jack the Ripper was. Or why he killed. Or why he stopped killing."

Sir Guy was silent. Obviously he expected some comment from me.

"You tell the story well," I remarked. "Though with a slight emotional bias."

"I've got all the documents," said Sir Guy Hollis. "I've made a collection of existing data and studied it."

I stood up. "Well," I yawned, in mock fatigue, "I've enjoyed your little bedtime story a great deal, Sir Guy. It was kind of you to abandon your duties at the British Embassy to drop in on a poor psychiatrist and regale him with your anecdotes."

Goading him always did the trick.

"I suppose you want to know why I'm interested?" he snapped.

"Yes. That's exactly what I'd like to know. Why are you interested?"

"Because," said Sir Guy Hollis, "I am on the trail of Jack the Ripper now. I think he's here—in Chicago!"

I sat down again. This time I did the blinking act.

"Say that again," I stuttered.

"Jack the Ripper is alive, in Chicago, and I'm out to find him."

"Wait a minute," I said. "Wait—a—minute!"

He wasn't smiling. It wasn't a joke.

"See here," I said. "What was the date of these murders?"

"August to November, 1888."

"1888? But if Jack the Ripper was an able-bodied man in 1888, he'd surely be dead today! Why look, man—if he were merely *born* in that year, he'd be 55 years old today!"

"Would he?" smiled Sir Guy Hollis. "Or should I say, 'Would she?' Because Jack the Ripper may have been a woman. Or any number of things."

"Sir Guy," I said. "You came to the right person when you looked me up. You definitely need the services of a psychiatrist."

"Perhaps. Tell me, Mr. Carmody, do you think I'm crazy?"

I looked at him and shrugged. But I had to give him a truthful answer.

"Frankly—no."

"Then you might listen to the reasons I believe Jack the Ripper is alive today."

"I might."

"I've studied these cases for thirty years. Been over the actual ground. Talked to officials. Talked to friends and acquaintances of the poor drabs who were killed. Visited with men and women in the neighborhood. Collected an entire library of material touching on Jack the Ripper. Studied all the wild theories or crazy notions.

"I learned a little. Not much, but a little. I won't bore you with my conclusions. But there was another branch of inquiry that yielded more fruitful returns. I have studied unsolved crimes. Murders.

"I could show you clippings from the papers of half the world's great cities. San Francisco. Shanghai. Calcutta. Omsk. Paris. Berlin. Pretoria. Cairo. Milan. Adelaide.

"The trail is there, the pattern. Unsolved crimes. Slashed throats of women. With the peculiar disfigurations and removals. Yes, I've followed a trail of blood. From New York westward across the continent. Then to the Pacific. From there to Africa. During the World War of 1914–18 it was Europe. After that, South America. And since 1930, the United States again. Eighty-seven such murders—and to the trained criminologist, all bear the stigma of the Ripper's handiwork.

"Recently there were the so-called Cleveland torso slayings. Remember? A shocking series. And finally, two recent deaths in Chicago. Within the past six months. One out on South Dearborn. The other somewhere up on Halsted. Same type of crime, same technique. I tell you, there are unmistakable indications in all these affairs—indications of the work of Jack the Ripper!"

I smiled.

"A very tight theory," I said. "I'll not question your evidence at all, or the deductions you draw. You're the criminologist, and I'll take your word for it. Just one thing remains to be explained. A minor point, perhaps, but worth mentioning."

"And what is that?" asked Sir Guy.

"Just how could a man of, let us say, 85 years commit these crimes? For if Jack the Ripper was around 30 in 1888 and lived, he'd be 85 today."

Sir Guy Hollis was silent. I had him there. But—

"Suppose he didn't get any older?" whispered Sir Guy.

"What's that?"

"Suppose Jack the Ripper didn't grow old? Suppose he is still a young man today?"

"All right," I said. "I'll suppose for a moment. Then I'll stop supposing and call for my nurse to restrain you."

"I'm serious," said Sir Guy.

"They all are," I told him. "That's the pity of it all, isn't it? They *know* they hear voices and see demons. But we lock them up just the same."

It was cruel, but it got results. He rose and faced me.

"It's a crazy theory, I grant you," he said. "All the theories about the Ripper are crazy. The idea that he was a doctor. Or a maniac. Or a woman. The reasons advanced for such beliefs are flimsy enough. There's nothing to go by. So why should my notion be any worse?"

"Because people grow older," I reasoned with him. "Doctors, maniacs, and women alike."

"What about—*sorcerers?*"

"Sorcerers?"

"Necromancers. Wizards. Practicers of Black Magic?"

"What's the point?"

"I studied," said Sir Guy. "I studied everything. After awhile I began to study the dates of the murders. The pattern those dates formed. The rhythm. The solar, lunar, stellar rhythm. The sidereal aspect. The astrological significance."

He *was* crazy. But I still listened.

"Suppose Jack the Ripper didn't murder for murder's sake alone? Suppose he wanted to make—a sacrifice?"

"What kind of a sacrifice?"

Sir Guy shrugged. "It is said that if you offer blood to the dark gods they grant boons. Yes, if a blood offering is made at the proper time—when the moon and the stars are right—and with the proper ceremonies—they grant boons. Boons of youth. Eternal youth."

"But that's nonsense!"

"No. That's—Jack the Ripper."

I stood up. "A most interesting theory," I told him. "But Sir Guy—there's just one thing I'm interested in. Why do you come here and tell it to me? I'm not an authority on witchcraft. I'm not a police official or criminologist. I'm a practicing psychiatrist. What's the connection?"

Sir Guy smiled.

"You are interested, then?"

"Well, yes. There must be some point."

"There is. But I wished to be assured of your interest first. Now I can tell you my plan."

"And just what is that plan?"

Sir Guy gave me a long look. Then he spoke.

"John Carmody," he said, "you and I are going to capture Jack the Ripper."

That's the way it happened. I've given the gist of that first interview in all its intricate and somewhat boring detail, because I think it's important. It helps to throw some light on Sir Guy's character and attitude. And in view of what happened after that—

But I'm coming to those matters.

Sir Guy's thought was simple. It wasn't even a thought. Just a hunch.

"You know the people here," he told me. "I've inquired. That's why I came to you as the ideal man for my purpose. You number among your acquaintances many writers, painters, poets. The so-called intelligentsia. The Bohemians. The lunatic fringe from the near north side.

"For certain reasons—never mind what they are—my clues lead me to infer that Jack the Ripper is a member of that element. He chooses to pose as an eccentric. I've a feeling that with you to take me around and introduce me to your set, I might hit upon the right person."

"It's all right with me," I said. "But just how are you going to look for him? As you say, he might be anybody, anywhere. And you have no idea what he looks like. He might be young or old. Jack the Ripper—a Jack of all trades? Rich man, poor man, beggar man, thief, doctor, lawyer—how will you know?"

"We shall see." Sir Guy sighed heavily. "But I must find him. At once."

"Why the hurry?"

Sir Guy sighed again. "Because in two days he will kill again."

"Are you sure?"

"Sure as the stars. I've plotted his chart, you see. All 87 of the murders correspond to certain astrological rhythm patterns. If, as I suspect, he makes a blood sacrifice to renew his youth, he must murder within two days. Notice the pattern of his first crimes in London. August 7th. Then August 31. September 8th. September 30th. November 9th. Intervals of 24 days, 9 days, 22 days—he killed two this time—and then 40 days. Of course there were crimes in between. There had to be. But they weren't discovered and pinned on him.

"At any rate, I've worked out a pattern for him, based on all my data. And I say that within the next two days he kills. So I must seek him out, somehow, before then."

"And I'm still asking you what you want me to do."

"Take me out," said Sir Guy. "Introduce me to your friends. Take me to parties."

"But where do I begin? As far as I know, my artistic friends, despite their eccentricities, are all normal people."

"So is the Ripper. Perfectly normal. Except on certain nights." Again that faraway look in Sir Guy's eyes. "Then he becomes an ageless pathological monster, crouching to kill, on evenings when the stars blaze down in the blazing patterns of death."

"All right," I said. "All right. I'll take you to parties, Sir Guy. I want to go myself, anyway. I need the drinks they'll serve there, after listening to your kind of talk."

We made our plans. And that evening I took him over to Lester Baston's studio.

As we ascended to the penthouse roof in the elevator I took the opportunity to warn Sir Guy.

"Baston's a real screwball," I cautioned him. "So are his guests. Be prepared for anything and everything."

"I am." Sir Guy Hollis was perfectly serious. He put his hand in his trousers pocket and pulled out a gun.

"What the—" I began.

"If I see him I'll be ready," Sir Guy said. He didn't smile, either.

"But you can't go running around at a party with a loaded revolver in your pocket, man!"

"Don't worry, I won't behave foolishly."

I wondered. Sir Guy Hollis was not, to my way of thinking, a normal man.

We stepped out of the elevator, went toward Baston's apartment door.

"By the way," I murmured, "just how do you wish to be introduced? Shall I tell them who you are and what you are looking for?

"I don't care. Perhaps it would be best to be frank."

"But don't you think that the Ripper—if by some miracle he or she is present—will immediately get the wind up and take cover?"

"I think the shock of the announcement that I am hunting the Ripper would provoke some kind of betraying gesture on his part," said Sir Guy.

"You'd make a pretty good psychiatrist yourself," I conceded. "It's a fine theory. But I warn you, you're going to be in for a lot of ribbing. This is a wild bunch."

Sir Guy smiled.

"I'm ready," he announced. "I have a little plan of my own. Don't be shocked by anything I do," he warned me.

I nodded and knocked on the door.

Baston opened it and poured out into the hall. He teetered back and forth regarding us very gravely. He squinted at my square-cut homburg hat and Sir Guy's mustache.

"Aha," he intoned. "The Walrus and the Carpenter."

I introduced Sir Guy.

"Welcome," said Baston, gesturing us inside with over-elaborate courtesy. He stumbled after us into the garish parlor.

I stared at the crowd that moved restlessly through the fog of cigarette smoke.

It was the shank of the evening for this mob. Every hand held a drink. Every face held a slightly hectic flush. Over in one corner the piano was going full blast.

Sir Guy got a monocle-full right away. He saw LaVerne Gonnister, the poetess, hit Hymie Kralik in the eye. He saw Hymie sit down on the floor and cry until Dick Pool accidentally stepped on his stomach as he walked through to the dining room for a drink.

He heard Nadia Vilinoff the commercial artist tell Johnny Odcutt that she thought his tattooing was in dreadful taste.

His zoological observations might have continued indefinitely if Lester Baston hadn't stepped to the center of the room and called for silence by dropping a vase on the floor.

"We have distinguished visitors in our midst," bawled Lester, waving his empty glass in our direction. "None other than the Walrus and the Carpenter. The Walrus is Sir Guy Hollis, a something-or-other from the British Embassy. The Carpenter, as you all know, is our own John Carmody, the prominent dispenser of libido-liniment."

He turned and grabbed Sir Guy by the arm, dragging him to the middle of the carpet. For a moment I thought Hollis might object, but a quick wink reassured me. He was prepared for this.

"It is our custom, Sir Guy," said Baston, loudly, "to subject our new friends to a little cross-examination. Just a little formality at these very formal gatherings, you understand. Are you prepared to answer questions?"

Sir Guy nodded and grinned.

"Very well," Baston muttered. "Friends—I give you this bundle from Britain. Your witness."

Then the ribbing started. I meant to listen, but at that moment Lydia Dare saw me and dragged me off into the vestibule for one of those Darling-I-waited-for-your-call-all-day routines.

By the time I got rid of her and went back, the impromptu quiz session was in full swing. From the attitude of the crowd, I gathered that Sir Guy was doing all right for himself.

Then Baston himself interjected a question that upset the applecart.

"And what, may I ask, brings you to our midst tonight? What is your mission, oh Walrus?"

"I'm looking for Jack the Ripper."

Nobody laughed.

Perhaps it struck them all the way it did me. I glanced at my neighbors and began to *wonder*.

LaVerne Gonnister. Hymie Kralik. Harmless. Dick Pool. Nadia Vilinoff. Johnny Odcutt and his wife. Barclay Melton. Lydia Dare. All harmless.

But what a forced smile on Dick Pool's face! And that sly, self-conscious smirk that Barclay Melton wore!

Oh, it was absurd, I grant you. But for the first time I saw these people in a new light. I wondered about their lives—their secret lives beyond the scenes of parties.

How many of them were playing a part, concealing something?

Who here would worship Hecate and grant that horrid goddess the dark boon of blood?

Even Lester Baston might be masquerading.

The mood was upon us all, for a moment. I saw questions flicker in the circle of eyes around the room.

Sir Guy stood there, and I could swear he was fully conscious of the situation he'd created, and enjoyed it.

I wondered idly just what was *really* wrong with him. Why he had this odd fixation concerning Jack the Ripper. Maybe he was hiding secrets, too. . . .

Baston, as usual, broke the mood. He burlesqued it.

"The Walrus isn't kidding, friends," he said. He slapped Sir Guy on the back and put his arm around him as he orated. "Our English cousin is really on the trail of the fabulous Jack the

Ripper. You all remember Jack the Ripper, I presume? Quite a
cutup in the old days, as I recall. Really had some ripping good
times when he went out on a tear.

"The Walrus has some idea that the Ripper is still alive,
probably prowling around Chicago with a Boy Scout knife. In
fact"—Baston paused impressively and shot it out in a rasping
stage-whisper—"in fact, he has reason to believe that Jack the
Ripper might even be right here in our midst tonight."

There was the expected reaction of giggles and grins. Baston
eyed Lydia Dare reprovingly. "You girls needn't laugh," he smirked.
"Jack the Ripper might be a woman, too, you know. Sort of a
Jill the Ripper."

"You mean you actually suspect one of us?" shrieked LaVerne
Gonnister, simpering up to Sir Guy. "But that Jack the Ripper
person disappeared ages ago, didn't he? In 1888?"

"Aha!" interrupted Baston. "How do you know so much about
it, young lady? Sounds suspicious! Watch her, Sir Guy—she may
not be as young as she appears. These lady poets have dark pasts."

The tension was gone, the mood was shattered, and the whole
thing was beginning to degenerate into a trivial party joke.

Then Baston caught it.

"Guess what?" he yelled. "The Walrus has a gun."

His embracing arm had slipped and encountered the hard outline of the gun in Sir Guy's pocket. He snatched it out before
Hollis had the opportunity to protest.

I stared hard at Sir Guy, wondering if this thing had carried
far enough. But he flicked a wink my way and I remembered he
had told me not to be alarmed.

So I waited as Baston broached a drunken inspiration.

"Let's play fair with our friend the Walrus," he cried. "He came
all the way from England to our party on this mission. If none
of you is willing to confess, I suggest we give him a chance to
find out—the hard way."

"What's up?" asked Johnny Odcutt.

"I'll turn out the lights for one minute. Sir Guy can stand here
with his gun. If anyone in this room is the Ripper he can either
run for it or take the opportunity to—well, eradicate his pursuer.
Fair enough?"

It was even sillier than it sounds, but it caught the popular
fancy. Sir Guy's protests went unheard in the ensuing babble. And
before I could stride over and put in my two cents' worth, Lester
Baston had reached the light switch.

"Don't anybody move," he announced, with fake solemnity.

"For one minute we will remain in darkness—perhaps at the mercy of a killer. At the end of that time, I'll turn up the lights again and look for bodies. Choose your partners, ladies and gentlemen."

The lights went out.

Somebody giggled.

I heard footsteps in the darkness. Mutterings.

A hand brushed my face.

The watch on my wrist ticked violently. But even louder, rising above it, I heard another thumping. The beating of my heart.

Absurd. Standing in the dark with a group of tipsy fools. And yet there was real terror lurking here, rustling through the velvet blackness.

Jack the Ripper prowled in darkness like this. And Jack the Ripper had a knife. Jack the Ripper had a madman's brain and a madman's purpose.

But Jack the Ripper was dead, dead and dust these many years—by every human law.

Only there are no human laws when you feel yourself in the darkness, when the darkness hides and protects and the outer mask slips off your face and you feel something welling up within you, a brooding shapeless purpose that is brother to the blackness.

Sir Guy Hollis shrieked.

There was a grisly thud.

Baston had the lights on.

Everybody screamed.

Sir Guy Hollis lay sprawled on the floor in the center of the room. The gun was still clutched in his hand.

I glanced at the faces, marveling at the variety of expressions human beings can assume when confronting horror.

All the faces were present in the circle. Nobody had fled. And yet Sir Guy Hollis lay there . . .

LaVerne Gonnister was wailing and hiding her face.

"All right."

Sir Guy rolled over and jumped to his feet. He was smiling.

"Just an experiment, eh? If Jack the Ripper *were* among those present, and thought I had been murdered, he would have betrayed himself in some way when the lights went on and he saw me lying there.

"I am convinced of your individual and collective innocence. Just a gentle spoof, my friends."

Hollis stared at the goggling Baston and the rest of them crowding in behind him.

"Shall we leave, John?" he called to me. "It's getting late, I think."

Turning, he headed for the closet. I followed him. Nobody said a word.

It was a pretty dull party after that.

I met Sir Guy the following evening as we agreed, on the corner of 29th and South Halsted.

After what had happened the night before, I was prepared for almost anything. But Sir Guy seemed matter-of-fact enough as he stood huddled against a grimy doorway and waited for me to appear.

"Boo!" I said, jumping out suddenly. He smiled. Only the betraying gesture of his left hand indicated that he'd instinctively reached for his gun when I startled him.

"All ready for our wild goose chase?" I asked.

"Yes." He nodded. "I'm glad that you agreed to meet me without asking questions," he told me. "It shows you trust my judgment." He took my arm and edged me along the street slowly.

"It's foggy tonight, John," said Sir Guy Hollis. "Like London."

I nodded.

"Cold, too, for November."

I nodded again and half-shivered my agreement.

"Curious," mused Sir Guy. "London fog and November. The place and the time of the Ripper murders."

I grinned through darkness. "Let me remind you, Sir Guy, that this isn't London, but Chicago. And it isn't November, 1888. It's over fifty years later."

Sir Guy returned my grin, but without mirth. "I'm not so sure, at that," he murmured. "Look about you. These tangled alleys and twisted streets. They're like the East End. Mitre Square. And surely they are as ancient as fifty years, at least."

"You're in the poor neighborhood off South Clark Street," I said, shortly. "And why you dragged me down here I still don't know."

"It's a hunch," Sir Guy admitted. "Just a hunch on my part, John. I want to wander around down here. There's the same geographical conformation in these streets as in those courts where the Ripper roamed and slew. That's where we'll find him, John.

Not in the bright lights of the Bohemian neighborhood, but down here in the darkness. The darkness where he waits and crouches."

"Is that why you brought a gun?" I asked. I was unable to keep a trace of sarcastic nervousness from my voice. All of this talk, this incessant obsession with Jack the Ripper, got on my nerves more than I cared to admit.

"We may need the gun," said Sir Guy, gravely. "After all, tonight is the appointed night."

I sighed. We wandered on through the foggy, deserted streets. Here and there a dim light burned above a doorway. Otherwise, all was darkness and shadow. Deep, gaping alleyways loomed as we proceeded down a slanting side street.

We crawled through that fog, alone and silent, like two tiny maggots floundering within a shroud.

When that thought him me, I winced. The atmosphere was beginning to get *me,* too. If I didn't watch my step I'd go as loony as Sir Guy.

"Can't you see there's not a soul around these streets?" I said, tugging at his coat impatiently.

"He's bound to come," said Sir Guy. "He'll be drawn here. This is what I've been looking for. A *genius loci.* An evil spot that attracts evil. Always, when he slays, it's in the slums.

"You see, that must be one of his weaknesses. He has a fascination for squalor. Besides, the women he needs for sacrifice are more easily found in the dives and stewpots of a great city."

I smiled. "Well, let's go into one of the dives or stewpots," I suggested. "I'm cold. Need a drink. This fog gets into your bones. You Britishers can stand it, but I like warmth and dry heat."

We emerged from our side street and stood upon the threshold of an alley.

Through the white clouds of mist ahead, I discerned a dim blue light, a naked bulb dangling from a beer sign above an alley tavern.

"Let's take a chance," I said. "I'm beginning to shiver."

"Lead the way," said Sir Guy. I led him down the alley passage. We halted before the door of the dive.

"What are you waiting for?" he asked.

"Just looking in," I told him. "This is a tough neighborhood, Sir Guy. Never know what you're liable to run into. And I'd prefer we didn't get into the wrong company."

"Good idea, John."

I finished my inspection through the doorway. "Looks deserted," I murmured. "Let's try it."

We entered a dingy bar. A feeble light flickered above the counter and railing, but failed to penetrate the further gloom of the back booths.

A gigantic Negro lolled across the bar. He scarcely stirred as we came in, but his eyes flickered open quite suddenly and I knew he noted our presence and was judging us.

"Evening," I said.

He took his time before replying. Still sizing us up. Then he grinned.

"Evening, gents. What's your pleasure?"

"Gin," I said. "Two gins. It's a cold night."

"That's right, gents."

He poured, I paid, and took the glasses over to one of the booths. We wasted no time in emptying them. The fiery liquor warmed.

I went over to the bar and got the bottle. Sir Guy and I poured ourselves another drink. The big Negro went back into his doze, with one wary eye half-open against any sudden activity.

The clock over the bar ticked on. The wind was rising outside, tearing the shroud of fog to ragged shreds. Sir Guy and I sat in the warm booth and drank our gin.

He began to talk, and the shadows crept up about us to listen.

He rambled a great deal. He went over everything he'd said in the office when I met him, just as though I hadn't heard it before. The poor devils with obsessions are like that.

I listened very patiently. I poured Sir Guy another drink. And another.

But the liquor only made him more talkative. How he did run on! About ritual killings and prolonging life unnaturally—the whole fantastic tale came out again. And, of course, he maintained his unyielding conviction that the Ripper was abroad tonight.

I suppose I was guilty of goading him.

"Very well," I said, unable to keep the impatience from my voice. "Let us say that your theory is correct—even though we must overlook every natural law and swallow a lot of superstition to give it any credence.

"But let us say, for the sake of argument, that you are right. Jack the Ripper was a man who discovered how to prolong his own life through making human sacrifices. He did travel around the world as you believe. He is in Chicago now and he is planning to kill. In other words, let us suppose that everything you claim is gospel truth. So what?"

"What do you mean, 'so what'?" said Sir Guy.

"I mean—so what?" I answered. "If all this is true, it still doesn't prove that by sitting down in a dingy gin-mill on the South Side, Jack the Ripper is going to walk in here and let you kill him, or turn him over to the police. And come to think of it, I don't even know now just what you intend to *do* with him if you ever did find him."

Sir Guy gulped his gin. "I'd capture the bloody swine," he said. "Capture him and turn him over to the government, together with all the papers and documentary evidence I've collected against him over a period of many years. I've spent a fortune investigating this affair, I tell you, a fortune! His capture will mean the solution of hundreds of unsolved crimes, of that I am convinced.

"I tell you, a mad beast is loose on this world! An ageless, eternal beast, sacrificing to Hecate and the dark gods!"

In vino veritas. Or was all this babbling the result of too much gin? It didn't matter. Sir Guy Hollis had another. I sat there and wondered what to do with him. The man was rapidly working up to a climax of hysterical drunkenness.

"One other point," I said, more for the sake of conversation than in any hopes of obtaining information. "You still don't explain how it is that you hope to just blunder into the Ripper."

"He'll be around," said Sir Guy. "I'm psychic. I know."

Sir Guy wasn't psychic. He was maudlin.

The whole business was beginning to infuriate me. We'd been sitting here an hour, and during all this time I'd been forced to play nursemaid and audience to a babbling idiot. After all, he wasn't a regular patient of mine.

"That's enough," I said, putting out my hand as Sir Guy reached for the half-emptied bottle again. "You've had plenty. Now I've got a suggestion to make. Let's call a cab and get out of here. It's getting late and it doesn't look as though your elusive friend is going to put in his appearance. Tomorrow, if I were you, I'd plan to turn all those papers and documents over to the F.B.I. If you're so convinced of the truth of your wild theory, they are competent to make a very thorough investigation and find your man."

"No." Sir Guy was drunkenly obstinate. "No cab."

"But let's get out of here anyway," I said, glancing at my watch. "It's past midnight."

He sighed, shrugged, and rose unsteadily. As he started for the door, he tugged the gun free from his pocket.

"Here, give me that!" I whispered. "You can't walk around the street brandishing that thing."

I took the gun and slipped it inside my coat. Then I got hold of his right arm and steered him out of the door. The Negro didn't look up as we departed.

We stood shivering in the alleyway. The fog had increased. I couldn't see either end of the alley from where we stood. It was cold. Damp. Dark. Fog or no fog, a little wind was whispering secrets to the shadows at our backs.

The fresh air hit Sir Guy just as I had expected it would. Fog and gin fumes don't mingle very well. He lurched as I guided him slowly through the mist.

Sir Guy, despite his incapacity, still stared apprehensively at the alley, as though he expected to see a figure approaching.

Disgust got the better of me.

"Childish foolishness," I snorted. "Jack the Ripper, indeed! I call this carrying a hobby too far."

"Hobby?" He faced me. Through the fog I could see his distorted face. "You call this a hobby?"

"Well, what is it?" I grumbled. "Just why else are you so interested in tracking down this mythical killer?"

My arm held him. But his stare held me.

"In London," he whispered. "In 1888 . . . one of those women the Ripper slew . . . was my mother."

"What?"

"My father and I swore to give our lives to find the Ripper. My father was the first to search. He died in Hollywood in 1926—on the trail of the Ripper. They said he was stabbed by an unknown assailant in a brawl. But I know who that assailant was.

"So I've taken up his work, do you see, John? I've carried on. And I will carry on until I do find him and kill him with my own hands.

"He took my mother's life and the lives of hundreds to keep his own hellish being alive. Like a vampire, he battens on blood. Like a ghoul, he is nourished by death. Like a fiend, he stalks the world to kill. He is cunning, devilishly cunning. But I'll never rest until I find him, never!"

I believed him then. He wouldn't give up. He wasn't just a

drunken babbler any more. He was as fanatical, as determined, as relentless as the Ripper himself.

Tomorrow he'd be sober. He'd continue the search. Perhaps he'd turn those papers over to the F.B.I. Sooner or later, with such persistence—and with his motive—he'd be successful. I'd always known he had a motive.

"Let's go," I said, steering him down the alley.

"Wait a minute," said Sir Guy. "Give me back my gun." He lurched a little. "I'd feel better with the gun on me."

He pressed me into the dark shadows of a little recess.

I tried to shrug him off, but he was insistent.

"Let me carry the gun now, John," he mumbled.

"All right," I said.

I reached into my coat, brought my hand out.

"But that's not a gun," he protested. "That's a knife."

"I know."

I bore down on him swiftly.

"John!" he screamed.

"Never mind the 'John'," I whispered, raising the knife. "Just call me . . . Jack."

10

The Treasure Hunt

Edgar Wallace

There is a tradition in criminal circles that even the humblest of detective officers is a man of wealth and substance, and that his secret hoard was secured by thieving, bribery, and blackmail. It is the gossip of the fields, the quarries, the tailor's shop, the laundry, and the bake-house of fifty county prisons and three convict establishments, that all highly placed detectives have by nefarious means laid up for themselves sufficient earthly treasures to make work a hobby and their official pittance the most inconsiderable portion of their incomes.

Since Mr. J. G. Reeder had for more than twenty years dealt exclusively with bank robbers and forgers, who are the aristocrats and capitalists of the underworld, legend credited him with country houses and immense secret reserves. Not that he would have a great deal of money in the bank. It was admitted that he was too clever to risk discovery by the authorities. No, it was hidden somewhere: it was the pet dream of hundreds of unlawful men that they would some day discover the hoard and live happily ever after. The one satisfactory aspect of his affluence (they all agreed) was that, being an old man—he was over 50—he couldn't take his money with him, for gold melts at a certain temperature and gilt-edged stock is seldom printed on asbestos paper.

The Director of Public Prosecutions was lunching one Saturday at his club with a judge of the King's Bench—Saturday being one of the two days in the week when a judge gets properly fed. And the conversation drifted to a certain Mr. J. G. Reeder, the chief of the Director's sleuths.

"He's capable," he confessed reluctantly, "but I hate his hat. It is the sort that So-and-so used to wear," he mentioned by name an eminent politician; "and I loathe his black frockcoat—people who see him coming into the office think he's a coroner's officer—but he's capable. His side whiskers are an abomination, and I have a feeling that, if I talked rough to him, he would burst into tears—a gentle soul. Almost too gentle for my kind of work. He apologizes to the messenger every time he rings for him!"

The judge, who knew something about humanity, answered with a frosty smile.

"He sounds rather like a potential murderer to me," he said cynically.

Here, in his extravagance, he did Mr. J. G. Reeder an injustice, for Mr. Reeder was incapable of breaking the law—quite. At the same time there were many people who formed an altogether wrong conception of J. G.'s harmlessness as an individual. And one of these was a certain Lew Kohl, who mixed counterfeiting with elementary burglary.

Threatened men live long, a trite saying but, like most things trite, true. In a score of cases, where Mr. J. G. Reeder had descended from the witness stand, he had met the baleful eye of the man in the dock and had listened with mild interest to colorful promises as to what would happen to him in the near future. For he was a great authority on forged bank notes and he had sent many men to penal servitude.

Mr. Reeder, that inoffensive man, had seen prisoners foaming at the mouth in their rage, he had seen them white and livid, he had heard their howling execrations and he had met these men after their release from prison and had found them amiable souls half ashamed and half amused at their nearly forgotten outbursts and horrific threats.

But when, in the early part of 1914, Lew Kohl was sentenced for ten years, he neither screamed his imprecations nor registered a vow to tear Mr. Reeder's heart, lungs, and important organs from his frail body.

Lew just smiled and his eyes caught the detective's for the space

of a second—the forger's eyes were pale blue and speculative, and
they held neither hate nor fury. Instead, they said in so many
words:

"At the first opportunity I will kill you."

Mr. Reeder read the message and sighed heavily, for he disliked
fuss of all kinds, and resented, in so far as he could resent anything,
the injustice of being made personally responsible for the performance of a public duty.

Many years had passed, and considerable changes had occurred
in Mr. Reeder's fortune. He had transferred from the specialized
occupation of detecting the makers of forged bank notes to the
more general practice of the Public Prosecutor's bureau, but he
never forgot Lew's smile.

The work in Whitehall was not heavy and it was very interesting.
To Mr. Reeder came most of the anonymous letters which the
Director received in shoals. In the main they were self-explanatory,
and it required no particular intelligence to discover their motive.
Jealousy, malice, plain mischief-making, and occasionally a sordid
desire to benefit financially by the information which was conveyed,
were behind the majority. But occasionally:

Sir James is going to marry his cousin, and it's not three months
since his poor wife fell overboard from the Channel steamer crossing to
Calais. There's something very fishy about this business. Miss Margaret
doesn't like him, for she knows he's after her money. Why was I sent
away to London that night? He doesn't like driving in the dark, either.
It's strange that he wanted to drive that night when it was raining like
blazes.

This particular letter was signed "A Friend." Justice has many
such friends.

"Sir James" was Sir James Tithermite, who had been a director
of some new public department during the war and had received
a baronetcy for his services.

"Look it up," said the Director when he saw the letter. "I seem
to remember that Lady Tithermite was drowned at sea."

"On the nineteenth of December last year," said Mr. Reeder
solemnly. "She and Sir James were going to Monte Carlo, breaking
their journey in Paris. Sir James, who has a house near Maidstone,
drove to Dover, garaging the car at the Lord Wilson Hotel. The
night was stormy and the ship had a rough crossing—they were
halfway across when Sir James came to the purser and said that
he had missed his wife. Her baggage was in the cabin, her pass-

port, rail ticket, and hat, but the lady was not found, indeed was never seen again."

The Director nodded.

"I see you've read up the case."

"I remember it," said Mr. Reeder. "The case is a favorite speculation of mine. Unfortunately, I see evil in everything and I have often thought how easy—but I fear that I take a warped view of life. It is a horrible handicap to possess a criminal mind."

The Director looked at him suspiciously. He was never quite sure whether Mr. Reeder was serious. At that moment, his sobriety was beyond challenge.

"A discharged chauffeur wrote that letter of course," he began.

"Thomas Dayford, of 179 Barrack Street, Maidstone," concluded Mr. Reeder. "He is at present in the employ of the Kent Motor-Bus Company, and has three children, two of whom are twins and bonny little rascals."

The Chief laughed helplessly.

"I'll take it that you know!" he said. "See what there is behind the letter. Sir James is a big fellow in Kent, a Justice of the Peace, and he has powerful political influences. There is nothing in this letter, of course. Go warily, Reeder—if any kick comes back to this office, it goes on to you—doubled!"

Mr. Reeder's idea of walking warily was peculiarly his own. He traveled down to Maidstone the next morning, and finding a bus that passed the lodge gates of Elfreda Manor, he journeyed comfortably and economically, his umbrella between his knees. He passed through the lodge gates, up a long and winding avenue of poplars, and presently came within sight of the gray manor house.

In a deep chair on the lawn he saw a girl sitting, a book on her knees, and evidently she saw him, for she rose as he crossed the lawn and came toward him eagerly.

"I'm Miss Margaret Letherby—are you from—?" She mentioned the name of a well-known firm of lawyers, and her face fell when Mr. Reeder regretfully disclaimed connection with those legal lights. She was as pretty as a perfect complexion and a round, not too intellectual face could, in combination, make her.

"I thought—do you wish to see Sir James? He is in the library. If you ring, one of the maids will take you to him."

Had Mr. Reeder been the sort of man who could be puzzled by anything, he would have been puzzled by the suggestion that any girl with money of her own should marry a man much older than herself against her own wishes. There was little mystery in the matter now. Miss Margaret would have married any strong-willed man who insisted.

"Even me," said Mr. Reeder to himself, with a certain melancholy pleasure.

There was no need to ring the bell. A tall, broad man in a golfing suit stood in the doorway. His fair hair was long and hung over his forehead in a thick flat strand; a heavy tawny mustache hid his mouth and swept down over a chin that was long and powerful.

"Well?" he asked aggressively.

"I'm from the Public Prosecutor's office," murmured Mr. Reeder. "I have had an anonymous letter."

His pale eyes did not leave the face of the other man.

"Come in," said Sir James gruffly.

As he closed the door he glanced quickly first toward the girl and then toward the poplar avenue.

"I'm expecting a fool of a lawyer," he said, as he flung open the door of what was evidently the library.

His voice was steady; not by a flicker of eyelash had he betrayed the slightest degree of anxiety when Reeder had told his mission.

"Well—what about this anonymous letter? You don't take much notice of that kind of trash, do you?"

Mr. Reeder deposited his umbrella and flatcrowned hat on a chair before he took a document from his pocket and handed it to the baronet, who frowned as he read. Was it Mr. Reeder's vivid imagination, or did the hard light in the eyes of Sir James soften as he read?

"This is a cock and bull story of somebody having seen my wife's jewelry on sale in Paris," he said. "There is nothing in it. I can account for every one of my poor wife's trinkets. I brought back the jewel case after that awful night. I don't recognize the handwriting: who is the lying scoundrel who wrote this?"

Mr. Reeder, who had thought it best to prepare an entirely new letter to show Sir James, had never before been called a lying scoundrel, but he accepted the experience with admirable meekness.

"I thought it untrue," he said, shaking his head. "I followed the details of the case very thoroughly. You left here in the afternoon—"

"At night," said the other brusquely. He was not inclined to discuss the matter, but Mr. Reeder's appealing look was irresistible. "It is only eighty minutes' run to Dover. We got to the pier at eleven o'clock, about the same time as the boat train, and we went on board at once. I got my cabin key from the purser and put her ladyship and her baggage inside."

"Her ladyship was a good sailor?"

"Yes, a very good sailor; she was remarkably well that night. I left her in the cabin dozing, and went for a stroll on the deck—"

"Raining very heavily and a strong sea running," nodded Reeder, as though in agreement with something the other man had said.

"Yes—I'm a pretty good sailor—anyway, that story about my poor wife's jewels is utter nonsense. You can tell the Director that, with my compliments."

He opened the door for his visitor, and Mr. Reeder was some time replacing the letter and gathering his belongings.

"You have a beautiful place here, Sir James—a lovely place. An extensive estate?"

"Three thousand acres." This time he did not attempt to disguise his impatience. "Good afternoon."

Mr. Reeder went slowly down the drive, his remarkable memory at work.

He missed the bus, which he could easily have caught, and pursued an apparently aimless way along the winding road which marched with the boundaries of the baronet's property. A walk of a quarter of a mile brought him to a lane shooting off at right angles from the main road, and marking, he guessed, the southern boundary. At the corner stood and old stone lodge, on the inside of a forbidding iron gate. The lodge was in a pitiable state of neglect and disrepair. Tiles had been dislodged from the roof, the windows were grimy or broken, and the little garden was overrun with rocks and thistles. Beyond the gate was a narrow, weed-covered drive that trailed out of sight into a distant plantation.

Hearing the clang of a mailbox closing, he turned to see a postman mounting his bicycle.

"What place is this?" asked Mr. Reeder, arresting the postman's departure.

"South Lodge—Sir James Tithermite's property. It's never used now. Hasn't been used for years—I don't know why; it's a short cut if they happen to be coming this way."

Mr. Reeder walked with him toward the village. He was a skilful pumper of wells, however dry, and the postman was not dry by any means.

"Yes, poor lady! She was very frail—one of those sort of invalids that last out many a healthy man."

Mr. Reeder put a question at random and scored most unexpectedly.

"Yes, her ladyship was a bad sailor. I know, because every time

she went abroad she used to get a bottle of that stuff people take
for seasickness. I've delivered many a bottle till Raikes, the druggist, stocked it—'Pickers' Travelers' Friend,' that's what it was
called. Mr. Raikes was only saying to me the other day that he'd
got half a dozen bottles on hand, and he didn't know what to do
with them. Nobody in Climbury ever goes to sea."

Mr. Reeder went on to the village and idled his precious time
in most unlikely places. At the drugstore, at the blacksmith shop,
at the modest lumber yard. He caught the last bus back to Maidstone, and by great good luck the last train to London.

And, in his vague way, he answered the Director's query the next
day with: "Yes, I saw Sir James: a very interesting man."

This was on Friday. All day Saturday he was busy. The Sabbath
brought him a new interest.

On this bright Sunday morning, Mr. Reeder, attired in a flowered
dressing gown, his feet encased in black velvet slippers, stood at
the window of his house in Brockley Road and surveyed the deserted
thoroughfare. The bell of a local church had rung for early Mass,
and there was nothing living in sight except a black cat that lay
asleep in a patch of sunlight on the top step of the house opposite.
The hour was 7:30, and Mr. Reeder had been at his desk since six,
working by artificial light, the month being October toward the
close.

From the half-moon of the window bay he regarded a section
of the Lewisham High Road and as much of Tanners Hill as
can be seen before it dips past the railway bridge into sheer Deptford.

Returning to his table, he opened a carton of the cheapest cigarettes and, lighting one, puffed in an amateurish fashion. He smoked
cigarettes rather like a woman who detests them but feels that it is
the correct thing to do.

"Dear me," said Mr. Reeder feebly.

He was back at the window, and he had seen a man turn out of
Lewisham High Road. He had crossed the road and was coming
straight to Daffodil House—which frolicsome name appeared on the
door posts of Mr. Reeder's residence. A tall, straight man, with a
somber brown face, he came to the front gate, passed through and
beyond the watcher's range of vision.

"Dear me!" said Mr. Reeder, as he heard the tinkle of a bell.

A few minutes later his housekeeper tapped on the door.

"Will you see Mr. Kohl, sir?" she asked.

Mr. J. G. Reeder nodded.

Lew Kohl walked into the room to find a middle-aged man in a flamboyant dressing gown sitting at his desk, a pair of pince-nez set crookedly on his nose.

"Good morning, Kohl."

Lew Kohl looked at the man who had sent him to seven and a half years of hell, and the corners of his thin lips curled.

" 'Morning, Mr. Reeder." His eyes flashed across the almost bare surface of the writing desk on which Reeder's hands were lightly clasped. "You didn't expect to see me, I guess?"

"Not so early," said Reeder in his hushed voice, "but I should have remembered that early rising is one of the good habits which are inculcated by penal servitude."

He said this in the manner of one bestowing praise for good conduct.

"I suppose you've got a pretty good idea of why I have come, eh? I'm a bad forgetter, Reeder, and a man in Dartmoor has time to think."

The older man lifted his sandy eyebrows, the steel-rimmed glasses on his nose slipped further askew.

"That phrase seems familiar," he said, and the eyebrows lowered in a frown. "Now let me think—it was in a melodrama, of course, but was it 'Souls in Harness' or 'The Marriage Vow'?"

He appeared genuinely anxious for assistance in solving this problem.

"This is going to be a different kind of play," said the long-faced Lew through his teeth. "I'm going to get you, Reeder—you can go along and tell your boss, the Public Prosecutor. But I'll get you sweet! There will be no evidence to swing me. And I'll get that nice little stocking of yours, Reeder!"

The legend of Reeder's fortune was accepted even by so intelligent a man as Kohl.

"You'll get my stocking! Dear me, I shall have to go barefooted," said Mr. Reeder, with a faint show of humor.

"You know what I mean—think that over. Some hour and day you'll go out, and all Scotland Yard won't catch me for the killing! I've thought that out—"

"One has time to think in Dartmoor," murmured Mr. J. G. Reeder encouragingly. "You're becoming one of the world's thinkers, Kohl. Do you know Rodin's masterpiece—a beautiful statue throbbing with life—"

"That's all." Lew Kohl rose, the smile still trembling at the corner of his mouth. "Maybe you'll turn this over in your mind, and in a day or two you won't be feeling so gay."

Reeder's face was pathetic in its sadness. His untidy sandy-gray hair seemed to be standing on end; the large ears, that stood out at right angles to his face, gave the illusion of quivering movement.

Lew Kohl's hand was on the door knob.

"Womp!"

It was the sound of a dull weight striking a board; something winged past his cheek, before his eyes a deep hole showed in the wall, and his face was stung by flying grains of plaster. He spun round with a whine of rage.

Mr. Reeder had a long-barrelled Browning in his hand, with a barrel-shaped silencer over the muzzle, and he was staring at the weapon open-mouthed.

"Now how on earth did that happen?" he asked in wonder.

Lew Kohl stood trembling with rage and fear, his face yellow-white.

"You—you swine!" he breathed. "You tried to shoot me!"

Mr. Reeder stared at him over his glasses.

"Good gracious—you think that? Still thinking of killing me, Kohl?"

Kohl tried to speak but found no words, and flinging open the door, he strode down the stairs and through the front entrance. His foot was on the first step when something came hurtling past him and crashed to fragments at his feet. It was a large stone vase that had decorated the window sill of Mr. Reeder's bedroom. Leaping over the debris of stone and flower mold, he glared up into the surprised face of Mr. J. G. Reeder.

"I'll get you!" he spluttered.

"I hope you're not hurt?" asked the man at the window in a tone of concern. "These things happen. Some day and some hour—"

As Lew Kohl strode down the street, the detective was still talking.

Mr. Stan Bride, late of Dartmoor, was at his morning ablutions when his friend and sometime prison associate came into the little room that overlooked Fitzroy Square.

Stan Bride, who bore no resemblance to anything virginal, being a stout and stumpy man with a huge red face and many chins, stopped in the act of drying himself and gazed over the edge of the towel.

"What's the matter with you?" he asked sharply. "You look as if you'd been chased by a cop. What did you go out so early for?"

Lew told him, and the jovial countenance of his roommate grew longer and longer.

"You poor fish!" he hissed. "To go after Reeder with that stuff! Don't you think he was waiting for you? Do you suppose he didn't know the very moment you left the Moor?"

"I've scared him, anyway," said the other, and Mr. Bride laughed.

"Good scout!" he sneered. "If he's as white as you, he *is* scared! But he's not. Of course he shot past you— if he'd wanted to shoot you, you'd have been stiff by now. But he didn't. Thinker, he—he's given you somep'n' to think about."

"Where that gun came from I don't—"

There was a knock at the door and the two men exchanged glances.

"Who's there?" asked Bride, and a familiar voice answered.

"It's that dick from the Yard," whispered Bride, and opened the door.

The "dick" was Sergeant Allford, C.I.D., an affable and portly man and a detective of some promise.

" 'Morning, boys—not been to church, Stan?"

Stan grinned politely.

"How's trade, Lew?"

"Not so bad." The forger was alert, suspicious.

"Come to see you about a gun—got an idea you're carrying one, Lew—Colt automatic R.7/94318. That's not right, Lew—guns don't belong to this country."

"I've got no gun," said Lew sullenly.

Bride had suddenly become an old man, for he also was a convict on parole, and the discovery might send him back to serve his unfinished sentence.

"Will you take a little walk to the station, or will you let me go over you?"

"Go over me," said Lew, and put out his arms stiffly while the detective frisked him.

"I'll have a look around," said the detective, and his "look around" was very thorough.

"Must have been mistaken," said Sergeant Allford. And then, suddenly: "Was that what you chucked into the river as you were walking along the Embankment?"

Lew started. It was the first intimation he had received that he had been tailed that morning.

Bride waited till the detective was visible from the window crossing Fitzroy Square; then he turned in a fury on his companion.

"Clever, ain't you! That old hound knew you had a gun—knew

the number. And if Allford had found it you'd have been pulled
in, and me too!"

"I threw it in the river," said Lew sulkily.

"Brains—not many but some!" said Bride, breathing heavily.
"You lay off Reeder—he's poison, and if you don't know it you're
deaf! Scared him? You big stiff! He'd cut your throat and write
a hymn about it."

"I didn't know they were tailing me," growled Kohl, "but I'll get
him! And his money too."

"Get him from another lodging," said Bride curtly. "A crook I
don't mind, a murderer I don't mind, but a talking jackass makes
me sick. Get his stuff if you can—I'll bet it's all invested in real
estate, and you can't lift houses—but don't talk about it. I like you,
Lew, up to a point; you're miles before the point and out of sight.
I don't like Reeder—I don't like snakes, but I keep away from the
Zoo."

So Lew Kohl went into new lodgings on the top floor of a house
in Dean Street, and here he had leisure and inclination to brood
upon his grievances and to plan afresh the destruction of his enemy.
And new plans were needed, for the schemes which had seemed so
watertight in the quiet of a Devonshire cell showed daylight through
many crevices.

Lew's homicidal urge had undergone considerable modification.
He had been experimented upon by a very clever psychologist—
though he never regarded Mr. Reeder in this light, and, indeed,
had the vaguest idea as to what the word meant. But there were
other ways of hurting Reeder, and his mind fell constantly back to
the dream of discovering the detective's hidden treasure.

It was nearly a week later that Mr. Reeder invited himself into
the Director's private office, and that great official listened spell-
bound while his subordinate offered his outrageous theory about
Sir James Tithermite and his dead wife. When Mr. Reeder had
finished, the Director pushed back his chair from the table.

"My dear man," he said, a little irritably, "I can't possibly give
a warrant on the strength of your surmises—not even a search
warrant. The story is so fantastic, so incredible, that it would be
more at home in the pages of a sensational story than in a Public
Prosecutor's report."

"It was a wild night, and yet Lady Tithermite was not ill," suggested the detective gently. "That is a fact to remember, sir."

The Director shook his head.

"I can't do it—not on the evidence," he said. "I should raise a storm that'd swing me into Whitehall. Can't you do anything—unofficially?"

Mr. Reeder shook his head.

"My presence in the neighborhood has been remarked," he said primly. "I think it would be impossible to—er—cover up my traces. And yet I have located the place, and could tell you within a few inches—"

Again the Director shook his head.

"No, Reeder," he said quietly, "the whole thing is sheer deduction on your part. Oh, yes, I know you have a criminal mind—I think you have told me that before. And that is a good reason why I should not issue a warrant. You're simply crediting this unfortunate man with your ingenuity. Nothing doing!"

Mr. Reeder sighed and went back to his bureau, not entirely despondent, for there had intruded a new element into his investigations.

Mr. Reeder had been to Maidstone several times during the week, and he had not gone alone; though seemingly unconscious of the fact that he had developed a shadow, for he had seen Lew Kohl on several occasions, and had spent an uncomfortable few minutes wondering whether his experiment had failed.

On the second occasion an idea had developed in the detective's mind, and if he were a laughing man he would have chuckled aloud when he slipped out of Maidstone station one evening and, in the act of hiring a cab, had seen Lew Kohl negotiating for another.

Stan Bride was engaged in the tedious but necessary practice of so cutting a pack of cards that the ace of diamonds remained at the bottom, when his former co-lodger burst in upon him, and there was a light of triumph in Lew's cold eye which brought Mr. Bride's heart to his boots.

"I've got him!" said Lew.

Bride put aside the cards and stood up.

"Got who?" he asked coldly. "And if it's killing, you needn't answer, but get out!"

"There's no killing."

Lew sat down squarely at the table, his hands in his pockets, a real smile on his face.

"I've been trailing Reeder for a week, and that fellow wants some trailing!"

"Well?" asked the other, when he paused dramatically.

"I've found where he hides his cash."

Bride scratched his chin, and was half convinced.

"You have?"

Lew nodded.

"He's been going to Maidstone a lot lately, and driving to a little village about five miles out. There I always lost him. But the other night, when he came back to the station to catch the last train, he slipped into the waiting room and I found a place where I could watch him. What do you think he did?"

Mr. Bride hazarded no suggestion.

"He opened his bag," said Lew impressively, "and took out a wad of notes as thick as that! He'd been drawing on his private bank! I trailed him up to London. There's a restaurant in the station and he went in to get a cup of coffee, with me keeping well out of his sight. As he came out of the restaurant he took out his handkerchief and wiped his mouth. He didn't see the little book that dropped, but I did. I was scared sick that somebody else would see it, or that he'd wait long enough to find it himself. But he went out of the station and I got that book before you could say 'knife.' Look!"

It was a well-worn little notebook, covered with faded red morocco. Bride put out his hand to take it.

"Wait a bit," said Lew. "Are you in this with me fifty-fifty, because I want some help?"

Bride hesitated.

"If it's just plain thieving, I'm with you," he said.

"Plain thieving—and sweet," said Lew exultantly, and pushed the book across the table.

For the greater part of the night they sat together talking in low tones, discussing impartially the methodical bookkeeping of Mr. J. G. Reeder and his exceeding dishonesty.

The Monday night was wet. A storm blew up from the southwest, and the air was filled with falling leaves as Lew and his companion footed the five miles which separated them from the village. Neither carried any impedimenta that was visible, yet under Lew's waterproof coat was a kit of tools of singular ingenuity, and Mr. Bride's coat pockets were weighted down with the sections of a powerful jemmy.

They met nobody in their walk, and the chuch bell was striking eleven when Lew gripped the bars of the South Lodge gates, on the estate of Sir James Tithermite, pulled himself up to the top and dropped lightly on the other side. He was followed by Mr. Bride, who, in spite of his bulk, was a singularly agile man. The ruined lodge showed in the darkness, and they passed through the creaking gates to the door and Lew flashed his lantern upon the keyhole before he began manipulation with the implements which he had taken from his kit.

The door was opened in ten minutes and a few seconds later they stood in a low-roofed little room, the principal feature of which was a deep, grateless fireplace. Lew took off his mackintosh and stretched it over the window before he spread the light in his lamp, and, kneeling down, brushed the debris from the hearth, examining the joints of the big stone carefully.

"This work's been botched," he said. "Anybody could see that."

He put the claw of the jemmy into a crack and levered up the stone, and it moved slightly. Stopping only to dig a deeper crevice with a chisel and hammer, he thrust the claw of the jemmy farther down. The stone came up above the edge of the floor and Bride slipped the chisel underneath.

"Now together," grunted Lew.

They got their fingers beneath the hearthstone and with one heave hinged it up. Lew picked up the lamp and, kneeling down, flashed a light into the dark cavity. And then:

"Oh, my God!" he shrieked.

A second later two terrified men rushed from the house into the drive. And a miracle had happened, for the gates were open and a dark figure stood squarely before them.

"Put up your hands, Kohl!" said a voice, and, hateful as it was to Lew Kohl, he could have fallen on the neck of Mr. Reeder.

At twelve o'clock that night Sir James Tithermite was discussing matters with his bride-to-be: the stupidity of her lawyer, who wished to safeguard her fortune, and his own cleverness and foresight in securing complete freedom of action for the girl who was to be his wife.

"These blackguards think of nothing but their fees," he began, when his footman came in unannounced, and behind him the Chief Constable of the county and a man he remembered seeing before.

"Sir James Tithermite?" said the Chief Constable unnecessarily, for he knew Sir James very well.

"Yes, Colonel, what is it?" asked the baronet, his face twitching.

"I am taking you into custody on a charge of wilfully murdering your wife, Eleanor Mary Tithermite."

"The whole thing turned upon the question as to whether Lady Tithermite was a good or a bad sailor," explained J. G. Reeder

to his chief. "If she were a bad sailor, it was unlikely that she would be on the ship, even for five minutes, without calling for the stewardess. The stewardess did not see her ladyship, nor did anybody on board, for the simple reason that she was not on board!

"She was murdered within the grounds of the Manor; her body was buried beneath the hearthstone of the old lodge, and Sir James continued his journey by car to Dover, handing over his packages to a porter and telling him to take them to his cabin before he returned to put the car into the hotel garage. He had timed his arrival so that he passed on board with a crowd of passengers from the boat train, and nobody knew whether he was alone or whether he was accompanied, and, for the matter of that, nobody cared.

"The purser gave him his key, and he put the baggage, including his wife's hat, into the cabin, paid the porter and dismissed him. Officially, Lady Tithermite was on board, for he surrendered her ticket to the collector and received her landing voucher. And then he discovered she had disappeared. The ship was searched, but of course the unfortunate lady was not found. As I remarked before—"

"You have a criminal mind," said the Director good-humoredly. "Go on, Reeder."

"Having this queer and objectionable trait, I saw how very simple a matter it was to give the illusion that the lady was on board, and I decided that, if the murder was committed, it must have been within a few miles of the house. And then the local builder told me that he had given Sir James a little lesson in the art of mixing mortar. And the local blacksmith told me that the gate had been damaged, presumably by Sir James's car—I had seen the broken rods and all I wanted to know was when the repairs were made. That she was beneath the fireplace hearth in the lodge I was certain. Without a search warrant it was impossible to prove or disprove my theory, and I myself could not conduct a private investigation without risking the reputation of our department—if I may say 'our'," he said apologetically.

The Director was thoughtful.

"Of course, you induced this man Kohl to dig up the hearth by pretending you had money buried there. I presume you revealed that fact in your notebook? But why on earth did he imagine that you had a hidden treasure?"

Mr. Reeder smiled sadly.

"The criminal mind is a peculiar thing," he said, with a sigh. "It harbors illusions and fairy stories. Fortunately, I understand that mind. As I have often said . . ."

11

The Man Who Knew How

Dorothy L. Sayers

For the twentieth time since the train had left Carlisle, Pender glanced up from *Murder at the Manse* and caught the eye of the man opposite.

He frowned a little. It was irritating to be watched so closely, and always with that faint, sardonic smile. It was still more irritating to allow oneself to be so much disturbed by the smile and the scrutiny. Pender wrenched himself back to his book with a determination to concentrate upon the problem of the minister murdered in the library.

But the story was of the academic kind that crowds all its exciting incidents into the first chapter, and proceeds thereafter by a long series of deductions to a scientific solution in the last. Twice Pender had to turn back to verify points that he had missed in reading. Then he became aware that he was not thinking about the murdered minister at all—he was becoming more and more actively conscious of the other man's face. A queer face, Pender thought.

There was nothing especially remarkable about the features in themselves; it was their expression that daunted Pender. It was a secret face, the face of one who knew a great deal to other people's disadvantage. The mouth was a little crooked and tightly tucked in at the corners, as though savoring a hidden amusement. The eyes, behind a pair of rimless pince-nez, glittered curiously; but that was possibly due to the light reflected in the glasses. Pender wondered what the man's profession might be. He was dressed in a dark lounge suit, a raincoat and a shabby soft hat; his age was perhaps about forty.

Pender coughed unnecessarily and settled back into his corner, raising the detective story high before his face, barrier-fashion. This was worse than useless. He gained the impression that the man saw through the maneuver and was secretly entertained by it. He wanted to fidget, but felt obscurely that his doing so would in some way constitute a victory for the other man. In his self-consciousness he held himself so rigid that attention to his book became a sheer physical impossibility.

There was no stop now before Rugby, and it was unlikely that any passenger would enter from the corridor to break up this disagreeable *solitude à deux*. Pender could, of course, go out into the corridor and not return, but that would be an acknowledgment of defeat. Pender lowered *Murder at the Manse* and caught the man's eye again.

"Getting tired of it?" asked the man.

"Night journeys are always a bit tedious," replied Pender, half relieved and half reluctant. "Would you like a book?"

He took *The Paper-Clip Clue* from his briefcase and held it out hopefully. The other man glanced at the title and shook his head.

"Thanks very much," he said, "but I never read detective stories. They're so—inadequate, don't you think so?"

"They are rather lacking in characterization and human interest, certainly," said Pender, "but on a railway journey——"

"I don't mean that," said the other man. "I am not concerned with humanity. But all these murderers are so incompetent—they bore me."

"Oh, I don't know," replied Pender. "At any rate they are usually a good deal more imaginative and ingenious than murderers in real life."

"Than the murderers who are found out in real life, yes," admitted the other man.

"Even some of those did pretty well before they got pinched," objected Pender. "Crippen, for instance; he need never have been caught if he hadn't lost his head and run off to America. George Joseph Smith did away with at least two brides quite successfully before fate and the *News of the World* intervened."

"Yes," said the other man, "but look at the clumsiness of it all; the elaboration, the lies, the paraphernalia. Absolutely unnecessary."

"Oh, come!" said Pender. "You can't expect committing a murder and getting away with it to be as simple as shelling peas."

"Ah!" said the other man. "You think that, do you?"

Pender waited for him to elaborate this remark, but nothing came of it. The man leaned back and smiled in his secret way at the roof of the carriage; he appeared to think the conversation not worth going on with. Pender found himself noticing his companion's hands. They were white and surprisingly long in the fingers. He watched them gently tapping upon their owner's knee—then resolutely turned a page—then put the book down once more and said:

"Well, if it's so easy, how would *you* set about committing a murder?"

"I?" repeated the man. The light on his glasses made his eyes quite blank to Pender, but his voice sounded gently amused. "That's different; *I* should not have to think twice about it."

"Why not?"

"Because I happen to know how to do it."

"Do you indeed?" muttered Pender, rebelliously.

"Oh, yes; there's nothing to it."

"How can you be sure? You haven't tried, I suppose?"

"It isn't a case of trying," said the man. "There's nothing uncertain about my method. That's just the beauty of it."

"It's easy to say that," retorted Pender, "but what *is* this wonderful method?"

"You can't expect me to tell you that, can you?" said the other man, bringing his eyes back to rest on Pender's. "It might not be safe. You look harmless enough, but who could look more harmless than Crippen? Nobody is fit to be trusted with *absolute* control over other people's lives."

"Bosh!" exclaimed Pender. "I shouldn't think of murdering anybody."

"Oh yes you would," said the other man, "if you really believed it was safe. So would anybody. Why are all these tremendous artificial barriers built up around murder by the Church and the law? Just because it's everybody's crime and just as natural as breathing."

"But that's ridiculous!" cried Pender, warmly.

"You think so, do you? That's what most people would say. But I wouldn't trust 'em. Not with sulphate of thanatol to be bought for two pence at any chemist's."

"Sulphate of what?" asked Pender sharply.

"Ah! you think I'm giving something away. Well, it's a mixture of that and one or two other things—all equally ordinary and cheap. For ninepence you could make up enough to poison the entire Cabinet. Though of course one wouldn't polish the whole lot at once; it might look funny if they all died simultaneously in their baths."

"Why in their baths?"

"That's the way it would take them. It's the action of the hot water that brings on the effect of the stuff, you see. Any time from a few hours to a few days after administration. It's quite a simple chemical reaction and it couldn't possibly be detected by analysis. It would just look like heart failure."

Pender eyed him uneasily. He did not like the smile; it was not only derisive, it was smug, it was almost gloating, triumphant! He could not quite put the right name to it.

"You know," pursued the man, pulling a pipe from his pocket and beginning to fill it, it is very odd how often one seems to read of people being found dead in their baths. It must be a very common accident. Quite temptingly so. After all, there is a fascination about murder. The thing grows upon one—that is, I imagine it would, you know."

"Very likely," said Pender.

"I'm sure of it. No, I wouldn't trust anybody with that formula— not even a virtuous young man like yourself."

The long white fingers tamped the tobacco firmly into the bowl and struck a match.

"But how about you?" said Pender, irritated. (Nobody cares to be called a virtuous young man.) "If nobody is fit to be trusted——"

"I'm not, eh?" replied the man. "Well, that's true, but it can't be helped now, can it? I know the thing and I can't unknow it again. It's unfortunate, but there it is. At any rate you have the comfort of knowing that nothing disagreeable is likely to happen to *me*. Dear me! Rugby already. I get out here. I have a little bit of business to do at Rugby."

He rose and shook himself, buttoned his raincoat about him, and pulled the shabby hat more firmly down about his enigmatic glasses. The train slowed down and stopped. With a brief goodnight and a crooked smile the man stepped onto the platform. Pender watched him stride quickly away into the drizzle beyond the radius of the gas light.

"Dotty or something," said Pender, oddly relieved. "Thank goodness, I seem to be going to have the compartment to myself."

He returned to *Murder at the Manse,* but his attention still kept wandering from the book he held in his hand.

"What was the name of that stuff the fellow talked about? Sulphate of what?"

For the life of him he could not remember.

It was on the following afternoon that Pender saw the news item. He had bought the *Standard* to read at lunch, and the word "Bath" caught his eye; otherwise he would probably have missed the paragraph altogether, for it was only a short one.

WEALTHY MANUFACTURER DIES IN BATH

WIFE'S TRAGIC DISCOVERY

A distressing discovery was made early this morning by Mrs. John Brittlesea, wife of the well-known head of Brittlesea's Engineering Works at Rugby. Finding that her husband, whom she had seen alive and well less than an hour previously, did not come down in time for his breakfast, she searched for him in the bathroom, where the engineer was found lying dead in his bath, life having been extinct, according to the medical men, for half an hour. The cause of the death is pronounced to be heart-failure. The deceased manufacturer . . .

"That's an odd coincidence, said Pender. "At Rugby. I should think my unknown friend would be interested—if he is still there, doing his bit of business. I wonder what his business is, by the way."

It is a very curious thing how, when once your attention is attracted to any particular set of circumstances, that set of circumstances seems to haunt you. You get appendicitis: immediately the newspapers are filled with paragraphs about statesmen suffering from appendicitis and victims dying of it; you learn that all your acquaintances have had it, or know friends who have had it and either died of it, or recovered from it with more surprising and spectacular rapidity than yourself; you cannot open a popular magazine without seeing its cure mentioned as one of the triumphs of modern surgery, or dip into a scientific treatise without coming across a comparison of the vermiform appendix in men and monkeys. Probably these references to appendicitis are equally frequent at all times, but you only notice them when your mind is attuned to the subject. At any rate, it was in this way that Pender accounted to himself for the extraordinary frequency with which people seemed to die in their baths at this period.

The thing pursued him at every turn. Always the same sequence of events: the hot bath, the discovery of the corpse, the inquest. Always the same medical opinion: heart failure following immersion in too hot water. It began to seem to Pender that it was scarcely safe to enter a hot bath at all. He took to making his own bath cooler and cooler every day, until it almost ceased to be enjoyable.

He skimmed his paper each morning for headlines about baths before settling down to read the news; and was at once relieved and vaguely disappointed if a week passed without a hot-bath tragedy.

One of the sudden deaths that occurred in this way was that of a young and beautiful woman whose husband, an analytical chemist, had tried without success to divorce her a few months previously. The coroner displayed a tendency to suspect foul play, and put the husband through a severe cross-examination. There seemed, however, to be no getting behind the doctor's evidence. Pender, brooding over the improbable possible, wished, as he did every day of the week, that he could remember the name of that drug the man in the train had mentioned.

Then came the excitement in Pender's own neighborhood. An old Mr. Skimmings, who lived alone with a housekeeper in a street just around the corner, was found dead in his bathroom. His heart had never been strong. The housekeeper told the milkman that she had always expected something of the sort to happen, for the old gentleman would always take his bath so hot. Pender went to the inquest.

The housekeeper gave her evidence. Mr. Skimmings had been the kindest of employers, and she was heartbroken at losing him. No, she had not been aware that Mr. Skimmings had left her a large sum of money, but it was just like his goodness of heart. The verdict of course was accidental death.

Pender, that evening, went out for his usual stroll with the dog. Some feeling of curiosity moved him to go around past the late Mr. Skimmings' house. As he loitered by, glancing up at the blank windows, the garden gate opened and a man came out. In the light of a street lamp, Pender recognized him at once.

"Hullo!" he said.

"Oh, it's you, is it?" said the man. "Viewing the site of the tragedy, eh? What do *you* think about it all?"

"Oh, nothing very much," said Pender. "I didn't know him. Odd, our meeting again like this."

"Yes, isn't it? You live near here, I suppose."

"Yes," said Pender; and then wished he hadn't. "Do you live in these parts too?"

"Me?" said the man. "Oh, no. I was only here on a little matter of business."

"Last time we met," said Pender, "you had business at Rugby." They had fallen into step together, and were walking slowly down to the turning Pender had to take in order to reach his house.

"So I had," agreed the other man. "My business takes me all over the country. I never know where I may be wanted next, you see."

"It was while you were at Rugby that old Brittlesea was found dead in his bath, wasn't it?" remarked Pender carelessly.

"Yes. Funny thing, coincidence." The man glanced up at him sideways through his glittering glasses. "Left all his money to his wife, didn't he? She's a rich woman now. Good-looking girl—a lot younger than he was."

They were passing Pender's gate. "Come in and have a drink," said Pender, and again immediately regretted the impulse.

The man accepted, and they went into Pender's bachelor study.

"Remarkable lot of these bath deaths lately," observed Pender as he squirted soda into the tumblers.

"You think it's remarkable?" said the man, with his irritating trick of querying everything that was said to him. "Well, I don't know. Perhaps it is. But it's always a fairly common accident."

"I suppose I've been taking more notice on account of that conversation we had in the train." Pender laughed, a little self-consciously. "It just makes me wonder—you know how one does —whether anybody else had happened to hit on that drug you mentioned—what was its name?"

The man ignored the question.

"Oh, I shouldn't think so," he said. "I fancy I'm the only person who knows about that. I only stumbled on the thing by accident myself when I was looking for something else. I don't imagine it could have been discovered simultaneously in so many parts of the country. But all these verdicts just show, don't they, what a safe way it would be of getting rid of a person."

"You're a chemist, then?" asked Pender, catching at the one phrase which seemed to promise information.

"Oh, I'm a bit of everything. Sort of general utility man. I do a good bit of studying on my own, too. You've got one or two interesting books here, I see."

Pender was flattered. For a man in his position—he had been

in a bank until he came into that little bit of money—he felt that he had improved his mind to some purpose, and he knew that his collection of modern first editions would be worth money some day. He went over to the glass-fronted bookcase and pulled out a volume or two to show his visitor.

The man displayed intelligence, and presently joined him in front of the shelves.

"These, I take it, represent your personal tastes?" He took down a volume of Henry James and glanced at the fly-leaf. "That your name? E. Pender?"

Pender admitted that it was. "You have the advantage of me," he added.

"Oh! I am one of the great Smith clan," said the other with a laugh, "and work for my bread. You seem to be very nicely fixed here."

Pender explained about the clerkship and the legacy.

"Very nice, isn't it?" said Smith. "Not married? No. You're one of the lucky ones. Not likely to be needing any sulphate of . . . any useful drugs in the near future. And you never will, if you stick to what you've got and keep off women and speculation."

He smiled up sideways at Pender. Now that his hat was off, Pender saw that he had a quantity of closely curled gray hair, which made him look older than he had appeared in the railway carriage.

"No, I shan't be coming to you for assistance yet awhile," said Pender, laughing. "Besides, how should I find you if I wanted you?"

"You wouldn't have to," said Smith. *"I* should find *you*. There's never any difficulty about that." He grinned, oddly. "Well, I'd better be getting on. Thank you for your hospitality. I don't expect we shall meet again—but we may, of course. Things work out so queerly, don't they?"

When he had gone, Pender returned to his own armchair. He took up his glass of whiskey, which stood there nearly full.

"Funny!" he said to himself. "I don't remember pouring that out. I suppose I got interested and did it mechanically." He emptied his glass slowly, thinking about Smith.

What in the world was Smith doing at Skimmings' house?

An odd business altogether. If Skimmings' housekeeper had known about that money . . . But she had not known, and if she had, how could she have found out about Smith and his sulphate of . . . the word had been on the tip of his tongue then.

"You would not need to find me. *I* should find *you.*" What had the man meant by that? But this was ridiculous. Smith was not the devil, presumably. But if he really had this secret—if he liked to put a price upon it—nonsense.

"Business at Rugby—a little bit of business at Skimmings' house." Oh, absurd!

"Nobody is fit to be trusted. *Absolute* power over another man's life . . . it grows on you. That is, I imagine it would."

Lunacy! And, if there was anything in it, the man was mad to tell Pender about it. If Pender chose to speak he could get the fellow hanged. The very existence of Pender would be dangerous.

That whiskey!

More and more, thinking it over, Pender became persuaded that he had never poured it out. Smith must have done it while his back was turned. Why that sudden display of interest in the book-shelves? It had had no connection with anything that had gone before. Now Pender came to think of it, it had been a very stiff whiskey. Was it imagination, or had there been something about the flavor of it?

A cold sweat broke out on Pender's forehead.

A quarter of an hour later, after a powerful dose of mustard and water, Pender was downstairs again, very cold and shivering, huddling over the fire. He had had a narrow escape—if he had escaped. He did not know how the stuff worked, but he would not take a hot bath again for some days. One never knew.

Whether the mustard and water had done the trick in time, or whether the hot bath was an essential part of the treatment, at any rate Pender's life was saved for the time being. But he was still uneasy. He kept the front door on the chain and warned his servant to let no strangers into the house.

He ordered two more morning papers and the *News of the World* on Sundays, and kept a careful watch upon their columns. Deaths in baths became an obsession with him. He neglected his first editions and took to attending inquests.

Three weeks later he found himself at Lincoln. A man had died of heart failure in a Turkish bath—a fat man, of sedentary habits. The jury added a rider to their verdict of accidental death to the effect that the management should exercise a stricter super-vision over the bathers and should never permit them to be left unattended in the hot room.

As Pender emerged from the hall he saw ahead of him a shabby hat that seemed familiar. He plunged after it, and caught

Mr. Smith about to step into a taxi.

"Smith," he cried, gasping a little. He clutched him fiercely by the shoulder.

"What, you again?" said Smith. "Taking notes of the case, eh? *Can I do anything for you?*"

"You devil!" said Pender. "You're mixed up in this! You tried to kill me the other day."

"Did I? Why should I do that?"

"You'll swing for this," shouted Pender menacingly.

A policeman pushed his way through the gathering crowd.

"Here!" said he. "What's all this about?"

Smith touched his forehead significantly.

"It's all right, officer," said he. "The gentleman seems to think I'm here for no good. Here's my card. The coroner knows me. But he attacked me. You'd better keep an eye on him."

"That's right," said a bystander.

"This man tried to kill me," said Pender.

The policeman nodded.

"Don't you worry about that, sir," he said. "You think better of it. The 'eat in there has upset you a bit. All right, *all* right."

"But I want to charge him," said Pender.

"I wouldn't do that if I was you," said the policeman.

"I tell you," said Pender, "that this man Smith has been trying to poison me. He's a murderer. He's poisoned scores of people."

The policeman winked at Smith.

"Best be off, sir," he said. "I'll settle this. Now, my lad"—he held Pender firmly by the arms—"just you keep cool and take it quiet. That gentleman's name ain't Smith nor nothing like it. You've got a bit mixed up like."

"Well, what is his name?" demanded Pender.

"Never mind," replied the constable. "You leave him alone, or you'll be getting yourself into trouble."

The taxi had driven away. Pender glanced around at the circle of amused faces and gave in.

"All right, officer," he said. "I won't give you any trouble. I'll come round with you to the police station and tell you about it."

"What do you think o' that one?" asked the inspector of the sergeant when Pender had stumbled out of the station.

"Up the pole an' 'alf-way round the flag, if you ask me," replied his subordinate. "Got one o' them ideez fix what they talk about."

"H'm!" replied the inspector. "Well, we've got his name and address. Better make a note of 'em. He might turn up again.

Poisoning people so as they die in their baths, eh? That's a pretty good 'un. Wonderful how these barmy ones thinks it all out, isn't it?"

The spring that year was a bad one—cold and foggy. It was March when Pender went down to an inquest at Deptford, but a thick blanket of mist was hanging over the river as though it were November. The cold ate into your bones. As he sat in the dingy little court, peering through the yellow twilight of gas and fog, he could scarcely see the witnesses as they came to the table. Everybody in the place seemed to be coughing. Pender was coughing too. His bones ached, and he felt as though he were about due for a bout of influenza.

Straining his eyes, he thought he recognized a face on the other side of the room, but the smarting fog which penetrated every crack stung and blinded him. He felt in his overcoat pocket, and his hand closed comfortably on something thick and heavy. Ever since that day in Lincoln he had gone about armed for protection. Not a revolver—he was no hand with firearms. A sandbag was much better. He had bought one from an old man wheeling a pushcart. It was meant for keeping out drafts from the door—a good, old-fashioned affair.

The inevitable verdict was returned. The spectators began to push their way out. Pender had to hurry now, not to lose sight of his man. He elbowed his way along, muttering apologies. At the door he almost touched the man, but a stout woman intervened. He plunged past her, and she gave a little squeak of indignation. The man in front turned his head, and the light over the door glinted on his glasses.

Pender pulled his hat over his eyes and followed. His shoes had crêpe rubber soles and made no sound on the pavement. The man went on, jogging quietly up one street and down another, and never looking back. The fog was so thick that Pender was forced to keep within a few yards of him. Where was he going? Into the lighted streets? Home by bus or tram? No. He turned off to the left, down a narrow street.

The fog was thicker here. Pender could no longer see his quarry, but he heard the footsteps going on before him at the same even pace. It seemed to him that they were two alone in the world—pursued and pursuer, slayer and avenger. The street began to slope more rapidly. They must be coming out somewhere near the river.

Suddenly the dim shapes of the houses fell away on either

side. There was an open space, with a lamp vaguely visible in the middle. The footsteps paused. Pender, silently hurrying after, saw the man standing close beneath the lamp, apparently consulting something in a notebook.

Four steps, and Pender was upon him. He drew the sandbag from his pocket.

The man looked up.

"I've got you this time," said Pender, and struck with all his force.

Pender had been quite right. He did get influenza. It was a week before he was out and about again. The weather had changed, and the air was fresh and sweet. In spite of the weakness left by the malady he felt as though a heavy weight had been lifted from his shoulders. He tottered down to a favorite bookshop of his in the Strand, and picked up a D. H. Lawrence "first" at a price which he knew to be a bargain. Encouraged by this, he turned into a small chophouse chiefly frequented by newspaper men, and ordered a grilled cutlet and a half-tankard of bitter.

Two journalists were seated at the next table.

"Going to poor old Buckley's funeral?" asked one.

"Yes," said the other. "Poor devil! Fancy his getting bashed on the head like that. He must have been on his way down to interview the widow of that fellow who died in a bath. It's a rough district. Probably one of Jimmy the Card's crowd had it in for him. He was a great crime-reporter—they won't get another like Bill Buckley in a hurry."

"He was a decent sort, too. Great old sport. No end of a practical joker. Remember his great stunt sulphate of thanatol?"

Pender started. *That* was the word that had eluded him for so many months. A curious dizziness came over him.

". . . looking at you as sober as a judge," the journalist was saying. "No such stuff, of course, but he used to work off that wheeze on poor boobs in railway carriages to see how they'd take it. Would you believe that one chap actually offered him——"

"Hullo!" interrupted his friend. "That bloke over there has fainted. I thought he was looking a bit white."

12

The Dilemma of Grampa Dubois

Clayre and Michel Lipman

Although it was not yet noon, Grampa Jean Dubois locked and barred the door of his dusty printing shop, and pulled down the shades. He went to the engraving desk under the green-shaded light and took out the drawer with steady hands. From it he removed the thousand-dollar bill, carefully concealed in a secret hiding place that he had made in the back panel.

The ink was dry at last, he noticed, as he examined the bill with a strong lens, then sighed with pride and satisfaction. He knew his craft, did Grampa Dubois, and this perfect counterfeit was the proof. The United States Treasury made nothing finer. Paper, silk threads, the multitude of fine unbroken lines. All perfect. Yes, and he could make dozens more if he wished.

But he wouldn't make any more. Just this one, for he was an honest, law-abiding American citizen.

It was only that his beloved granddaughter Annette needed the piano. The so-beautifully toned piano they'd looked at in Mr. Frierly's Music, Instrument & Greeting Card Shop on Carondelet Street. For Annette had more than usual talent. She would go far on the concert stage, Madame Lausanne said—if only the child had a good instrument on which to practice.

Grampa, who lived in the little back room of their house on St. Charles, knew that Annette's papa and mamma could hardly afford the lessons. And though his presses and tools were the best he could import from France forty years ago, a couple of hundred dollars would be the most he could get for them in New Orleans today.

Besides, the shop was his living. A slim living, to be sure, for who cares about fine engraving these days? He'd thought about the piano for Annette until his head ached, and finally, with the aid of a photograph, began work on a steel plate.

The result was this perfect one-thousand-dollar bill.

He folded and unfolded it several times; then placed it in his wallet. He'd already burned the rough proofs over a gas jet. He put the steel plate into a jar of acid, and his dark eyes, sharper than many a younger man's, watched unblinkingly as the beautiful engraving was slowly eaten away. At last he straightened up, a short, solid, white-haired man with curling iron-gray mustaches, and a kindly, humorous face that belied the ferocity of his high-bridged Gallic nose.

There was, nonetheless, a sense of discomfort in Grampa Dubois. It was not that he lacked confidence in his masterpiece, nor that he feared detection. Rather, it was that the entire neighborhood— which was more like a small town than a parish of the big city— considered Grampa Dubois an exceptionally honest man.

And he did not lack a certain pride in the label.

He knew the government's attitude toward unauthorized manufacturing of money. But that, he told himself, was only with respect to inferior copies and therefore understandable. It did not apply to *his* work, which surpassed any mere imitation and was, in substance, another original!

He told himself that he was not depriving anyone of anything. On the contrary, he was helping the country gain a great new concert pianist.

Yet the sense of unhappiness persisted in him, even when he left his own door and proceeded up Carondelet Street to Mr. Frierly's Music, Instrument & Greeting Card Shop.

"This style's gone from $795 to $929.50 since you and the little girl looked at it last fall, Mr. Dubois," Frierly said. "With tax."

"It does not matter," Grampa said grandly, producing his crisp thousand-dollar bill. "I will purchase it."

Frierly turned the bill in his fingers. "I—I don't know about this," he said.

"It is a good one," Grampa Dubois said jocularly. "Made it myself."

"Ho!" Frierly said. "You! I c'n imagine. No; it isn't that. I hear the gov'ment's checking up on thousand-dollar bills, that's all. Lot of guys who made big money in the black market can't move the big fellas now. I hear you can buy them there thousand-dollar bills for seven, eight hundred dollars."

"Tosh," Grampa said. "Do not sell the piano. I return."

He walked a block to the bank on the corner.

"I will take hundreds and two fifties," he told young Danny Robertson.

Danny shook his head, looked around cautiously, and leaned forward. "Look, Mr. Dubois, I know *you're* okay on a deal like this, but the government's been getting awfully fussy lately on these thousands. We have to make a record, take the serial number, fill out forms and send everything to Washington. Then they check back, and—"

"I do not care to disturb Washington," Grampa said with dignity, replacing the bill in his wallet. "The government must already employ enough people to worry about the affairs of other people." He explored his pockets and fished up a half dollar. "Will you kindly give me some change, that I may make a telephone call?"

"You bet, Mr. Dubois."

He took the coins that were slid out to him and started for the telephone booths. Automatically, he glanced at the change in his hand, then turned back. He waited patiently while Mrs. Gilley from the Savemore Variety Store down the street made her bulky nickel and dime deposit. Then he stepped again to the wicket.

"You have given me an extra ten cents, Danny," he chided. "You must be more careful, or the bank will soon go broke."

"That's right! Thanks. If I need someone to watch the cash sometime, I'll give you a ring."

Thoughtfully, Grampa dropped a nickel in the phone and dialed a number. Frierly had been right. He hadn't supposed there'd be so much trouble about changing a large bill. But was he, Jean Pierre Dubois, to be thus discountenanced? Never. There were ways. A good American citizen, to be sure, but he was not Parisian-born for nothing. He was—as they say—a man who knew his way around.

There was no response to his ring. Very well; he would go there personally. Even if he had to take seven or eight hundred dollars for his bill, he might still raise the balance for Annette's piano.

He turned in at the Green Cat on Milan.

"Where is Mr. del Muto?" he asked the barman.

"Who wants to know?"

"Jean Dubois. I print some cards and menus for him last month."

"Upstairs. Third door, left."

Grampa found the owner in his office and produced his masterpiece.

"Where'd you get it, Gramp?"

"I—I found it."

Del Muto chewed the stub of his unlit cigar, glanced up through the black fuzz of his eyebrows, and then back to the bill. "From you, Gramp, I'll take that pitch."

"Help me out, will you not? Take it for seven hundred fifty."

"Listen, I got a bunch of these bills myself I can't sell now for stage money. And with business the way it is—You want a tip? Tear it up."

Sweat ran down Grampa Dubois' face as he left the Green Cat. He couldn't even *give* it away! He could hide it, but he had no really safe place. And he couldn't tear it up. It would be like destroying the Mona Lisa. What *could* he do?

He returned to St. Charles. Officer Norton was directing noon-hour traffic as he crossed toward his shop.

"Hiya, Mr. Dubois," Officer Norton called. "Annette still practicing hard for those concerts?"

"Very hard," Gramp assured him gravely, "except on the notes of G-sharp and B, which are lacking on her instrument."

Officer Norton made ferocious gestures at a truck driver. "She'll make out. A gen-u-ine artist c'n rise above a missing G-sharp and B."

"Perhaps you are right," Grampa said without conviction. His mind wrestled futilely with his problem. How was he to dispose of that accursed bill?

For a moment he considered giving himself up to Officer Norton. Then a better idea popped into his mind. He would act at once.

He was almost running when he reached the police station.

"I—I thought it was a dollar bill laying there in the gutter," he told Sergeant Withers. "And when I picked it up—I—I nearly fainted!"

"Don't wonder," Sergeant Withers said, examining the thousand-dollar bill. "Isn't every man would turn in a find like this."

"Once an honest man, always an honest man!" Corporal Finnegan said.

Jean Dubois shrugged. "The law says found property has to

be turned over to the police. I merely obey the law. Besides, I wager it is not authentic."

The two officers smiled. "I kin spot a phony a mile off," Corporal Finnegan said. "If the owner turns up, he should pay you a good fat reward."

"That would be nice," Grampa said, and went sadly home. It had been a trying day, but at least he'd never again have to worry about that devil of a counterfeit. He wished he'd had the courage to burn it, but that was impossible. He'd done the next best thing; if someone was fool enough to claim it, well and good. If not, let it rot in the authorities' safe.

And as—in the weeks that followed—he listened to Annette's steady improvement, he became less conscious of the piano's defects; more appreciative of the child's growing ability. Officer Norton was right; a genuine artist can rise above a missing G-sharp and B.

By June, he'd all but forgotten the counterfeit bill. So when the two police officers and the men with the cameras were ushered into the living room, Grampa Dubois' inner muscles contracted with painful intensity.

François and Delphine, his son and daughter-in-law, looked mildly embarrassed. Annette hammered a conclusive chord and stared wide-eyed.

Sergeant Withers' voice was abrupt and unnecessarily loud. "About that thousand-dollar bill you found three months ago."

"Oh, that." Grampa Dubois waited for the jangle of handcuffs. He might have known they'd find out somehow. If only it did not have to be in front of his family—in front of Annette. . . .

"It's a very unusual case, so the Chief sent us over special." Carefully Sergeant Withers extracted the thousand-dollar bill. Grampa closed his eyes. "Here!" the officer said. "It's yours! That's the law. If no one claims the object for ninety days, it belongs to the finder."

"I—I didn't know that," Grampa stammered.

Flashbulbs splayed brief lightning as he stood with the bill in his hand.

Someone asked, "What are you going to do with all that money, Grampa?"

"I—I'm not sure yet." Dazed though he was, one fact was clear. The bill had received official sanction; the newspapers would carry the story. He could go to the bank; he could go to Frierly, and

they would take it without question. At last Annette could have her fine new piano.

He heard someone ask François, "Have you any plans to help your father spend his money?" And François, good son that he was, replied. "The money belongs to him. I should never think of questioning his use of it."

Another inquisitive voice: "Mr. Dubois, what was it that prompted you to take this fortune to the police, when you might easily have kept it for yourself, and no one would be the wiser?"

Grampa moistened his dry lips; the conscience he'd thought dormant had revived and was knifing him painfully. "Wh—what m-made me—?" he fumbled. What could he say? What possible answer could he give?

Unexpectedly, Annette answered, her voice sharp, sweet, clear and brimmed with unrestrained pride. "Mister, didn't you ever hear about George Washington and Abraham Lincoln when you went to school? My grampappa is just like Washington and Lincoln. *My grampappa is an honest man . . . !*"

When they had gone, Grampa Dubois sat alone in his room, listening through the thin walls to Annette's nimble, happy melodies, and watching a small flame rise and die away on the grate. There was a smile on his lips. Yes, it would have been so easy to order the new piano. All the obstacles had been removed. All but his conscience. And Annette's pride in him.

And there was the parish, like a village in New Orleans, where everyone knew—from one side to the other—that Grampa Jean Dubois was an honest man.

13

P. Moran, Diamond-Hunter

Percival Wilde

TELEGRAM.
CHIEF INSPECTOR,
ACME INTERNATIONAL DETECTIVE CORRESPONDENCE SCHOOL,
SOUTH KINGSTON, N. Y.
TELEGRAPHING YOU ONE DOLLAR PLEASE DESCRIBE HOW TO
FIND DIAMONDS.

OPERATIVE P. MORAN

From Chief Inspector, Acme International Detective Correspondence School, South Kingston, N. Y.,
To: Operative P. Moran, c/o Mr. R. B. McRae, Surrey, Conn.

Your telegram is not clear by which we mean it might mean this or also that and then again it might mean something else, and if you paid for more than ten words we might know which. We deduct you want to find diamonds. If they are lost, advertize for them, offering a reward. If they are stolen, a good detective should be hired right away, but since nobody would take you for a good detective and hire you as same, we deduct they are not stolen.

Perhaps you would be satisfied if you found any diamonds, blue ones or yellow ones, big ones or small ones. So would we, because diamonds are worth money. We have looked in the ency-clopedia. It says diamonds are found in mines in S. Africa. They are also found in S. America. They have also been found in S. Carolina, N. ditto, Ga., and Va. Observation tells us you also find them in jewelry stores, and our secretary, who likes what she calls good music which we can't stand because it makes our ears ring, says you will see many diamonds coming in during the second act of the opera—any opera. Observation also tells us they are plentiful on chorus girls, actresses, saloon-keepers, oil men, gamblers, race-track touts, prizefighters and big-shot politi-cians, but that is only when the graft is good and people are hiring offices on the 40th floor for the view, not for jumping. When times are hard diamonds are most generally lost for adver-tising, but they may be fakes.

We think it would be a good idea if you took a trip to S. America or S. Africa, preferably S. Africa because it is farther away, to find some diamonds. Let us know when you start.

P.S. We are keeping the One Dollar which Western Union handed us because it pays for the time we wasted answering your fool telegram.

J. J. O'B.

From: Operative P. Moran, c/o Mr. R. B. McRae, Surrey, Conn.
To: Chief Inspector, Acme International Detective Correspondence School, South Kingston, N. Y.

Well, you certainly had a nerve keeping my One Dollar, be-cause your letter was not worth it and your time ditto, and Marry-lin, which is the name of the new hired girl we have taken on at the house because she is working her way through college, and the dough she makes in the summer sees her through the winter, read your letter and she laughed and she says she will bet another Dollar this is the first time you ever opened an encyclopedia and you should break a bottle of wine on the bow and crissen it. Marrylin is a smart girl and she is quick as a flash; but maybe I should tell you about Mr. Burton Findlay and Mr. William Underwood Junior and Mr. & Mrs. Arnold Gaylord and Mr. Cutler and Mr. A. E. Erskine-Bevin and the other amebas and the eleven rose-diamonds.

Sunday morning the boss sends for me. "Peter," he says, "come in, close the door, and keep it under your hat."

I says, "Yes, Mr. McRae."

"Peter, are you acquainted with Mr. Burton Findlay?"

"Yes, sir."

"What do you know about him?"

"Well, sir, he is a rich man, and he has done lots of hunting."

The boss screws up his face in a way he has. "Peter, he is more than a hunter: he is an ameba."

I didn't know that about Mr. Findlay, though he has owned a big house right here in Surrey for a good many years. I says, "Mr. McRae, he always registers as a Republican."

"That may well be, Peter, for Republican amebas are more abundant than Democratic ones. Do you know what an ameba is? It is a round animal. When it sees something it wants, it surrounds it—and it wants everything it sees." The boss puts two ashtrays on his desk. "One of these is the ameba; it doesn't matter which. The other is the object. The ameba flows up to it. It throws out part of its body on the left. Then it throws out part of its body on the right. Do you follow me, Peter?"

"Yes, sir: I deduct the ameba is left-handed."

The boss laughs. "Could be; could be; but whichever part reaches the object first, meets the other part, capturing the object, which may be a work of art, or a country house, or somebody else's wife."

"What happens to the object, Mr. McRae?"

"It becomes part of the ameba, which digests it. Then the ameba sees something else it wants because it is always wanting something, and it repeats the process ad infinitum, and it becomes a very big ameba. That is why the Hobby Club met at Mr. Findlay's last night."

I waited for him to go on. "Yes, sir."

"The Hobby Club is a club of people who collect things. They are small amebas. They meet at Mr. Findlay's because he is the biggest ameba. Mr. Seymour collects stamps. He showed four he bought at auction and they are worth a lot because the airplane has been flying upside down for years and the pilot hasn't fallen out yet. Mr. Cutler collects buttons. He showed some which belonged to George Washington he said but I would not believe it if George swore to it himself. Mr. William Underwood Junior collects etchings. He bought two which Whistler left unfinished so they are worth more than if he had finished them, which teaches us never to do today what we can put off till tomorrow. Mr. Pomeroy, who plays the stock market, showed eleven rose-diamonds which he always carries in his pocket to bring him luck. I wish he had broken his neck and had stayed home. Mr. Erskine-Bevin had a particularly rare first edition: he collects them. So does Mr. Jones. He exhibited his, and they said they were friendly rivals, which means one of them will not stick a knife into the other excepting on a dark night. I have the sporting prints you may have seen in this room. I brought them. Arnold Gaylord, who married one of Findlay's granddaughters, doesn't collect anything because the great-grandchildren have been coming pretty fast and it takes every cent he makes to keep them in shoes: I hear Findlay gives them nothing but free board and lodging over the summer. They thought it would be a good joke on the rest, so they showed their newest baby. Mr. & Mrs. Gaylord are not amebas."

"No, sir, anybody could see that right off."

"We all had dinner."

"The baby, too?"

"Yes—privately. After that it gurgled and smiled and shook its rattle, and we all loved it. Then Mr. Findlay, who collects everything—stamps, and etchings, and paintings, and first editions—not to mention stocks and bonds, and is a great hunter and a great fisherman besides, showed some motion pictures he had taken when he was collecting fish in the Gulf Stream, which he would collect also only it is too wet. The pictures were exciting: there was one in which a shark almost collected Mr. Findlay, and I was disappointed when the shark lost out. The butler worked the motion-picture projector."

"Hewitt, sir?"

"You know him?"

"He is a big man in village politics."

"So I have heard. After the lights went on again we all applauded, and Mr. Pomeroy went up to Mr. Findlay and told him quietly that his eleven rose-diamonds, which had been left on a table with the other exhibits, were missing."

"Oh!"

"What would you have done, Peter?"

"If those diamonds had belonged to me I would not have been quiet, Mr. McRae. I would have hollered blue murder."

"Mr. Pomeroy speculates in Wall Street, and he takes his losses without bawling about them. I mean, what would you have done next?"

"I would have locked the door, and I would have searched the members of the Hobby Club."

"We discussed that and we decided against it. It is done in all good detective stories, and they never find the loot that way. No, Peter, we decided we would not be primitive. First we invited the guilty person, whoever he was, to put the stones on the table from which he had taken them while we turned out the lights again.

When that didn't do any good, we concluded a search would be undignified, and fruitless."

"Which, Mr. McRae?"

"Mr. Pomeroy spoke for all of us when he said, 'The man who took the diamonds is prepared to be searched. Therefore they are not hidden on him, or in his pockets, or anywhere we might expect to find them. If we search each other, we'll find nothing, and we'll annoy the ladies, who won't want to be searched, even by the other ladies. Why waste the time?' "

"I wouldn't call it wasted time, Mr. McRae."

"The opinion seemed to be unanimous, Peter. We looked here and there: under the rugs; in the upholstery of the furniture; under the table. We searched just one human being: the baby, and we did that because somebody might have planted the stones on it in the dark. After that it was all we could do to get the ladies to dress it again: it is only five months old, and if we had left them alone, the ladies would have spent the night playing 'This little piggie went to market' with its toes."

"I deduct you didn't find the diamonds, Mr. McRae."

"Your deduction is correct, Peter."

"Maybe Mr. Pomeroy put them back in his pockets without thinking."

"Somebody suggested that, so Pomeroy turned his pockets inside out. Everything was very polite and dignified."

"I can see that, sir."

"Unfortunately there are no detectives in the Hobby Club. We're all afraid there'll be a story in the papers if Mr. Findlay hires a regular detective. How would you like to run over and see him?"

I thought quick, like I always do. "Is there a reward?"

"We haven't discussed it, but you can depend on us to do the right thing. But if I were you, Peter, I would ask Mr. Findlay to pay you for your time by the hour, win, lose, or draw. After more than a dozen bright men and women tried to find those stones and gave up, surely you can't expect to be successful."

I says, "Mr. McRae, like you told me, there are not any detectives in the Hobby Club. I am all through with this case already, and I am busy thinking about the next."

He says, "Holy Smoke!"

I says, "Yes, sir, because that is the way my mind works, especially after I got 60 per cent on Lesson II, which is Observation."

The boss gives me a queer look. "I don't know what you could have observed because you weren't there, and I have just been telling you the story in my own way and I have doubtless left out some of the most essential details; but if it is as easy as you say, you must lose no time making tracks to Mr. Findlay's house, where Mr. Findlay will be delighted to see you."

I says, "I am not so sure of that, but I will hurry right back," and I mean it, because I have got a date to take Marrylin to the movies they are having at the Stuart Theatre in Lakeville the same afternoon which is Sunday, but the boss only says, "Now I will ring up Mr. Findlay and tell him you are on your way."

Well, Jim Hewitt lets me in, and he says, "Gosh, Pete, I certainly am glad you are here, and maybe I wasn't excited last night when they talked about searching everybody!"

I says, "Jim, I hear they didn't search anybody excepting the baby."

"That's right."

"Not Mr. Findlay?"

"Why should they search the boss?"

"Or Mr. Pomeroy?"

"He turned his pockets inside out, and we all watched, you can bet." Jim gives me a dig in the ribs. "I was sorry they didn't search Mr. Seymour. I know the colored lady that does his laundry, and she says he is so stingy he makes her sew big patches on his underwear till it falls apart. Now I am not like that, Pete. I change right down to the skin once a week whether I need it or not, and you can bet there are not any holes in my union suits."

I says, "That is neither here nor there, my good man. You may now lead me to your master."

He says, "You are snootier than you used to be before you became a detective," but he knocks on the door of the living room which is locked, and when somebody growls, "Confound it, what is it, humpf?" he answers, "Mr. Findlay, Moran has come."

I says, "Mr. Moran, you dumb cluck," but Hewitt kicks me on the shin accidental on purpose, and then I hear the lock opening and Mr. Findlay says, "Come in, Moran, come in! Confound it, don't stand there in the doorway making a draft! Come in and I will lock the door behind you."

Well, Mr. Burton Findlay does not look like a ameba, because he is about 75, and he is tall and bony, and he has skinny hands and also bushy white eyebrows which look like he knitted them himself; and he is smoking a cigar which cost One Dollar straight if it cost a cent, and he does not offer one to me though I can see plenty more in his outside pocket. And the room is pretty messy, with ashtrays everywhere full of cigar stumps and cigarette butts, and dirty highball glasses and bottles of Scotch and siphons and some of those bottles have not been opened yet, and the movie machine is set up at one end of the room with the screen at the other, and there is a baby carriage in the corner. There are some flowers wilting in a tall green-blue glass which is on a table and there are some silver trays with sandwiches and they do not look so hot because they are dried out and curling up at the edges, and the baby's bedding and the baby's toys are in the baby carriage, and there are some buttons and some stamps and some books and Mr. McRae's prints and some other things on another table, and the windows are shut and the air is so thick you could cut it with a knife. And the room looks like a museum, with thick carpets, and glass cases with more books, and jars, and vases, and clocks, and there are also statues and paintings which do not have any clothes on them so I do not look at them except when Mr. Findlay is not watching.

He says, "Come in, Moran, confound it, humpf!" and he talks a blue streak while we are walking around. "You will see everything exactly as it was last night excepting the guests have gone home if that was where they went when they left here though I would not put it past some of them to go to the Green Lantern or the Brookside Tavern to have a few drinks and chew the rag. These are the buttons Cutler showed: he offered to leave them because they unscrew and they have been used to smuggle precious stones. We took them apart and you can see they are empty. Here are Seymour's stamps: you couldn't hide a diamond in a stamp, could you?—and I've got rarer stamps in my own albums. Here are McRae's sporting prints: don't tell him, but I've got better ones. Here are the first editions two of the members brought: they aren't a marker on those in the bookcases right behind you. Sometimes the insides of a book are scooped out so you can smuggle dope in it: these are regular books, and we know because we looked. We searched the ladies' handbags, and we made them take them home with them, though they offered to leave them. There is the baby carriage which was occupied by my great-grandchild: I asked to have it left here, and it was left. The motion-picture screen is exactly where it was last night. There is the projector, with the film still on the reel. There are the cans of film Hewitt showed first: we've gone all through them. The gadget next to the projector is the splicer: if the film breaks, you mend it right there. The can on the splicer used to hold cement: we opened it and poured out the little there was left to be sure there was nothing else in it, and you can bet your life it is empty."

I says, "Mr. Findlay, I can deduct you suspected Hewitt."

He hoists his shoulders up and down. "Confound it, we suspected everybody, humpf!"

"What's this little pile of pebbles near the movie machine?"

"Out of one of the pots, I suppose. You'll see plants growing at
all of the windows."

"Have you looked through the cigar and cigarette butts?"

"No, but you can if you want to. Confound it, how can a man
hide a diamond in a cigar and then put the ash back on top of
it?"

"Have you examined the sandwiches?"

"Moran, eat as many as you wish, if that's what you're hinting
at."

Well, I eat eight or ten of those sandwiches, and he goes on
talking: "After the guests left I locked the doors of this room and
I slept on the sofa. Hewitt put my breakfast outside the door on
a tray and I have just eaten it: see the shells of the soft-boiled eggs?
Nothing that came into this room yesterday has gone out of it
except the people, and we agreed there was no use in searching
them as I believe Mr. McRae has told you. That door there opens
on a bathroom: that's where I'm going to shave and clean my
teeth if I ever get around to it.

"Well, Moran, speak up! McRae tells me you can name the
guilty man. Who is he?"

I says, "First I got some questions to ask."

"Shoot!"

"How much is the reward?"

"Humpf! Humpf! Well, the eleven diamonds were worth about
five thousand dollars: the rose-cut kind isn't as valuable as the
others. I offered him six for them."

"Wait a minute! You offered him six—who?"

"Yes—when he lost them—Pomeroy. I would have paid him to
keep quiet and have no scandal. He wouldn't accept."

"You mean he wanted more than six thousand bucks?"

"Confound it, man, he didn't want money! He wanted the
diamonds: he's superstitious about them. He says that before he
buys or sells anything he puts his hand in his pocket, picks up
some stones, and counts them. If the number is odd, he follows his
hunch; if it's even he does the opposite. Since eleven is an odd
number, he generally follows his hunches, and he's generally hard
up. . . . Moran, shall we say that a one-thousand dollar reward,
one-fifth the value of the diamonds, will satisfy you?"

"O.K.—if you put it in writing."

He does that, while I walk around the room, looking at the

hundreds and hundreds of things he has got in it, and eating some more sandwiches. "It would take a year to search this place."

"Yes, confound it! Well, here's my agreement to pay you the reward—*if* you find the stones. Now tell me the man's name."

I fold the paper careful and I put it away in a safe place because I remember what the boss said about amebas, and I do not want Mr. Burton Findlay surrounding that there paper. "Mr. Findlay, I says, "you collect things."

"Yes."

"What things?"

"I've told you about them, and you've seen them here: paintings; sculpture; vases; books; prints—"

"Rose-diamonds, too?"

"I've got a couple."

"Show me one."

He puts two fingers in his vest pocket, and he shoots a big stone to me like it was a marble. "That's a rose-diamond."

I look him straight in the eyes. "O.K. Where's the other ten?"

"What do you mean?"

"Probably you tried to buy Mr. Pomeroy's diamonds before last night."

"No: they're not good enough."

"When he missed them, you tried to buy them again."

"As I told you, I would have paid well to prevent a scandal."

"In the dark, when you were having the movies, you could have found the table where he left the stones, because this is your living room and you know it like you know the palm of your hand."

"Confound it, Moran, what are you getting at?"

"When somebody says, 'Let's search everybody,' you says, 'No, don't do it.' "

"It was Pomeroy who said that."

"It was you who agreed. Well, come across: maybe you could fool the Hobby Club which has not got any detectives in it, but you cannot fool Operative P. Moran. Give 'em here!"

For a minute I think he is going to bite me. Then he starts to laugh, and it is a real laugh or I will eat my hat. "Moran," he says, "I should have guessed what was in your mind before you spoke. I saw it coming, and I just couldn't believe it. But you're barking up the wrong tree, my good man! Moran, do you know what a carrot is?"

"They grow in gardens."

"Not this kind. This kind is used to weigh diamonds. Pomeroy's diamonds were little ones, one carrot apiece or thereabouts. This one here is more than nine carrots: I mean it weighs nearly as much as all of Pomeroy's put together, and what is more, it is a famous stone which was worn by a cardinal five hundred years ago. Why, there are dozens of experts who will identify it."

Sometimes you just know when a guy is telling the truth, and I could see this was one of them. I says, "Oh!"

"That isn't all, Moran," he goes on. "You said the room was dark while the pictures were being shown. Well, it was, in a manner of speaking, because the only light came from the projector. But I was standing next to the screen all the time, telling the members of the club what the pictures were about, and if I had moved, everybody in the room would have noticed it. The others could have gone where they pleased: I couldn't." He is just as friendly as a big ameba can be, I guess. "Don't be too cressfallen, Moran. *We* couldn't find the diamonds either; it is too much to expect you would succeed."

I was feeling pretty low in my spirits. "I guess," I says, "I guess I better give up."

Mr. Findlay walks over and slaps me on the back. "Confound it, Moran, never say die! I think better of you because you accused me right to my face. You are a brave man, and you rushed in where angels fear to tread." He goes on with a queer grin: "In many ways you remind me of a gorilla that walked up to me so slow and so friendly that I was almost ashamed to shoot the poor thing. But even my enemies will tell you that while I might steal a bank or a railroad, I would draw the line at a handful of small diamonds."

He was too much for me. "Mr. Findlay," I says, "I guess you had better send for a regular detective."

He stops grinning mighty quick. "Moran, I'll shoot the first that sticks his ugly nose in this place, so help me God, I will! There is a gun room in this house, and if one of those professional gum-shoes shows himself around here, I will fill him full of copper-jacketed bullets! Remember, Moran: no publicity; no scandal! The reward holds good. Call again when you have got a better idea: I mean one that works. And by the way, give me back my big rose-diamond before you go. I know you're taking it with you absently-mindedly, but I will relieve you of it in the same absent-minded fashion."

After that I slink out of the house, and if I was a dog, my tail would be between my legs. I have got a date to take Marrylin to the movies, like I wrote, but it is O. K. with me when the boss says, "Peter, I'm sorry if I'm interfering with any plans, but you'll have to drive me to the train this afternoon." Then he says, "Oh, by the way, how did you make out at Mr. Findlay's?" and I says, "I report progress, Mr. McRae," which is not true, but it is the best thing to say.

Please send me a telegram that a regular detective is coming right away.

TELEGRAM.
PETER MORAN C/O MR. B. MCRAE, SURREY, CONN.
COLLECT TO BE SHOT QUESTION MARK NO THANK YOU PERIOD.
  CHIEF INSPECTOR, ACME INTERNATIONAL
  CORRESPONDENCE SCHOOL.

From: Operative P. Moran c/o Mr. R. B. McRae, Surrey, Conn., To: Chief Inspector, Acme International Detective Correspondence School, South Kingston, N. Y.

Well, I kind of figured in advance you would not send a detective or maybe come yourself if you were not sure you would get paid, but the reward is bigger now than it was at first and I guess you will change your mind when you know about that.

Your telegram did not come till pretty late this afternoon which is Monday, and I was out driving the missus so Marrylin took it over the telephone and she wrote it out for me, and when she gave it to me she was all set to ask questions, but I read it over three or four times first, and then I had my dinner, and then I had to drive the missus to a party, and when I put the car away it was near midnight, and there was Marrylin and she was waiting in the garage.

She says, "Well, Peter?" and I says, "Marrylin, I am in trouble and I need a friend," and she says, "What kind of trouble?" and I says, "Rose-diamond trouble," and I spill the story.

I can see her eyes shining while I am talking, and she does not ask any questions till I am all through, because all she is saying is "Peter, go on! Don't you dare stop! Oh, Peter, go on!"

Then when I am finished, she says, "Peter, how perfectly divine and how lucky you came to me with your little problem! When I was a junior last year in the college they have got for girls in Mt. Holyoke, Mass., I took a cause in the Art and Craft of the Detective Story, and this sounds like one of the tests they used to spring on us juniors when we were least expecting it."

I says, "Isn't that fine, Marrylin? Well, who swiped the diamonds?"

She hoists her shoulders up and down. "Elementary, my dear Peter, elementary!"

"Is it? Then how did he do it?"

"You make me laugh. Peter, I am almost ashamed to put my little gray cells to work because it is so easy."

"O.K., so it's easy, because I figured it out myself; but where did he hide them?"

"That Peter, is the crux." I have not heard that word before, so she spells it out for me, like she spells out the names she starts shooting at me in a couple of minutes. "I can see everything in my mind's eye. Oh, Peter, it is really so simple! I just want to ask you one question."

"Go ahead."

"Who wrote the story?"

I wasn't sure I was hearing her right, so I made her repeat it.

"Who wrote the story?" she says.

"Why, Marrylin, what story?"

She laughs, and I must say she has a nice laugh. "Peter, after three years of college, don't ask me to believe stories write themselves! Any girl who is innocent enough to believe that would get suet in her eyes looking for Sandy Claws in the chimney at Christmas! Tell me who wrote the story, and I will tell you where the diamonds are hidden. If it is by Conan Doyle, there is one answer; if it is by Dashiell Hammett there is another; if it is by Ellery Queen there is a third. For instance—Wait a minute, Peter! You said Mr. Findlay has a gun room."

"That's right."

"With guns in it?"

"What would you expect to find in a gun room? Pianos?"

"And a cannon? Now if Ellery Queen wrote that story, the jewels would be in the shell Mr. Findlay is going to put in that cannon when he lowers the flag every sunset, and he will fire the shell into the river where a confederate is waiting to pick it up which they arranged in advance."

"You mean the diamonds will be in a shell and he will shoot that same shell?"

"That's the idea, Peter. Isn't it super?"

I thought a couple of seconds. "It's no good, Marrylin."

"Why not?"

"I wouldn't put it past a big ameba like Mr. Findlay to have a cannon because he has got about everything else there is in the world, but if he shot it off early in the morning folks would be kicking about the noise because folks are like that in New Eng-

land, and anyhow there is not any river in Surrey, and there are
not any confederates on this side of Mason and Dixie's line."

That doesn't stop her long. "Peter, does Mr. Findlay keep
geese?"

"Geese?"

"Especially a white goose with a barred tail?"

I says, "No. He don't keep geese for the same reason he don't
shoot a cannon, and you cannot put silencers on poultry."

"That is too bad," she says, "because if he kept geese, and if
Conan Doyle wrote that story, you would find the blue carbuncle
—I mean the rose-diamonds—in the crop of the goose I told you
about which is a good three pounds lighter than the other goose, I
mean the big white one they fattened especially for Christmas."

I says, "What's the use of talking, Marrylin? There were just
amebas at that meeting of the Hobby Club, which are round
animals and left-handed."

But she is just beginning. "Peter, tell me quick: is there a stuffed
wildcat over the mantel?"

"Maybe there is a stuffed wildcat over the mantel in the gun
room where I have not been, but on the mantel in the living room
there is just the head of a gentleman with a very white face."

"What a pity! I'm sorry there isn't any stuffed wildcat because
if John Dickson Carr wrote the story that is where you would find
the diamonds or maybe it would be the bullet the wife of the
German scientist shot through the window before she shot the
German scientist with another bullet. But wait a minute, Peter!
My little gray cells!"

I wait.

She laughs that nice laugh of hers. "I have got it, Peter, and
just like I said, it is obvious."

"You said that before and it didn't help."

"I mean I have found the solution of this case."

"That makes two people that have soluted it, only it don't stay
like that."

"That is because you have not been to college, Peter. Have you
got your little note-book handy? Well, make believe I'm the per-
fessor, and make notes while I'm lecturing . . . ." She talks for
more than an hour, I guess, and now and then she reads things
she gets out of books she has brought with her to study on her
vacation, she says. "And now, Peter, do you think Mr. Burton
Findlay will be glad to see you when you ring his bell?"

I look at my watch. It is almost two A.M. in the morning, so
I am driving past his house first till I see there is a light in the

living room, and then he answers the door himself. "Confound it," he says, "so it's you, Moran? Come in, come in, humpf! Don't keep me standing here in the draft where I'll catch my death of cold. I suppose you want to go to the living room?"

"Yes, sir."

He unlocks the door and he locks it again after we are inside. "Speak up, Moran! Don't keep me on tender hooks!"

I says, "Mr. Burton Findlay, I have found the answer to this case."

"Again?"

"This time it is for keeps." I look at my notes which I wrote while Marrylin was lecturing, and I says, "Mr. Findlay, have you got a clean white cloth?"

"Will a towel answer?"

"If it is a clean white cloth." We spread it on a table, and I lift up the head of the gentleman with the white face which is over the mantel and I put it on the clean white cloth.

"And now?" he says, looking at me hard. "And now?"

I look at my notes. "If Mr. Doyle wrote this story, like it says in what I have got written here, this would be a bust of Napoleon."

"It is a bust of Napoleon."

I have put a heavy hammer in my coat pocket before I started out. I bring it down on the head of that bust, good and hard, and Napoleon breaks into more than a dozen pieces, I guess, though I do not count them because I am busy catching all those pieces in the towel.

Mr. Findlay screams, "My God!"

I says, "That is correct, because it says in my notes, 'He gave a loud shout of triumph.'"

He screams, "That wasn't triumph, you confounded idiot!"

I says, "Wait a minute," and I read from my notes: "'The famous black pearl of the Borgias was fixed in one splinter like a plum in a pudding.'"

"Well, is it?"

By now I have finished mashing up all the big pieces into little pieces, and I do not see any pearls or any diamonds. "Mr. Doyle did not write this story."

Mr. Findlay drops into a chair and holds his head in his hands. "I paid nine hundred dollars for that bust at auction."

I didn't waste time. By one of the windows is a plant which is growing in a red vase, and the leaves of that plant are turned away from the window and not toward it. "'If the story was written by Mr. Wallace there could be a long line of pots and when you

see the leaves of one plant turned away from the light you will know somebody turned it when he hid the diamonds there because if you leave a plant alone it will turn its leaves to the light like a regular plant.' "

He says, "Stop, Moran!" but I am too quick for him.

Whang!

Mr. Findlay jumps about four feet which is a pretty good jump for an old guy who is not in training. He says, "Moran, do you realize what have you done? You have smashed a sang de beef vase right out of the finest Ming period! The Metropolitan Museum tried to buy that vase from me but I would not sell it, and the leaves of the plant are turned away from the light because it is an artificial plant!"

But I am not listening to him. I am hunting through the pieces of the vase and the pot which was inside the vase and the dirt which was inside the pot for the eleven rose-diamonds, and I guess Mr. Wallace did not write the story because all I am finding is one bottle cap and two worms.

Mr. Findlay is kneeling near the window picking up the pieces, but I am reading in my notes, " 'There is a story by Mr. Chesterton and you can't see the diamonds because they are in the water in a glass, and sometimes diamonds are invisible when they are under water, but always in detective stories.' " Well, you remember the tall blue-green glass and the flowers that were wilting in that glass the last time I was here, because I wrote about those flowers and if you have forgotten you can read my letter again.

Whang!

I guess Mr. Chesterton did not write this story, because all there is is hunks of glass and flowers and water and more hunks of glass, and I am lucky I have not cut my hand. Mr. Findlay is on his knees like I said, but he turns to me and he looks like he was going to bust out crying. "Moran," he says, and this time he is real quiet, "Venetian glass—yes. Venetian glass—sixteenth century. A piece which simply cannot be replaced."

"I am sorry," I says, "but you are talking to a student in the Acme International Detective Correspondence School which is in South Kingston, N. Y., and our motto is, 'Let the Chips Fall Where They May.' " I do not know if we have got a motto like that, but the idea came to me just then and I think it is a good idea.

Mr. Findlay comes over, and he is handing me one of those One Dollar straight cigars. "Light this, Moran, and let me take care of your hammer for just a couple of minutes. I am afraid you will damage it if you are not careful." He strikes a match for me himself. "Moran, yesterday I offered you a thousand dollars to find the eleven rose-diamonds."

"Yes, Mr. Findlay, that is true."

"Today I will offer you two thousand dollars not to find them."

"What?"

"That is my offer."

"Mr. Findlay, let me get this straight——"

"Moran, you heard me right the first time. I'm offering you twice the amount of the reward to drop the case here and now."

I couldn't make head or tail out of that. I says, "Why should you do such a thing, Mr. Findlay? It does not sound honest to me."

"I mean to be honest."

"Are you going to give back the diamonds you swiped?"

He gives a sigh. "Moran, I repeat I did not steal them."

"Maybe you would not call it stealing. . . ."

"I didn't take them. I didn't touch them. I don't know where they are."

"Then why are you making me that offer, Mr. Findlay?"

He gives me a funny look. "Moran, if you cannot guess why, after you have destroyed some of my most cherished works of art, I am not sure I can explain. Do you see that painting on the wall back of you? It is worth a couple of pecks of rose-diamonds. Do you see that marble statue in the corner? No, don't look at it, please! I would not like you to smash it up next because Nick Carter, the Demon Detective, once found some jewelry hidden in the body of such a statue."

"Why not?"

He opens a drawer in his desk and he locks up the hammer in it first. "Look, I will put my offer in writing. . . . No, I will do better than that: I will write you a check for two thousand dollars if you will solemnly swear never to darken my door again. Is it a bargain?"

I like two thousand dollars, which is more than one thousand dollars, but I do no want to take it because you will blow me up like you did once before when you wrote, "Accepting money makes you an accomplice if a crime is contemplated," and I do not know what crime a big ameba like Mr. Findlay is contemplating, so I says, "Before I take that check I will have to get permission from the Chief Inspector."

"The Chief Inspector? A regular detective?"

"Yes, sir; in South Kingston, N. Y."

"A regular detective coming here and spilling the whole story to the newspapers—after what you've done already?"

"I am afraid there is no help for it."

He laughs. "You are right to be afraid, Moran! Come with me. Come, Moran!" He unlocks the door, locking it after us, and he takes me into a room which is down the hall. "My gun room," he says. "I have used these guns to shoot everything from antelopes to zebras, from chipmunks to crocodiles. This is my Ross thirty-thirty. It shoots a bullet which expands which means it gets larger after it hits you, so it makes a small hole when it goes in but it takes your liver with it when it goes out. This is my elephant gun which I used in Burma, where I shot both cobras and elephants. You will see it has two barrels. One barrel is for the female elephant and the other is for the male which always coils up in the same spot when you have killed its mate. I have not shot an elephant recently, so I would get back into form gradually, starting with the Chief Inspector and saving the second barrel for you. This here is a four-oh-five automatic rifle. It is a brutal weapon but any jury would acquit me. This is a Russian bazooka which will nail the Chief Inspector even if he comes in a tank. I have lots of ammunition. And now, Moran, let me escort you to the front door, which will be locked, bolted, and chained after you go out."

I says, "Mr. Findlay, you cannot scare the Chief Inspector! I guess you do not know that guy!"

He licks his lips like he was hungry. "I look forward to meeting him. He will look pretty over the sights of the bazooka. Mention that when you write, and add that I may drive over to South Kingston one of these days even if he doesn't come here. Good-by, Moran."

Please telegraph me right away when you will arrive so I can wise you up about Mr. Findlay who is a peculiar man and I think I should tell you more about him.

Please telegraph right away.

TELEGRAM.

PETER MORAN, C/O MR. R. B. MCRAE, SURREY, CONN. CHIEF INSPECTOR LEFT TO ATTEND HIS GRANDMOTHER'S FUNERAL IN MEXICO IMMEDIATELY AFTER READING YOUR LETTER AND DATE OF HIS RETURN IS UNCERTAIN STOP A COPY OF THIS TELEGRAM GOES TO MR. BURTON FINDLAY STOP I AM SIGNING IT BECAUSE OF MY LOYALTY TO CHIEF INSPECTOR COMMA MR. FINDLAY COMMA BUT I AM A DEFENCELESS WOMAN AND I APPEAL TO YOUR CAVALRY.

M. M. O'R, SECRETARY TO J. J. O'B.

From: Operative P. Moran c/o Mr. R. B. McRae, Surrey Conn.,
To: Chief Inspector, Acme International Detective Correspondence School,
  South Kingston, N. Y. Please forward.

Well, I showed your secretary's telegram to Marrylin, and I says, "What does she mean, 'Your cavalry'? Mr. Findlay has not got any horses," and she says, "She meant 'chivalry,' " and I says, "I do not know that word," and she says, "No, I did not think you did or you would have told me what happened before you wrote that long letter, and then you nearly drove me mad by refusing to open your mouth until the telegram came in reply."

Well, I wipe off a chair in my office which is the garage, and she asks me more than a million questions, and I have got to tell her my story over and over again, and it is lucky I got 60% on Lesson II which is Observation or I would be saying, "I do not know" oftener than I am saying it which is pretty often.

By and by she shakes her head and she says, "If this was part of that cause I have been taking in college I guess they would give me 'F' which stands for Flunk. Peter, why did you have to be so drastic? You could have examined the bust of Napoleon without smashing it to bits."

"Mr. Holmes smashed his, it says in my notes."

"Yes, but he paid for it first."

"Don't be ridiculous, Marrylin. Where would I get nine hundred dollars, and if I had it do you think I would spend it all for the head of a gentleman with a pale face?"

"Then, too, you could have examined the earth about the plant without ruining the vase, and you could have turned the tall Venetian glass upside down very carefully and poured the water out of it."

I says, "Here are my notes which I made while you were lecturing, and the fellows in those stories were not extra careful."

"But Peter, you are not a regular detective, and I expected you to have more common sense! When I think of the beautiful things you have destroyed, I could cry! Well, let's get going."

"To the Green Lantern—or to the Brookside Tavern?"

"No. To Mr. Findlay's."

"Marrylin, are you crazy?"

"Maybe I was when I didn't read those notes you were making, but I batted out an 'A' in 'the Art and Craft of the Detective Story,' and I am not crazy now. What a fool I was not to think of her!"

"Her?"

"Dorothy Sayers, silly! Everything about this story has a woman's touch. Come Peter."

"Not on your life."

"Are you a quitter, like the Chief Inspector?"

"You bet I am."

"Well, 'fraid cat, I won't need you. I can drive a car myself."

"O.K. Here are the keys."

"For the last time, Peter, are you coming?"

"For the last time, Marrylin, I am staying right here, where Mr. Findlay cannot draw a bead on me with that elephant gun."

"Good-by, Peter."

"Good-by, Marrylin."

So five minutes later we are ringing the bell at Mr. Findlay's house. Jim Hewitt, the butler, is opening the door.

He says, "Pete, I am under strict orders not to let you in."

Marrylin says, "He's with me."

Jim shakes his head. "Orders is orders. If I see you I am to set off the burglar alarm, and then I am to reload Mr. Findlay's rifles as fast as he fires them."

Marrylin says, "Peter has got no hammer with him this time."

"No, and I want to get mine back. Mr. Findlay locked it up in his desk, and I will be needing that there hammer."

"So it's you again, Moran, humpf?" The door of the living room opens about an inch, and I can see Mr. Findlay looking out. "Moran, remember what I said!"

Marrylin pipes up, "Mr. Findlay, it's only me."

"Good Heavens! The Chief Inspector—a woman?"

"I'm not the Chief Inspector, Mr. Findlay, or any other kind of inspector—and I could have cried when Peter told me what he had done."

"Well, what do you want?"

"I think I can find the diamonds for you. Peter, put your hands up."

"My hands up?"

"And keep them up. That way you won't do any more damage."

Mr. Findlay opens the door of the living room further. "That is the first sensible word that has been spoken to me since Moran darkened my threshold. Hewitt, you may let them in."

We go into the living room and he locks the door after us. Marrylin looks hard at the movie machine, which I do not understand, because I did not touch that at all; and then she looks at what is left of Napoleon—and the sang de beef vase—and the Venetian glass. "Oh, Peter, I could kill you!"

Mr. Findlay bobs his head up and down like he was pleased. "That is the second sensible word. Shall I lend you a rifle, Miss— Miss—?"

"Don't call me 'Miss,' Mr. Findlay. Call me Marrylin. Surely you must have heard of me through your granddaughter Helen, who is my classmate at Mt. Holyoke."

The old man smiles. "Of course! Of course! She has mentioned you in nearly every letter. You play on the basketball team together."

"That's right."

"And you are members of the same fraternity—or is it sorority?"

"That's right, too."

I says, "Can I take my hands down now? My arms are getting tired."

They both yell "No!" and Marrylin says, "Keep away from the walls, Peter, because you might touch one of the paintings. Just stand in the middle of the room, and act like the Statue of Liberty holding torches in both hands." She turns to Mr. Findlay. "Mr. Findlay, the mistake Peter made is obvious."

"He made nothing but mistakes."

"He did not recognize, as I do, that this story has a woman's touch."

He looks at her from under his bushy eyebrows. "Say that again—slowly. This story—"

"—has a woman's touch."

He shakes his head, because he is not understanding any more than I am understanding, and that is not anything.

"Dorothy Sayers wrote a story how the stolen pearls are pinned to the mistletoe and they look like extra berries. Nobody notices them."

Mr. Findlay is still shaking his head. "My dear young lady, we are not concerned with pearls, and it is not customary in New England to put up mistletoe in August."

"I am just explaining the general idea, Mr. Findlay. If Dorothy Sayers wrote this story, we will find the eleven diamonds in a place so obvious that you would never think of looking there."

"Such as?"

"Peter mentioned a little heap of rounded pebbles—small pebbles, all about the same size—lying on the stand next to the motion-picture projector."

"I saw them."

"Are they still there?"

"Everything that was in this room Sunday is still here."

Marrylin walks over and comes back with the pebbles. "All about the same size, as Peter noticed. Could I ask you, Mr. Findlay, if they are just a little larger than the missing diamonds?"

Now I am getting the idea, also, but Mr. Findlay beats me to it. "Marrylin," he says, "since you want me to call you that, they are indeed just a little larger."

They are nodding and smiling at each other. "Mr. Findlay, a hammer might do damage."

"It has already done damage."

"How about an instrument with which we might crack one of these stones?"

He hurries to a side table. "Would a nutcracker answer?"

"We'll try it."

Their heads are close together, and I hear the stone go "Crack!"

"It's just an ordinary stone!"

"Moran, keep your hands up!"

"Yes, sir."

"Let's crack the rest."

Well, they crack them, one after another, and when I look over their shoulders I can see the inside of those stones is like the outside, and you can find stones like that all over Connecticut.

Mr. Findlay shakes his head. "I'm sorry, Marrylin."

"So am I. What is worse, I'm ashamed. I did so well in that cause in college, Mr. Findlay."

"What cause?"

But she gives a little yelp. "Why didn't it come to me right off? The woman's touch! Another woman writer! Not Dorothy Sayers! Agatha Christie!"

Now Mr. Findlay is getting interested. "I, too, have read many of Miss Christie's books, but what is the point?"

Marrylin is getting excited. "In a Christie story, the guilty person is always the least likely suspect!"

I says, "What do you mean, Marrylin?" but she says, "Keep out of this, Peter."

Mr. Findlay nods. "I follow you now, but Moran, strange as it seems, has already acted on your theory. I have no reason to steal. I am the least likely suspect. Moran accused me of taking the diamonds."

"But dear Mr. Findlay, you are *not* the least likely suspect! Think back who was here Saturday night."

"All right." He checks them off on his fingers. "Mr. & Mrs. McRae. Mr. Seymour. Mr. & Mrs. Underwood, Mr. & Mrs.

Erskine-Bevin. Mr. & Mrs. Cutler. Mr. Jones. Mr. Pomeroy. Mr. & Mrs. Gaylord I."

"But it isn't all."

"Hewitt, my butler."

"That isn't all."

"I have mentioned every person who was in the room—"

"Except the least likely suspect!"

I get a bright idea, and I says, "Napoleon!" but Mr. Findlay says, "Marrylin, I give up. You mention him."

"The Gaylord Baby."

"My great-grandchild? How utterly ridiculous!"

"The least likely suspect!"

He swallows hard. "The baby was the only human being in the room who was searched. Why, the ladies took off every stitch of its clothing!"

But Marrylin has the bit in her teeth now, and there is no stopping her. "Then where do you think somebody—somehow—obtained the little pile of pebbles which we have just cracked, Mr. Findlay?"

They walk over to the baby carriage together.

Mr. Findlay says, "We searched it."

"I know. And you laid this to one side."

"What?"

They are carrying it back to Mr. Findlay's desk, and Marrylin is shaking it while she walks, because it makes a cheerful sound. "The baby's rattle," she says. "Look at it! It is celluloid, and it has been cemented together badly, because you can see where some of the cement spilled over in the dark! And remember that while you were looking at the motion pictures, it was just a few steps from the stand where the projector was running—automatic after you start it—to the baby carriage—and there was a can of celluloid cement handy!"

Mr. Findlay is not saying anything, but he is nodding, and he is breathing deep. He sits down at his desk, and he opens his penknife. He takes the rattle in one hand and the knife in the other—and then he stops. "Young lady," he says, "I believe it is your honor. . . ."

She slices through the rattle like it was so much putty. The halves of the ball spring open, and a shower of sparklers runs all over the desk. "Mr. Pomeroy's diamonds," she says.

"Eleven," says Mr. Findlay. "Count 'em."

It is no use trying to catch Jim Hewitt, because it turns out he had his ear at the keyhole, and he lit out when he saw the jig was up; and Mr. Findlay has written me a check for Five Hundred Dollars, and he has written another like it for Marrylin, and while it says on that paper I have got in my pocket he will pay me One Thousand Dollars if I find the diamonds, I guess I will not make a fuss, because Marrylin is just a young tot who is working her way through college, and she is not a detective who has had lots of important cases like me.

Mr. Findlay and Marrylin are sitting at his desk, laughing and drinking sherry, though I do not like to drink out of those little glasses which do not hold a man's sized drink, and besides, they break easy if you handle them rough, but it is all the same to me because they will not let me take my hands down and they are beginning to weigh a ton, especially the one which is holding the check.

Mr. Findlay is bobbing his head like he is satisfied. "So Hewitt stole them, with the baby's assistance."

"Or the baby stole them, with Hewitt's," she says.

He stares at her hard. "I can see that the pebbles, which were round, and small, and about the same size, obviously came from the baby's rattle—so obviously that nobody thought of it excepting you—and that Hewitt made the substitution in the dark, taking it for granted we wouldn't give the pebbles a second glance; but there must have been clues which told you who was the guilty man long before that."

"Peter supplied them."

I says, "Yes, I supplied the clues," but Mr. Findlay says, "Keep your hands up, Moran," and then he says, "Go on, Marrylin."

"Hewitt told Peter that while Mr. Seymour's underwear was in ribbons, he—Hewitt—was wearing a union suit which had no holes. In other words, long, long before the crime, he was ready to be searched."

Mr. Findlay bobs his head some more. "So he was, confound him!"

"If he was ready to be searched, he expected to be searched: therefore he wasn't a gentleman, don't you see? The gentlemen agreed at once that a search would be humiliating and useless. The one man who wasn't a gentleman hadn't foreseen that."

"Go on."

"He hid the stones in this room—obvious again. . . ."

"Yes, I was sure of that."

". . . . and he planned to recover them next week—next month —next year—whenever you got tired of keeping the room locked. Therefore he was a person who would have easy access to this room—alone! Now that we know where he hid the diamonds, the rest of the pattern fills itself in. Eventually the rattle would be given back to the baby, and the thief would steal it—or open it again, and make a second substitution. There were three or four different lines of reasoning, but they all led to the same man."

"Hewitt, confound him!"

"And Peter didn't believe when I told him I knew right off who was the thief."

"He wouldn't believe: naturally not!"

"No, naturally not."

They are both laughing, but they stop all of a sudden when I ask a question. "You will have to explain one thing, Marrylin! You said what put you on the right track was the woman's touch! Well, where was it?"

She folds Mr. Findlay's check and puts it away before she answers. "I made many inquiries before I came here," she says. "The baby—the least likely suspect—is a girl baby. After that, Peter, it was elementary."